JONATHAN CAPE
PAPERBACK
JCP 90

IN DEFENCE OF
ECONOMIC GROWTH

D1380821

In Defence of
Economic Growth

WILFRED BECKERMAN

*Professor of Political Economy in the University
of London, and Head of the Department of
Political Economy, University College London*

JONATHAN CAPE
THIRTY BEDFORD SQUARE LONDON

FIRST PUBLISHED 1974
THIS PAPERBACK EDITION FIRST PUBLISHED 1976
© 1974 BY WILFRED BECKERMAN

JONATHAN CAPE LTD, 30 BEDFORD SQUARE, LONDON WC1

ISBN 0 224 01223 1

Some of the contents of this book have
appeared previously in *Minerva* and the
Oxford Economic Papers. I am grateful to
the editors of these journals for their
kind permission to reproduce this material.

PRINTED AND BOUND IN GREAT BRITAIN BY
REDWOOD BURN LIMITED
TROWBRIDGE AND ESHER

Contents

Preface

The post-war years have seen unprecedented rates of growth in the Western world, Japan, the Soviet-bloc countries and certain of the developing nations. As conventionally measured by economic statisticians, national income per head in the advanced countries of the world is probably about twice as high as before the war (after allowing for price increases). Mass unemployment has been eliminated, and the pre-war trade cycle, which was the cause of so much anxiety and misery, has been replaced by, at worst, minor fluctuations around a generally high and rising level of economic activity. Before the war, when millions of ordinary people were rarely able to forget for long the shadow of unemployment which lay over their lives, and when even most of those in jobs could barely rise above the basic necessities of existence, it must have seemed that a general doubling of average incomes per head would be the greatest boon that mankind could expect. But now that this has been achieved, doubts are being cast on all sides as to whether it has been a boon after all. It is widely argued that the price that has been paid for economic progress has been too high if account is taken of various factors such as increasing pollution, general deterioration of the environment, the danger of running out of supplies of raw materials, the accelerating growth of world population, the destruction – in the name of economic growth – of essential spiritual and aesthetic values in society, and so on. And even if the achievements of the past are accepted, the feasibility and desirability of future economic growth has been increasingly questioned and challenged. The case against economic growth has become one of the most widely publicized – and widely accepted – of all indictments of modern society.

Indeed, to many people almost all the ills of modern society, ranging from inadequate drains to permissive sexual standards, crime, drugs, violence, youthful rebellion against parental authority, and so on, are ultimately attributable to economic growth and its alleged sacrifice of all that is best in life to the false god of higher national product.

As the title indicates, this book is not an attempt to present a survey of all the pros and cons of economic growth. The prosecution case has been put to the public over and over again in numerous forms; here I want to put the case for the defence – at least as I see it. I did not want to write a balanced *book*, for what is needed is a balanced *debate*, and so far the field has been occupied largely by the anti-growth cohorts. Some statement of the case for the defence will go some way to restore the balance of the discussion.

Inevitably, the argument of this book is polemical at many points. At the same time, the case for the defence does rest on the presentation and analysis of evidence. Some of this evidence is of a fairly detailed character, but none of it requires any special previous training in economics, science or any other subject. Where economic arguments are used, they are of an elementary character and well within the reach of the layman. (The reader who is not interested in the slightly more technical economic analysis of the pollution problem could skip Chapters 6 and 7.)

Finally, I should add that the defendant in the case – economic growth – was not given any opportunity to select his own defence counsel. The only reason why I find myself in this position is that, in the course of my service as a member of the Royal Commission on Environmental Pollution, I acquired a certain knowledge of the pollution aspect of economic growth that relatively few economists have had an opportunity to cultivate. From this I was able to see how weak was the pollution part of the prosecution's case against economic growth, and this naturally led to an interest in the rest of the case. But I do not regard myself as speaking for the economics profession. In the same way that the case for the prosecution calls on support from a wide variety of professions – including economists as well as scientists – the case for the defence can call on expert testimony of various kinds. I have merely come forward, for the reasons given above, in my capacity as an economist who has some special familiarity with certain of the issues involved, not as a self-appointed representative of the economics profession as a whole.

A superficial reading of some of the more polemical passages of this book may suggest that I see the issue as a battle between, on the one hand, myself as the self-appointed champion of the economics profession against, on the other hand, the assembled anti-growth dragons of the scientists, journalists, politicians, the Church, radical youth and almost everybody else. But this could hardly be further from the truth. Many economists are against economic growth. Conversely, many very distinguished scientists – such as Lord Zuckerman, Sir Eric (now Lord) Ashby, Professor Mellanby, Sir Frederick Dainton – have gone on record in opposition to some of the predictions of environmental disaster that form a large part of the anti-growth case. Hence, there is no battle between materialist, GNP-crazy economists who know nothing about the relevant scientific technicalities, on the one hand, and everybody else, including all the scientists, on the other. If anything, the dividing line is between those who – often for the most worthy of motives (such as lack of time) – are content with fairly vague and broad generalizations that seem to have some immediate superficial appeal, and those who want to take the time to probe a little further both the facts and the logic behind the anti-growth case. To revert to the court-room analogy, it is a difference between those who are prepared to convict the defendant on the basis of motive, opportunity and some circumstantial evidence – such as that economic growth has been accompanied, in the past at least, by an increase in certain forms of pollution – and those who want to test each single piece of evidence more carefully before reaching a verdict. And rarely has it been more important to weigh up the evidence carefully. A mistake in a criminal trial might mean imprisonment for one innocent man. A failure to maintain economic growth means continued poverty, deprivation, disease, squalor, degradation and slavery to soul-destroying toil for countless millions of the world's population.

1*

1 Introduction: An Economist's View of the Growth Issue

The Anti-Growth Movement

The goal of economic growth has been increasingly questioned during the last few years, at least in the advanced countries. The anti-growth movement has collected some very strange bedfellows, ranging from aristocratic conservationists worried about their salmon streams and grouse moors to extreme left-wing youth eager to condemn the soul-destroying consequences of capitalist greed and materialism. The many social groups that have climbed on to the anti-growth bandwagon over the last few years are portrayed in the next chapter. In this chapter I shall attempt to set out (a) two or three main strands of thought that they have in common, including the mistaken belief that the difference between the pro-growth and the anti-growth faction must correspond to a difference between the economist's and the non-economist's way of looking at things; and (b) what the economist's approach to the growth problem in general, and to the environmental problem in particular, really is. In subsequent chapters I shall examine in more detail the relationships between, on the one hand, economic growth, and, on the other hand, 'welfare', the 'quality of life', pollution, the exhaustion of resources, and so on.

There have been two main themes behind the widespread view that economic growth must be brought to a halt, or at least deliberately slowed down. The first is that growth does not make us any happier; indeed it is often argued that it makes us less happy and that the 'costs' of economic growth include a deterioration in the quality of life. The second is that growth cannot continue much longer anyway, since it will sooner or later come up against the limits set by the available resources or the accumulation of destructive and poisonous pollutants; 'So the growth which we have come to accept as normal cannot go on for ever. Unless we end it in a deliberate and controlled manner, it will simply be halted by a confrontation with environmental limits.'[1] One group of distinguished experts brought together by an international organization seems to suggest that we may even be approaching the limits of our capacity to absorb education.[2]

There is some overlap between these two themes. Those who maintain that economic growth leads to a decline in the 'quality of life' do so on various grounds, one of which is usually that the quality of life is being reduced by the increase in pollution, which, it is alleged, is inevitably associated with economic growth. And those who maintain that economic growth cannot be sustained much longer also often do so on the grounds that the rising pollution will eventually kill us off, unless such astronomic costs are incurred to prevent it that this would bring growth to a halt anyway. But the two themes can be treated separately, nevertheless, for they point to different conclusions even if they share some assumptions. One is saying that growth is bad for us whether we can have it or not. The other is saying that continued growth is impossible whether we like it or not. (Those who believe that growth is bad for us anyway should, of course, be relieved to learn that we can't have it much longer anyway, but they do not usually seem to be. After all, it would surely be far worse if we thought that continued economic growth was both unpleasant and inevitable.)

Lord Robbins has accurately described one of the anti-growth themes as follows: 'And now there is arising a ... school of thought which argues that ... growth itself is something which is intrinsically undesirable; and that to recommend anything on the ground that it will promote growth is simply to reveal an essentially philistine character, an indifference to all that makes life anxious and ugly in the present age and an insensitiveness to truly civilized values.'[3] For it is true that this part of the anti-growth argument generally takes the form of insisting that economic growth has involved an excessive concern with *material* output, particularly of a 'vulgar' kind, that often represents the gratification of artificially created needs by the advertising media in a 'consumer society' devoted to promoting 'the mushroom growth of television, automobile ownership, air travel and mass tourism',[4] and that the growth 'rat-race' destroys not merely the visual amenities of towns and country, but also our ability to communicate with our fellow-men, our sense of aesthetic and moral values, and even our pride in our work. 'All we can say in general is that the idea of work as a source of legitimate pride, as a source of gratification, forms no part of the ethos of an industrial civilization.'[5]

This notion of a contrast between the coarse materialism of the pro-growth school and the exquisitely refined sensibilities of the anti-growth school crops up over and over again. One of the founders of the anti-growth crusade in Britain, Sir Frank Fraser Darling, writes: ' ... the materialist's creed is that industry must not be handicapped by idealistic policies of pollution control'.[6] Another member of the Royal Commission on Environmental Pollution says: 'A new philosophy will not be achieved by ... allowing GNP, balance of payments, and the "national interest" to over-ride the more sensitive and less material instincts.'[7]

This distinction between the materialists who are in favour of growth and the men of sensitivity who see the sordid realities of modern economic growth is often accompanied by the notion that economists are, with two or three honourable exceptions like Dr Mishan, Kenneth Boulding, or Professor W. Kapp, in the materialist camp, and that ' ... for many years economic growth has been treated as an end in itself. Somewhere along the way economists forgot that increased GNP is a means [i.e. not an end in itself]'.[8] Accompanying this is the belief that the generally accepted objective of maximum growth of GNP (gross national product) now needs to be dethroned.[9] Thus, one of the working parties set up by the British Government to help with its contribution to the 1972 UNO Conference on the Human Environment at Stockholm stated: 'We have been driven by the evidence we have assembled to the conclusion that to devote our resources to the achievement of the highest possible growth rate, as conventionally measured, is no longer desirable';[10] or, as Dr Sicco Mansholt, who was recently President of the Commission of the European Economic Community, put it, 'To begin with, we should no longer orientate our economic system towards the pursuit of maximum growth, towards the greatest gross national product possible.'[11] Even one prominent politician, Mr Dick Taverne, who was a junior Minister at the Treasury during the 1964–1970 Labour Government, writes about the different attitudes that will be required, given 'the prospect of no longer pursuing the maximization of the growth of GNP', although he does concede that this cannot be achieved overnight and that 'Mr Barber should not aim for nil growth in his next budget.'[12]

Now economic growth is, presumably, a subject to which economists are likely to have given some thought. If those who are now proclaiming that, after extensive research and review of the evidence, they have discovered that maximum economic growth should *no longer* be society's objective had taken the trouble to consult almost any economist, they would have been told that not only would no economist support maximum economic growth as an objective *now*, but he would never have done so at any time in the past either. Maximum economic growth *per se* is simply a silly objective, as any economist would know. Those who apparently believed that it was a sensible objective until recently must be more growth-minded than almost all economists, who would never have held this view at any time. Elementary economic concepts can also illuminate discussions of some of the other related issues, such as how much of our national product should be devoted to pollution control.

In this chapter, therefore, it seemed advisable to try to explain at the outset the position of the economist with respect to the debate about growth and the environment, i.e., what sort of growth objective economists really subscribe to, and how it relates to the burning issue of economic growth versus the environment or the quality of life. For if knowledge of some elementary notions of economics is enough to dethrone the growth god, those who hold that economic growth is not the most important goal in life could profit by the knowledge. Furthermore, there are other aspects of the growth-versus-the-environment issue where the economist's way of looking at problems can be helpful.

Why maximum economic growth is a nonsensical objective

We might as well begin by explaining why maximum economic growth, without any qualification, has *never* been a sensible objective for society. Maximum 'welfare' is, presumably, a fairly acceptable starting point for what would be a sensible objective, but it does not get us very far since people will differ widely in their views as to what constitutes welfare. Some people may think that maximum economic growth is, or was, an overriding component of welfare to which all else should be sacrificed. Economists would not usually define welfare in these terms, nor would they be likely to attempt an exhaustive and complete definition of welfare in any terms. What they would do – as discussed in more detail later in the chapter – is to postulate that, subject to various well-known qualifications (particularly well-known to economists), *economic* welfare is a part of total welfare. Hence, subject to these qualifications, more economic welfare will contribute to more total welfare.

Furthermore, economic welfare can be regarded as having two dimensions; first, the size of the economic cake, and second, the way it is distributed. In fact, leaving aside the non-economic components of welfare, such as love of one's neighbours, tolerance, social peace and justice, and so on, the economist conceives of economic welfare as comprising the level of consumption and the equality of its distribution. Note the emphasis on consumption: not investment, or exports or the balance of payments, or anything else – just consumption. For that, in the end, is what we get out of the economic system in the way of goods and services that contribute directly to our economic welfare. But this doesn't mean that we should no longer use any resources for investment or for research into technical progress, and should immediately switch all our productive resources to the satisfaction of today's consumption.

For what about tomorrow? Or next year, and so on? A rational man tries to maximize consumption over some relevant period of time, such as his lifetime. To this end he will often be prepared to sacrifice some consumption now in order to have more consumption in the future.

The same applies to society. It may be perfectly rational for society to sacrifice some consumption now in order to enjoy a higher standard of living in the future. But it would be irrational to incur an unlimited sacrifice of current standards of living for this purpose. It would be absurd to cut current consumption by, say, 80 per cent, to reduce food supplies to subsistence levels, to allow people only the minimum essential clothing and heating, to send children down the mines, to introduce compulsory twelve-hour working days, and so on, in order to achieve the maximum possible investment rate simply to maximize the growth rate. For this clearly does not maximize *consumption* over the time-span relevant for society's decisions. The loss of welfare from such a cut in *current* consumption would far exceed any conceivable increase in welfare in later years obtained by the higher level of investment today. (This is not to say that such a policy has never been pursued in any country, since it is arguable that the Stalinist policy of forcing the build-up of heavy industry at the expense of consumption levels represented just such a choice between present and future consumption.) In other words, such an excessive diversion of resources from current consumption to future consumption would not achieve a sensible objective which would be to maximize consumption over some period of time, allowing for the extent to which the loss of consumption at present and the extra consumption in the future represent, respectively, subtractions from and additions to welfare.

This allowance must take account of the fact that a pound's worth of extra consumption in twenty years' time may not have the same value to society as a pound's worth of consumption today. To take an extreme case, for purposes of illustration, it would be folly for a starving man to sacrifice one loaf of bread now in order to have ten loaves next year; he would be dead by then. Even in less extreme cases the same principle holds. For

example, a young married man with a family and heavy mortgage payments to make on his house, who has not yet reached
his full potential earning capacity, may not want to put a lot of
money aside in order to have an even higher income when his
children have grown up and the mortgage is paid off. Much
will depend, therefore, on the level of consumption one enjoys
at present, and the level one expects to enjoy in the future, and
the uncertainty that has to be attached to the prospect of future
rewards in return for abstinence now.

But the essential point is that it is *consumption* over some
relevant time-period which should be maximized, not the
growth rate. Of course, if growth can be accelerated without
any sacrifice of current consumption, then it would be desirable
to take advantage of this costless means of adding to future
consumption. Such a policy could not fail to raise consumption
over the whole time-period in question. But if we can have
more in the future without giving up any welfare now there is
really no problem about making the correct choice. And if
there is no choice problem there is no economic problem,
because choice is what economics is about.

What economists advise society to go for is not maximum
growth, but *optimum* growth – i.e. that growth rate at which the
sacrifice of present consumption (or welfare, defined as widely
as one likes) in order to obtain faster growth is just offset by the
extra future consumption that this faster growth will permit.
This depends partly on society's relative valuation of present as
compared with future consumption, which must be a subjective
matter and is not one on which economists have any special
claim to pontificate. It must depend also on a purely technical,
factual consideration, namely, how much current consumption
actually has to be sacrificed in order to have more consumption
later on. Even our struggling young man might be prepared to
put aside some of his income for investment if he were offered
a really attractive proposition, yielding, say, 25 per cent per
annum. Given these two considerations – one a matter of subjective judgment and the other technical – there will be an
'optimum' growth rate that will achieve the objective of maximizing consumption over the time-period in question. And it

should be emphasized that in defining the economic objective in these terms, economists do not limit the definition of consumption to include only material goods. Not only does consumption include activities of all kinds, including such spiritual and aesthetic delights as listening to chamber music or admiring Raphael paintings, it also includes leisure and the conditions of work and living. It is for this reason, too, that maximizing measured economic growth *per se* must be a nonsensical objective; for, as indicated above, this would involve infringements of personal liberty and a drastic deterioration in working and living conditions that would constitute disproportionate reductions in standards of living for inadequate future gains.

Nor is there any special economist's preference concerning the way resources should be used at any moment of time; for instance, how much should be devoted to protecting the environment. This, too, is simply another dimension of choice, and the principles involved are basically the same as with the growth issue. But it is essential not to confuse the issue of how consumption should be spread over time, which is the growth issue, with that of how resources should be used at any moment of time. For example, many people believe that the existence of excessive traffic congestion or pollution provide arguments against economic growth, but in reality they only provide arguments for the view that resources may not be allocated optimally now. For example, Professor Galbraith, who ought to know better, associates the case against growth with the lack of public amenities (such as better public transport) and environmental nuisances such as the noise of jet planes. Others think that growth must be stopped or slowed down on account of the excessive pollution that can be seen around us or read about in the newspapers. But this is nothing to do with growth, this is a question of the misallocation of resources; in one case as between the private and the public sector, and in the other case as between the protection of the environment and other uses. Zero growth would not prevent this sort of resource misallocation; the private cars would not disappear to be replaced by adequate and prosperous public rail and road services. If anything, slower growth will merely make it more difficult for governments to achieve the desired switch in the way our national products are used.

The growth problem is a problem of how resources should be allocated over time. For in order to grow an economy must invest (either in physical capital, in human capital, or in research and development). If resources are used for investment they cannot be used for current consumption. To the economist, therefore, the costs of growth consist of the current consumption foregone. The optimum growth rate, therefore, is the one at which the additional sacrifice of current consumption is just worth while, given the addition to future output that will be obtained by the extra investment, and society's preference as between present and future consumption. Until recently it was fashionable to maintain that the free market economy failed to devote adequate resources to investment, so that the free market growth rate would be below the socially optimum growth rate. This view was, of course, subject to much dispute, but it was at least a recognizable economic argument. For it was generally based on the proposition that the costs of investment to private enterprise included many elements – notably a risk allowance – that were not true social costs. In other words, the social costs of investment (and hence of growth) were below private costs, so that, in the absence of special government measures, investment would only be pushed to the point where the private costs were covered, which would be below the socially optimum point. Nowadays, the mood has swung to the opposite extreme and it is maintained that, in the absence of special government measures, growth rates will be too high on account of the fact that growth involves many social costs that are not adequately allowed for in the calculations of the private-enterprise firms.

However, the symmetry between the two opposing doctrines does not go very far. The earlier view that growth was too slow did at least rest on a coherent theoretical analysis of the divergence between the private and social costs of *investment*, which is what matters in the context of the growth issue. The opposite view that growth is too fast, however, does not rest on any such clear theoretical basis. The external costs which are quoted in support of this view are costs such as environmental pollution. But these are not costs of *investment*, they are costs of production in general. This only implies that resources are misallocated at any given point of time – i.e. there is too much output of pollution-intensive goods and too little environmental protection in general. It has no implications at all for the growth rate, since it does not necessarily imply that the resource misallocation takes the form of inadequate investment.

Of course, it is true that there is too much pollution, and too much congestion of cities, and too many cars on the roads, and so on. These forms of resource misallocation exist in the un-regulated economy because of their associated external dis-economies: for example, the smoke from a factory chimney affects local residents and imposes costs on them that are not reflected in the costs of production of the firm that owns the factory. Most of these 'spillover effects', as they are often called, arise because of the fact that nobody has property rights in the environment. That is to say, nobody owns the clear air or clean water that is, in effect, 'used up' when it is polluted. But the fact that resources are misallocated at any moment of time on account of failure to correct for such externalities does not necessarily mean that the growth rate is wrong. To prove that the growth rate is wrong it is necessary to show that the resource misallocation at any point of time takes the form of inadequate investment.

Thus, choice depends on two considerations: one, a matter of tastes and preferences (for example, as between alternative goods or alternative time-periods), and the other a technical, factual matter of the amount of some goods that have to be sacrificed in order to have more of others.

Economists and social choice[13]

There is no such thing as 'the economist's' view as to how far society should prefer present to future consumption, only an economist's view as to how this should enter into the choice of a socially optimum growth rate. Economists, in their professional capacity at least, claim no special status in deciding the relative importance that society should attach to a pound's worth of consumption today as compared with a pound's worth of consumption in ten years' time, or any other aspect of society's preferences for that matter, such as the relative satisfactions society should obtain from an extra £1 spent on maternity homes, on schools, or on television sets. Economists do not claim to be the keepers of society's conscience in matters of relative tastes and preferences. They only claim to provide a guide as to *how* rational choice should be made, given these preferences and certain technical constraints. Thus, it would not be true, for example, that economists would choose faster growth than other people, or more pollution than other people.

Like other sciences, economics has two sides: the theories and the facts. The theory of choice in economics is of great generality in the sense that it applies to any choice problem, whether it be the choice between consumption now and consumption later, as discussed above, or the choice between allocating resources now between alternative uses, including the protection of the environment and the reduction of pollution, or the choice made by the reader of this book between reading it and reading something else or going to the cinema or spending his time in any other way. But the basic principles remain the same, as well as the neutrality of the economist concerning the relative preferences of the chooser which have to enter into the choice decision. Anybody who wishes to dissent from the economic principles bearing on the choice between alternative rates of growth or alternative levels of expenditure on pollution abatement, for example, should either say what is wrong with the basic economic principles of rational choice, or show why the criteria used by the economist to apply these principles to the particular problems of the environment or growth are inconsistent with the basic theory. For there is no other economist's contribution to the debate, apart from the fact that it will generally be the economist who is left to collect some of the data (for example, estimates of the costs or valuations of benefits) that, according to this logic of choice, as applied to the particular problem in hand, appear to be relevant. Of course, it is legitimate to discuss critically the data that the economists concerned may have collected; but this is no more a general criticism of the economist's contribution to the problem than would a critical discussion of some of the data collected by scientists be a criticism of scientific method.[14]

cost benefit analysis

Now what is this economic theory of choice? Basically, it begins with the trivial proposition that rational choice means weighing up the pros and cons of alternative courses of action. But economic theory has, of course, developed a much more precise and sophisticated analysis of what this means in terms of people's objectives, tastes and preferences, on the one hand, and the feasible alternatives on the other hand, and what they logically imply about rational behaviour, whether of an individual or a society, given certain very basic but trivial axioms, or definitions of rational behaviour. But there is no need to go into these in order to make the points at issue here. For this purpose we can manage with the simple and trivial results of the following kind.

Consider the time-honoured example of Robinson Crusoe on his island, and suppose that he is in a situation such that one banana gives him as much satisfaction as a pineapple, but he can find three pineapples in the time it would take him to find one banana. Obviously he would be well advised to spend more time looking for pineapples. It should be noticed that there is no need for money, or prices, to enter into this proposition. In the case of Robinson Crusoe on his island, it takes him three times as long to find a banana as to find a pineapple, so that his 'exchange rate' of bananas to pineapples is one banana to three pineapples. Since this ratio is less than the ratio of his relative preference of bananas to pineapples (one to one) the theory tells us that he would be well advised to spend more time collecting pineapples and less in collecting bananas. It can also easily be shown that he will have reached the optimum distribution of his time where the two ratios are equal, i.e., when his relative satisfactions from bananas and pineapples equal the relative amount of time required to obtain them.

It should also be noted that this basic proposition is not confined to material goods or needs. It applies equally well to spiritual or non-material satisfactions. Robinson Crusoe would

be well advised to apply the same principle even if he is choos-
ing between spending some more time collecting bananas and
spending the time admiring the sunset or listening to the parrots. Assuming that Robinson knows what he is doing it will
still be true that, at the margin, the value to him of one more
minute spent listening to the parrots on his island (i.e. one
minute of 'music') will be the same to him as the value of whatever he could catch in one minute in the way of, say, fish, or
what fruit he could find in one minute.

The economist does not, as a matter of principle, define
what enters Crusoe's pattern of relative preferences. These
might not even include, in Crusoe's case, *maximizing* current
food consumption; he might want to fast or to lose weight, or
to put aside some food in order to eat more later, or to make
offerings to the gods. In modern society most people might
include leisure among their objectives, and businessmen might
include power, or growth, or a quiet life. Again, much of the
popular criticism of what is thought to be the economist's
assumption of an economic man who is materialistic, or who
ought to be, is based on a misconception of the content of
economic theory. The formal rules of optimal choice apply
whatever objectives one is trying to maximize.

As pointed out above, money need not enter into the
optimization rules at all. It is only used because it happens to be
a convenient unit for expressing the amount of one good that
has to be sacrificed in order to get more of another. In Robinson
Crusoe's case, he would think in terms of *time*, since there
would be no money and no prices. Thus, there is absolutely
nothing necessarily 'materialistic' at all about the basic logic of
choice in economics. It would be just as valid if everything
were compared in terms of Beethoven quartets. The notion
that economists are somehow narrow, base, and commercial-
minded materialists, because they tend to be concerned with
monetary values, whereas conservationists and ecologists are
motivated by high-minded, virtuous, noble and spiritual
considerations, is a travesty of the truth.

Given the sort of conclusions that some extremist conservationists usually arrive at, frequently on the basis of alarmist and

contentious 'facts' or dubious logic, which always manage to come out in support of their pet prejudices and pastimes, irrespective of what the rest of society may have to sacrifice in the way of higher consumption of food, housing, education, medical care, and so on, my personal view is that they have absolutely nothing to be high-minded about. The middle classes, in particular, have always been very hot on morality, particularly when it coincides with their own interests. Hence, rather than come clean and say that they prefer to use resources for the purposes that they happen to approve of, even if the total value to society of these pursuits is less than the value of the other things that will have to be sacrificed, they naturally prefer to present the matter as one of high moral and spiritual values, by contrast with the base materialist approach of 'the economist'. Their intuition in picking on the economist is sound, for it is precisely the economist's logic of choice that tends to expose the fact that the extreme conservationist is asking the rest of society to make a sacrifice greater than the value of what society gets in return, simply in order to pander to the special preferences of one group of people.

To return to the basic principles of optimum choice, it should be noted that the economist as such does not take any view at all on what the relative tastes of Robinson Crusoe should be. He would not say to Robinson Crusoe: 'My dear chap, it is foolish of you to spend so much time listening to parrots instead of catching more fish since fish are delicious round here and I don't like parrot music myself.' The economist *may* have ideas about the relative value of these alternative ways of spending his own time that would differ from those of Robinson, but one cannot generalize about the way in which they would differ. Similarly, one cannot generalize about the relative importance that economists may attach to pollution, or material output, or nature. I know two distinguished economists who are fanatical ornithologists, and would tend to have unusual preferences as between watching birds and watching the television. But they would not dissent from the preceding analysis of the logic of choice and its application to the environment.

Another feature of Crusoe's choice problem, as with the growth problem discussed earlier, is that the optimum choice for the chooser depends on matching two things. First, to stick to Robinson Crusoe, there are his 'tastes' – that is, the pattern of his relative preferences as between fruit, fish and listening to birds singing; eating now or later; work or leisure; and so on. Secondly, his choice will depend on the technical opportunities open to him, namely, the technical matter of how much time he has to give up in order to satisfy each of these objectives – for example, the time it takes to catch one more fish compared with the time it takes to find one more banana.

Now if we had several islands, each with a Robinson Crusoe, there are obviously two reasons why they might differ in their choice as between the various ways they spend their time. First, the relative time required to catch fish or fruit or find birds with good voices might differ from island to island. Secondly, even if the relative time required to find fish or fruit were the same on all the islands, one Robinson, for example, might still spend more time catching fish than another – for he might simply like fish more than fruit. Each could allocate his time optimally, and the economist would not dream of saying that since they chose differently one or more of them must be wrong.

The economic advisers to the various Robinson Crusoes would only want to say to each: 'If that is your relative preference for fish and fruit and that is the time required to obtain each then *your* optimum choice would be such and such.' Now, on one island Man Friday may come along and think that inadequate time is spent on catching fish, because he rates fish more highly. But it would be wrong of him to accuse Robinson's economic adviser of having a bias against fish. If he did so, even after the situation had been patiently explained to him, one could only conclude that it was he, Man Friday, who was biased – in favour of fish. Similarly, in the context of the pollution problem, if economists tend to advocate that not so much should be spent on the environment as many extreme environmentalists or conservationists would like, this is not because the economist has some special set of preferences in which the environment carries relatively less weight than it does in the preferences of society as a whole. It will be because the economist knows that, given society's relative preferences for the environment *and* all other goods and services, and given the technical constraints determining how much other goods and services society has to sacrifice in order to get more environmental welfare, he judges that some compromise has to be reached at a point where the environment is still not as completely pure as the extreme conservationists would like.

It emerges from all this that there are only two possible grounds on which Man Friday may legitimately complain about the advice that the economist is giving to Robinson Crusoe. First, he may say that the economist has made a mistake in evaluating the relative priorities that Robinson attaches to his various objectives. Secondly, he may say that the economist has erred in measuring the technical relationships on the island – i.e. the relative costs, in terms of time, of pursuing one activity rather than another. For example, he may say that the economist has overlooked the existence of some stream where fish may be caught much more easily than had been thought. But he has no grounds for inferring that the economist must have a lower preference for fish than does Crusoe, and that he is being guided by this rather than by Crusoe's preferences.

Unfortunately, this is precisely the sort of criticism of the economist's contribution to the pollution debate that is frequently made by many conservationists, ecologists, and so on, who assume that the economist somehow or other attaches less importance to the preservation of the environment than does society, so that the economist's advice will mean a less than optimum devotion of effort to environmental preservation (from the point of view of society). What they rarely present is any hard reason or evidence for believing that the economist systematically errs in his estimation of society's preferences or of the technical relationships which enter into the choice decision. Where they do make some allusion to these aspects of the question they are usually simply mistaken about the way the economist does, in fact, evaluate these preferences. For example, they will frequently assert that the economist does not evaluate amenity, or evaluates it at below its true social costs, both of which assertions are untrue in principle, though in practice there will no doubt be mistakes of estimation in either direction.

Finally, an apparently completely different, and perhaps even simpler way of looking at the weakness of the extreme conservationist school of thought is as follows. Consider a simplified case where the value of the fish in some stretch of water was estimated at £5,000 (and there were no related secondary activities). Suppose it is argued that the present generation should have no right to pollute the area in question, even if the cost of avoiding the pollution were greater than this. But where do we stop? Suppose the value is only £5; or only 5p? Would it still be argued that the fish should be preserved? If so, this would imply turning over the whole of national product to the preservation of fish, for there must be an infinite number of cases where the value (or potential value in a thousand years' time) of some reduction in current pollution would be positive, even if estimated at only a few pence-worth. Now presumably nobody would go as far as this? But where does one stop? Or, to be more precise, what are the criteria for deciding where to stop? The economic theory set out above does at least make the criteria clear and explicit: you stop when the value to society of the improved environment is less than the value to society of the other things it will have to sacrifice in order to achieve the improved environment. Conservationists should either provide alternative criteria or demonstrate that the above criteria are wrongly applied. So far they have done neither.

The growth issue is simply another form of the choice problem. How should society choose between consumption today and consumption tomorrow? Those who would choose to stop economic growth must justify their stopping place. After all, what is special about the current level of national product? Why stop it here, rather than, say, at 0·5 per cent per annum growth? Should there even be some reduction in national product? What are the criteria that determine what is the optimum growth rate allowing for environmental pollution? Economists know what they are and how, at least in principle, they should be applied, but I have not yet heard any alternative criteria from the anti-growth school of thought.

The whole point is that 'all-or-nothing' solutions rarely make sense. It would be like Man Friday telling Robinson Crusoe that since he likes fish he should spend *all* his time fishing. Where objectives conflict some criteria have to be worked out for deciding on the optimum compromise between them. Only in the Garden of Eden are there no constraints on human choice. Economics shows what these criteria must be in general and what the empirical counterparts of these criteria are in special instances.

Growth versus the environment

It has been argued above that the growth problem is a problem of choice between consumption today and consumption tomorrow. How can this be reconciled with the belief that there is also a conflict between growth and the environment? Without entering into the controversy over the *desirability* of economic growth, or even the *feasibility* of sustained economic growth, it is worth repeating and developing the relatively non-controversial technical point made above. This is that the only economic cost of growth that really has to be incurred by any society is the consumption that has to be foregone in order to release resources for investment, since it is by investing that economies grow. If societies want to grow faster they must reduce consumption today (assuming that they are fully employed). The sacrifice of current consumption would no doubt be spread over innumerable components of final output (that is, gross national product), including food, clothing, health, education, and so on, and might also include some sacrifice of the resources currently devoted to protecting the environment. It is only in this sense, therefore, that it can be said that the environment is being sacrificed to economic growth; but this is a trivial and misleading way of putting the problem, for in this sense, it is also true that all other current uses of resources that have been cut have been sacrificed in the interests of faster growth. Hence, if it can be said that there is a conflict between growth and the environment, it is equally true that there is a conflict between growth and food consumption or clothing consumption, or any other ingredient of current standards of living. In other words, one does not choose between consumption tomorrow and the environment today; the choice is between consumption tomorrow and consumption today, irrespective of how consumption today or tomorrow is distributed between the environment and other uses of output.

This does not mean that there is no problem of choice concerning the environment. The environment itself forms a component of the standard of living, and is itself 'consumed'. It may well be that if more resources are devoted to investment now in order to protect the future environment future welfare would be raised more than it is cut at present. In other words, society can take advantage of a desirable investment opportunity today, like the struggling young man in my earlier example who should invest at the 25 per cent rate of return. But the young man in question should weigh up *all* his investment opportunities, in the same way that society should not single out for special treatment any one particular way in which the sacrifice of some consumption today will enable it to enjoy more consumption at a later date, whether this be in the form of improved environment, or in that of generally higher productive potential, which society may spend in any way it likes, including improving the environment. If an investment of £100 today would directly add to the future benefits of the environment by an amount valued (today) at more than £100 the investment should be made. But the same applies to any other investment, and in so far as such opportunities exist the growth rate should be raised by investing more now, that is, by cutting some other consumption. If a sacrifice of consumption today of £100 for purposes of investing in the environment can only yield an extra £90-worth of future welfare from the environment then it should not be undertaken.* The correct choice can

* There are, of course, enormous practical and conceptual problems involved in actually estimating the value people would attach to an improved environment. But these are quite irrelevant to the logic of the principle set out here.

only be made after analysis of the relative valuations that society places on the environment, the rate at which society compares future satisfactions of all kinds with present satisfactions, and the technical conditions determining how much investment now is, in fact, needed in order to achieve a given improvement in the environment in the future.

These are difficult things to evaluate, and no economist can pretend that the knowledge is available to make precise correct choices. The difficulties arise not merely on account of defects in the economic valuations of the items that must be considered. The required scientific and technical data are also not available in most cases. Extremist campaigns against 'materialist', 'myopic', 'complacent' or 'short-sighted' people, who want to allow economic growth to continue and who refuse to give absolute priority to the environment, add nothing to our knowledge of what we really want to know in order to arrive at those decisions that are best for society today and tomorrow.

Choice and income distribution

In the above Robinson Crusoe story the only role given to Man Friday was that of questioning Robinson's choice on the grounds that it may not have matched Man Friday's particular preference patterns. But the entry of Man Friday on to the scene is far more important than that. It introduces a completely new dimension into the whole problem of optimal social choice. When Crusoe is all alone the economic problem is relatively simple, namely, how to allocate his resources in such a way as to maximize his consumption over time. But as soon as there is more than one person involved there is a further new allocation problem to be considered. This is, how to allocate consumption between the various people; the problem of income distribution. In other words, we have the two basic economic objectives mentioned at the outset of this chapter: maximizing the size of the cake and achieving the desired share-out of the cake. This is extremely important in the context of

the environmental problem. For, as already indicated, some of
the pressures to allocate more resources to the environment
imply taking more away from certain members of the community than might be justified in terms of the welfare of society
taken as a whole.

This even has serious implications for the calculation of what
is the 'maximum' level of total consumption in general, and
what is the optimum level of environmental protection in particular. It is increasingly recognized that cost-benefit rules for
dealing with environmental protection should not be applied
mechanically. The economist is aware of the fact that the structure of the prices and costs that enter into these calculations
depends very much on the pattern of demand in society and
that this, in turn, depends very much on the income distribution. In respect of environmental policy, this is likely to be
extremely important. For although the poorer groups in society
are more likely to be the victims of a bad environment than are
the richer groups, who can more readily move away from
noisy or polluted localities, they are also likely to attach
relatively more importance to increased material consumption or better housing or better working conditions in factories
than the latter (see also Chapter 2, p. 56). At the same time,
in so far as the costs of greater environmental protection are
passed on in higher prices, the effect on income distribution
might well be regressive.[15]

To some extent even the growth problem is a problem of
income distribution. For the distribution of consumption over
time implies a distribution of consumption between different
generations of people. In deciding, therefore, to limit consumption now in order to improve the environment (or other components of consumption) in the future we are, to some extent,
deciding to re-distribute consumption away from present
generations in favour of future generations. It should not be
assumed, without question, that this is a more egalitarian distribution. Future generations may be much richer anyway. And
there is little doubt that a large proportion of the world's population alive today are very poor by any standards. Hence, the
principle of less consumption today or in the immediate future

in order to provide higher standards of living for remote future generations should not be accepted as being obviously on the side of virtue and the angels.

On the other hand, it may well be that faster growth is a necessary condition for shifting the income distribution in a more egalitarian direction. Clearly it is easier to raise the relative position of the poorer members of the communities when this does not have to involve an absolute cut in the standard of living of the more affluent members of society. The more the incomes of the latter can be maintained, or kept rising, the easier it will be to reduce their *share* in total income. This is one of the reasons why, in spite of some obvious disadvantages of growth for the middle classes, it would not be in their true interests to have zero growth, since the pressures for rising living standards by the less affluent would still persist, and the only way these pressures could be satisfied in a zero-growth context would be by means of cuts in the living standards of the more affluent. *

The case for faster growth to permit a more egalitarian income distribution is similar to the case for faster growth in the interests of a more egalitarian distribution of total national consumption, by means of an increase in public expenditure financed out of taxation. For Galbraith has a point, of course, particularly in the U.S.A., where public consumption has been relatively neglected.[16] Many European countries are now finding that the fast increase in demand for services – educational, medical, and environmental – raises problems of taxable limits. These may well be more imaginary than real; but, like nervous disorders, it is no comfort to the sufferer to be told that they are all in the mind. They are there, just the same, and in so far as political decisions are influenced by the view that we are approaching the limits of taxable capacity, faster growth may be essential in order to achieve the desired increase in public expenditure. In other words, although it is important to distinguish analytically between the growth problem and the problem of how resources and income should be distributed at any point in time, this does not mean that the two things are

* See also further discussions of this point in Chapter 2.

not related. In so far as faster growth helps to achieve the desired income distribution, this should be taken into account in deciding how far resources should be allocated to faster growth.

The environment is a serious problem

To conclude this chapter, therefore, it has been argued that the growth problem and the environment problem are serious matters of social choice. Economists have elaborated a technique for analysing these problems of choice. In the light of this analysis it appears that various criteria have to be taken into account, notably society's preferences as between consumption today and consumption tomorrow; the amount of the former that has to be sacrificed in order to have more of the latter; the way that output at any moment of time should be allocated to different kinds of consumption, including that of the environment; and the way in which choices affect income distribution. These are difficult criteria to apply. The information needed in order to apply them accurately is usually not available, and very little serious work on the economics of the environment is being carried out.

At the same time, it cannot be assumed that the environment will look after itself in the absence of appropriate government policies. As is explained in more detail in subsequent chapters, the characteristic feature of the environment is that, for most practical purposes, nobody owns it. Hence, it is used and misused by individuals, firms, and, for that matter, public bodies as well, without any automatic restraint in the form of some obligation to compensate the owners for its use or to pay some other form of fee for its use. To some extent the situation has been remedied in the past, particularly in Britain, by controls of one kind or another. But now that the environment is becoming an increasingly important ingredient in the welfare of the public, an *ad hoc* system of controls that is not clearly founded on any criteria of rational choice can no longer be allowed to suffice. Much more attention must now be given to

2

the elaboration of rational criteria for environmental policy and to the collection of the data needed to apply them. Furthermore, any policies to influence resource allocation will affect income distribution. In a democratic society, therefore, it is essential that environmental policies are not influenced solely by the more powerful and articulate, though possibly minority interests, for whom other needs, such as food, clothing, housing and working conditions, are now less important. The implementation of environmental policies raises important issues concerning the decision-making machinery to be used.

Another reason for public intervention in environmental matters is the 'public good' character of many of the measures needed in order to preserve and clean up the environment. That is to say, some of the environmental services needed are similar to traditional public services, such as the provision of basic hygiene facilities, the control of infectious diseases, the institutions of law and order, and so on. The market mechanism cannot be expected to supply the socially optimum amount of such services, so that the state has to fill the gap; but the gap will not be filled in the absence of well-informed and responsible public pressures. Extreme conservationist propaganda is not likely to cut much ice with politicians, who (i) know that no party could ever be elected to power on a zero-growth policy even if it were the right one, and (ii) are at least sufficiently in touch with the public to know that there are many serious needs other than the need to protect the environment that still have to be provided with resources.

It is much more debatable whether governments should intervene in the market for raw materials in order to ensure that growth will not be brought to a sudden halt by the exhaustion of such materials. While there is no doubt that the pollution problem arises largely out of a failure of the free-market mechanism to bring about the optimum allocation of resources to environmental protection and preservation, the same cannot be said of the problem of raw-material supply. There are usually clearly defined property rights in mineral resources, and, as argued at length in a later chapter, the market mechanism has, hitherto, usually ensured that, sooner or later, either increasing demand for materials has always been matched by increasing supplies, or that some other automatic adjustment mechanism has operated. In general government intervention has been desirable only in exceptional circumstances, such as those of war. The case for government intervention to ensure long-run supplies of raw materials would have to rest on the assumption that governments would be better than private industry at forecasting future trends in exploration, or in technologies for mining and extraction and for the use of the raw materials, or in technical changes determining the demand for the end-products, and so on. There is no reason to make such an assumption. This does not mean that private industry always gets it right; it doesn't, but it usually pays for its mistakes, and this is a better arrangement than if such mistakes were to become ammunition in political battles.

To conclude, the environmental problem and the growth problem are special cases of the general problem of resource allocation. They raise issues of the allocation of resources over time, and of the allocation of resources at any moment of time as between the environment and other uses, and as between different groups in society. The unaided free-market mechanism will not usually lead to a socially optimum allocation of resources to the environment, particularly as regards pollution, which is why a substantial section of this book is devoted to the problems of pollution, the policies needed to solve them, and the likely costs of such policies. But there is still a problem of how we use the growth of national product that we are likely to have, and that, in my view, society is probably well advised to pursue.

There is also a problem of how to achieve faster growth in Britain without excessive costs of one kind or another, but this book is chiefly about why economic growth is still an important source of increased welfare and why it can be safely pursued without fear of environmental catastrophe. The fact that not enough resources have been allocated to environmental protection in the past means neither that economic growth is too rapid nor that unlimited resources should be allocated to the environment in the present. The preservation of the environment is only one particular use of resources, which are still scarce in the fields of housing, working conditions, schools, hospitals, and so on. How the growth of the economy is to be used, therefore, is too serious a problem to be taken over by extremists of any kind.

2 Passengers on the Anti-Growth Bandwagon

In the following chapters it will be argued that much of the case for deliberate slowing down of economic growth is based on a series of errors of logic, distortions or ignorance of the facts, and special pleading of various kinds.* If all these strong assertions are true, it might be asked how it has been possible for the anti-growth movement to enjoy such wide support and achieve such prominence in the space of the last few years. The answer is that the strength of the movement does not depend on the validity of its arguments; it depends on the fact that it happens to appeal simultaneously to various very different groups and forces in society. The main groups seem to be as follows:

The mass media

Catastrophe is always good news. The public as a whole likes to hear about the imminence of disaster and about the fact that they are living on the edge of a precipice. Most people lead lives that are drab and monotonous and are confined to boring and routine jobs. The suggestion that, after all, they are living dangerously and that the world may go up in smoke any day adds a sort of *frisson* to their lives. Bad news has always been better for publicity than good news.

Some of the media of mass communications, therefore, blow up out of all proportion the magnitude of environmental problems or the obstacles and objections to sustained economic growth. One recent example of a failure to give all the relevant

* There are exceptions to this, of course. Some of the anti-growth writings of Dr Mishan are of a high technical level, as are also some of the contributions by Boulding, Galbraith, and others. See also, for example, *Toward a Steady-State Economy*, edited by Herman Daly (W. H. Freeman and Co., San Francisco, 1973).

facts and hence to prevent the average reader from drawing the wrong conclusions was an article in *The Observer* under the headline 'Cut in growth as price of clean air'. This article was a summary of a report produced by a team of experts on air pollution, for the O.E.C.D., concerning the costs of reducing air pollution.[1] The article stated that according to this report, 'For the O.E.C.D. area, the cost of reducing the 1980 sulphur-dioxide emissions to the 1968 level will be between $5,800 million and $15,600 million for capital investments and $2,200 million and $4,200 million for operating costs – all for the one year.'[2]

Now these figures may seem enormous to the layman, who might be expected to infer, presented with such sums, that the headline must be right and that expenditures of this order of magnitude must reduce economic growth.* In fact, however, compared with the size of the O.E.C.D. economies taken as a whole, the amounts involved are relatively insignificant. In the first place, the report explicitly stated that the capital costs were not annual requirements but were the amounts that would have to be spent by 1980, and it was suggested that they should be spread over about six years (1974 to 1980). Hence, if the total capital costs are spread over six years, as suggested in the report, one arrives at an annual figure for *all* costs (capital and current) of between $5·15 billion and $8·75 billion.†

But it would not have required much further research to have been able to report that the combined GNP of the O.E.C.D. countries was already over $2,000 billion in 1970. Given any reasonable expectation about growth rates by 1980, the average GNP during the years when the above expenditures would have to be carried out would be about $2,600 billion. This means that the vast programme to cut air pollution to

* The implication of the figures could be taken to be that they constitute a direct diversion of resources from investment, or consumption (in which case the profitability of investment would tend to be reduced and hence investment indirectly discouraged).

† This includes, in addition to the costs of reducing sulphur oxides mentioned above, the costs given in the report for reducing nitrogen oxides and other major air pollutants.

which the above figures refer would represent only about 0·2 per cent to 0·34 per cent of GNP. The article also failed to inform readers that *the report itself pointed out* that the capital costs of the programme in question only amounted to between 0·6 per cent and 1·0 per cent of total investment in the O.E.C.D. area. *

The bias shown by some of the media of mass communication over the environment issue is apparent over and over again. If a few hundred fish are found to have been killed by the accidental discharge of some toxic pollutant in a river there are headlines in some of the newspapers. But how far is the public kept informed of, for example, the sort of good news mentioned in Chapter 3 below such as the fall in the number of fatal factory accidents, the reductions in, or virtual elimination of, many diseases, and so on? How often is some scare story that has been prominently written up (such as the 'glasshouse' theory about the earth becoming too hot, or the one about all the oxygen in the atmosphere being used up, or the dangers of carbon monoxide concentrations in the streets caused by car exhausts) given further space when, as is often the case, it is shown by generally accepted scientific authorities to have been erroneous?[3]

The old slogan that good news is no news is partly responsible for the dissemination of undue alarm about environmental catastrophe. In 1972 some newspapers made a fuss about the danger of lead poisoning at the R.T.Z. zinc smelter at Avonmouth, and the public knew all about it. How much effort was put into informing the public that the subsequent inquiry into the matter showed that 'only mild symptoms were recorded and there was no evidence of serious or lasting damage to health', let alone other facts about industrial hazards, such as that total industrial accidents in 1970 were 40 per cent down on

---

* Furthermore, these figures are probably on the high side, for the truth of the matter is that one does not know how little or how much it will cost to reduce pollution once policies designed to achieve this objective have been put into operation. For the technology is quite new in many cases, so that the estimates available now, such as they are, tend to be conservative estimates by accountants and engineers on the basis of existing techniques, and without making allowance for the fact that, if a new technique is installed to reduce pollution, it will almost certainly embody other recent technical improvements as well.

the 1960 level, half of the 1950 level, and one-sixth of the 1900 levels?

Scientists

It is probably no accident that, although many eminent scientists have openly voiced strong criticisms of the eco-doomsters,* the leading eco-doomsters are often scientists of one kind or another. After all, they provide the apparently expert authority for the various scare stories about the accumulation of heavy metals or synthetic chemical compounds like PCBs (polychlorinated biphenyls) or DDT, or about the effects on health of lead in the atmosphere, or the effect on the climate of carbon-dioxide accumulation, and so on. It is not the layman or the social scientist who is going to think up this sort of anti-growth argument.

It is easy to understand, and hence to forgive, this tendency for many scientists to be highly critical of some of the uses to which applied science and technology has been put. The scientific community probably has a sort of collective guilt complex concerning certain scientific developments over the last two or three decades, notably the atom bomb, and also the increasing knowledge of even more destructive ways of wiping out mankind as a result of 'progress' in biological and botanical sciences. The public finds it easier to blame scientists for the use to which their knowledge has been put rather than to blame the politicians and hence the public who elect them. The scientific community has acquired, therefore, a reputation for having an inadequate sense of social responsibility, and for having failed to ensure that scientific expertise was never exploited for purposes that were against the interests of mankind. How much justice there is in this sort of allegation is not a question on which I am able to make an informed judgment. The point made here is simply that, rightly or wrongly, this view has been

* The 'eco-doomsters' are those who prophesy doom for the economy, the ecology, and the human race, unless economic growth is slowed down to some usually unspecified rate.

fairly widespread, and many scientists are no doubt conscious of it. Furthermore, until relatively recently science had come to occupy a revered position in society. The impressiveness of scientists' technical achievements meant that science became oversold; society began to believe that science and technology would solve all its problems. When, in addition to creating new problems arising out of the fearful means of destruction that had been developed, it became clear that science also had little to contribute – at least not yet – to other major social problems, such as the problems of inequality, crime, drugs, racial tolerance, and so on, the fickle public went too far and began to blame science and technology for all the ills of present-day society.

Consequently, there must be powerful, if subconscious, pressures on many scientists to demonstrate to the world that they are, in fact, oozing with moral fibre and very much alert to their social responsibilities. And what can demonstrate this more firmly than if scientists themselves come out against the economic growth that, to a large extent, is a by-product of their labours? It needs strong-minded scientists, proud of their contributions to man's knowledge and confident of their own value to society, to resist this temptation to be loved by the public. It is perhaps for this reason that, on the whole, it is not the more eminent scientists who have succumbed to the temptation to be loved by the laymen even at the cost of losing the respect of their colleagues.

In addition, there is, no doubt, a phenomenon of centrifugal force at work in the sciences as in any other discipline. This takes the form of ensuring that the weaker members of the profession, who cannot sustain the pace and pressures at the centre of their subject, get thrown out to the periphery, where they can survive happily because they are specialists in some esoteric field that nobody else knows anything about. It is easy there to get away with third-rate work. As Professor Petr Beckmann points out:

> Especially among the most radical apostles of apocalypse, one often finds the young and inexperienced ex-scientist

2*

who was a mediocrity in his original field. His theories are founded on such flimsy and one-sided evidence, and sometimes on no evidence at all, that one can soon discard the theory that his obsessions are rooted in dispassionate and patient scientific research. More likely, he is taking the short cut to glory. Death is frightening and interesting, and he is the man in the know; He becomes Medicine Man and Messiah in one. He does not use voodoo dolls, but digital computers ... [4]

But some eminent scientists have subscribed publicly to some of the most absurd examples of eco-doomster literature, such as the famous *Blueprint for Survival*, which was signed by five Fellows of the Royal Society and sixteen holders of science chairs in British universities.[5] One can only conclude that some scientists who may be world authorities on certain phenomena pertaining to the physical world do not have a minimal understanding of the way that the world of human beings operates in general, or, in particular, the way that society reacts to problems such as pollution and demands for raw materials.[6] After all, this requires a different sort of knowledge: a knowledge of the human being in his social context. Some scientists have, perhaps, become scientists precisely to shield themselves from these phenomena and to escape into a world where problems are not on a human scale, but microscopic or astronomic. These scientists cannot be expected to know much about what goes on outside their microscopes or telescopes or abstract mathematical manipulations, and there is no reason why they should. Some scientists may even be quite stupid outside their particular specialities, as is sometimes the case with specialists in any subject. But it is a pity that these particular scientists do not keep to their specialities and that they insist, instead, on showing that they, too, are interested in, and aware of, the problems of the world outside. Their technical expertise too readily guarantees them a hearing among the audience of those greedy for ammunition in the doomsday debate.

Radical Youth

Poor old radical youth; it is hard not to sympathize with them, for their intentions, too, are of the best. But they are often misguided; on this issue they have unwittingly been led into the reactionary camp, and have been diverted from the really important social issues of today. Again, this is perfectly understandable. Young people are more idealistic than the rest, perhaps; and part of their emancipation from childhood is a rejection of society's generally accepted values, together with a rejection of parental control. And rejection of the values expressed through the market mechanism is a highly convenient place to start since it fits very nicely with a general condemnation of the corrupting influence of capitalism and big business, and links up closely, so it is thought, with Marx's concept of alienation. What could be a better issue, therefore, than to attack economic growth in general and, in addition, press for more resources to be devoted to improving the environment and the 'quality of life'.

But all the poor countries of the world reject the anti-growth doctrine, since they know that poverty means degradation, misery and starvation. They also know that continued growth is not only essential in their own countries in order to eliminate abject poverty, but that it is also essential for them that the developed countries continue to grow in order to provide expanding markets for their products.

The workers in the advanced countries are not keen to slow down growth either, if this only means helping to preserve the salmon streams and grouse moors of the rich. They know that the environment that matters to them is chiefly the noise and stench and generally dismal surroundings in which most of them spend their working time, which is a good part of their lives, or the unsatisfactory housing conditions in which they spend most of their leisure.

At the Labour Party Conference in October 1972 one of the delegates (Mr Douglas Eden) said bluntly that the environmental issue was above all about slum housing, primitive working conditions, derelict and badly used land and depressing surroundings, which was an issue bearing hardest on the poor, and was not about preserving the grouse moors for Sir Alec Douglas-Home or yacht marinas for Mr Heath. Unfortunately, the more vociferous and extreme youthful environmentalists concentrate precisely on the 'glamorous' issues, like those of DDT, or the carbon-dioxide build-up, or the pollution of the oceans from heavy metals or synthetic chemical compounds which have very little bearing on the environment that the workers worry about.

It is a pity, too, that pollution of the environment cannot be truthfully attributed solely to the greed of capitalist society, in which production is purely for profit and where there is no social control over the use of resources. For there has been increasing awareness recently of the terrible pollution in the Soviet countries. In the U.S.S.R., for example, many of the worst instances of serious pollution have been publicized in the Soviet press, as well as documented by foreign experts, such as Marshall Goldman.[7] For example, the acute air-pollution crises in Soviet cities such as Sverdlovsk and Magnitogorsk in 1967 appeared to be worse than anything experienced in Britain for at least ten years. Similarly, an oil and chemical fire on the polluted Volga river, which required the firemen to 'put out the river', had to be publicized widely in the U.S.S.R. in order to generate support for a waste treatment programme. The serious damage done to Lake Baikal, which was once one of the most beautiful of the world's major lakes, is also common knowledge. This is a lake which once contained some unique forms of life and was of enormous interest to geologists, biologists and scientists of many kinds. But in the late 1950s some Soviet planners decided that it would be a perfect site for a group of cellulose plants, and cellulose is a process that requires pure water and huge timber supplies. By the late 1960s the serious damage to the lake became evident to the local ecologists, who were able to spark off a national outcry.[8]

There are innumerable other well-publicized instances of serious pollution and environmental damage in the U.S.S.R. Timber resources have been badly managed, leading to extensive erosion and other unfavourable environmental effects, which have been made famous in the novel *The Russian Forest*, by Leonid Leonov. Two great inland seas, the Caspian and the Aral sea, seem to be facing serious problems of water depletion as well as pollution. And it was recently officially stated that the amount of pollution entering into the country's waters would, in the absence of emergency action, increase six or sevenfold by 1980; and, according to an article in the weekly journal *Nedelya*, Siberia might be deprived of pure water in ten to fifteen years' time.[9] For it does not require the profit motive to make procedures ignore the environmental consequences of their activity. As Mr Kirillin, Deputy Prime Minister of the U.S.S.R., said in the course of the extremely frank discussion of environmental problems in the Supreme Soviet in September 1972, many firms had not taken account of the new anti-pollution regulations introduced back in 1963, since individual factory managers are constantly under pressure to fulfil quotas and make productive use of capital.[10] In other words, production goals can be as destructive of the environment as profit goals. If society does not attach much value to the environmental objectives no particular economic mechanism is likely to protect the environment.

Nor is pollution confined to the U.S.S.R. among the Soviet-bloc countries. Submissions made by national delegates to the United Nations Symposium on Environmental Problems in Prague, in May 1971, revealed similar severe pollution in the other Eastern European countries. For example, according to the Czechs, more than 40 per cent of the population living in the western half of the country are exposed to air pollution exceeding the legal limits. By 1967 the poisoning of air by chemical factories in North Bohemia reached such catastrophic proportions that the local authorities were temporarily obliged to evacuate the children. In Poland few communities have adequate sewage facilities, so that most rivers cannot serve as sources of drinking water and many will not support fish life. At the same time Polish air pollution is considered to be even worse than the water pollution. Similar reports come from East Germany, where 'as for the influential party organization in the factory, it will suffer no anti-pollution nonsense which would interfere with output and bonuses'.[11]

It is true, however, that the Eastern-bloc countries now appear to have begun to take the environment seriously. For example, under the present Five-Year Plan, Poland will build 800 new sewage-treatment plants. But the point is that, until very recently, the environment in the Soviet bloc had been neglected as much as, if not more than, in the greedy capitalist West. After all, the Polish director of the anti-pollution department in the new Environment Ministry stated in 1972: 'This is the first time that environmental considerations have been included as an integral part of Government policy, and are being treated on a par with economic factors in drawing up the five-year-plan.'[12]

Perhaps all this is just a sign that economic growth has been accompanied by increasing adoption of a bourgeois style of life in the Communist countries, apart from China, of course. For the Chinese may have succeeded far better than the U.S.S.R. and the Eastern bloc in protecting the environment up to now, judging by reports of the Chinese concern with urban conditions and the place of the motor-car, for example.[13] But that still does not put them in the anti-growth camp, by any means. 'The possibility of man's exploitation and utilization of natural resources is inexhaustible', according to the opening speech of the Chinese delegate to the 1972 UNO Conference on the Human Environment.

It is also a pity that the radical youth busy chalking up slogans and organizing recycling weeks and so on have got their facts so wrong. The well-meaning young men who chalk on the walls slogans like 'carbon monoxide refreshes', with cigarettes hanging out of the corners of their mouths, presumably don't know that the amount of carbon monoxide in the lungs of a cigarette smoker is about ten times as much as that in the lungs of a policeman on traffic duty in the centre of a city. Nor do they realize that the damage done to the environment from recycling paper (on account of the extra pollution generated in the various transport and production processes involved) is certainly far greater than any harm done through the controlled use of timber resources as carried out nowadays by most forestry operations. In fact, the latter are beneficial to the environment in various ways.[14]

But again, the determination of much of modern youth to feel guilty about the environment is also perfectly understandable. Most of them – at least in developed countries – suffer from a subconscious guilt complex about their relative affluence. We live in an age where one of the major social issues of our time – if not *the* major social issue of our time – is equality. There are various reasons for this, including, no doubt, the growing conflict between, on the one hand, the hierarchical structure of society that appears to be needed in the interests of 'efficiency' and, on the other hand, the increasing awareness of the ideal of equality. The latter has been strengthened in so far as it has become increasingly obvious that the nominal equality which most people have now acquired in the political sphere has not yet spread to the economic sphere, and hence, to the social sphere. Before the war, the most obvious means of raising the welfare of the mass of the population was to eliminate chronic unemployment and instability, and also to achieve sustained economic growth. But, now that these two goals have been more or less achieved, the emphasis has naturally shifted to concern with greater equality as a means of further raising the welfare of the poorer members of the community. This is also a cause which, to their credit, appeals to the idealism of many young people. Hence, those who are among the more affluent sections of the community – particularly if the community is defined widely to include the underdeveloped countries – feel guilty about their relative good fortune.

One way of expiating this guilt is to attack the very prosperity of which they are the 'victims' – that is, to attack economic output and economic growth. This has the added advantage of demonstrating one's liberation from the rat-race, and one's rejection of material prosperity, without actually having to do anything about it or to give up anything. Concern with misfortune thousands of miles away is highly commendable, but often it is a subconscious excuse for not being sufficiently concerned about the problem of one's next-door neighbour. In exactly the same way, it is less costly to be concerned about problems that are a hundred years removed in time. A passionate concern with prosperity gives one a nice, warm, virtuous glow without there being any danger that one might have to do anything about it today. It is all very natural and understandable, and morally more creditable no doubt than naked and deliberate determination to stop economic growth in order to preserve one's grouse moors and to prevent the servants getting uppity. It is all the more pity that this particular outlet for the idealism of youth is, in fact, merely serving to protect those bourgeois interests of which the young are, in general, most contemptuous.

Furthermore, this particular bourgeois interest has taken the form of an anti-growth movement which, in the past, was more the prerogative of the extreme political right. As Keith Pavitt has pointed out, in Europe

It has often been the landowners and the traditional 'bourgeoisie' that have been against economic growth because they rightly saw economic growth as eroding their privileges and power. This is exemplified best by the Vichy regime which was set up in France during the Second World War. It had the ideal of a stable agricultural society where everybody knows his place, where the national emblem was not 'liberty, equality and fraternity' but 'family, work and country' ... In other words, it had the characteristics that would satisfy many contemporary social critics of economic growth and technological change. But it was founded on ignorance, repression, prejudice and poverty.[15]

Back to nature and the old simple life, where workers are respectful and seek no change, where women know their place in the kitchen and nursery: it all has the familiar ring of Nazi Germany as well as of its Vichyite imitators. Discipline, sacrifice, and stagnation; these are the ways to preserve the privileges of the rich and of the bourgeois whose relative position is constantly being threatened in a world of change and challenge. As Lenin said, 'The petty bourgeois, "furious" over the horrors of capitalism, is a social phenomenon which, like anarchism, is characteristic of all capitalist countries. The instability of such revolutionism, its barrenness, its ability to become swiftly transformed into submission, apathy, phantasy, and even into "mad" infatuation with one or another bourgeois "fad" – all this is a matter of common knowledge.'[16] I don't think that radical youth will be duped for long, and I expect that they will soon climb off the anti-growth bandwagon. But they will leave behind the chief group, and the group whose presence has provided all the real force behind the anti-growth bandwagon: the middle classes.

The middle classes

For the heart of the matter is that the anti-growth movement and the excessive concern with the environment is basically middle class. Like the idealistic youth discussed above, the middle classes today feel more guilty about their relative affluence than has been the case in the past. But that probably makes only a small contribution to their anti-growth fervour. A more important reason is probably that as people become richer the environment moves up in their ranking of priorities. The poor man worried about getting a square meal next day does not worry much about the insecticides that might be used in order to raise food output. Nor does the worker in a factory, where the carbon-monoxide concentration is allowed to rise to 50 parts per million all day long, worry much about the fact that it may rise to 20 p.p.m. for about two minutes a day in some parts of the city at peak travel hours. But the middle classes, who mainly work in pleasant surroundings and who possess, in their homes, the goods to satisfy most of their needs, turn their attention to other, and more external, aspects of the quality of life, particularly those (such as the environment) where, for the reasons given in Chapter 5, there is no automatic mechanism to ensure that increased needs are matched by increased supplies. Again, there is nothing wrong with that; after all, the middle classes are part of society, and one of the functions of a well-organized society is to protect legitimate minority interests. But these must not be allowed to pass as everybody's interests.

Furthermore, it is likely that the middle-class opposition to growth reflects partly their sense that economic growth also brings a loss of various privileges. For it is strange that some of the more influential spokesmen of the anti-growth lobby seem to be obsessed with typically middle-class matters. For example, Mishan is probably very representative in his outright condemnation of the evils of too many motor-cars in the streets.[17] When only the middle classes had cars, nobody worried about them – except those who were too poor to buy them. Of course, it is perfectly true that too many cars are allowed on the roads in many areas at many times of the day. This is because the market mechanism fails to make car-users cover the full social costs of their use of the cars, including the external cost of congestion that they impose on other drivers. But this has nothing to do with the growth issue; it is a question of the misallocation of resources at any moment of time.

Another typically middle-class obsession of Mishan and many of his supporters is concern about the way in which economic growth and cheap mass travel has led to an overcrowding of hitherto pleasant holiday retreats, thereby reducing the pleasure obtained previously by the small minority able to seek out these retreats. What had hitherto been quiet Greek islands full of charm and local character have now been transformed into coarse versions of Blackpool or Miami Beach, where all the hotels are more or less the same and where one meets the same people that one met back home. According to Mishan, the mystery of travel to foreign parts has been destroyed, the world made narrower and its variety shattered by the advent of cheap fast jet travel. This is a typically middle-class concern, for the *really* rich are not worried about the congestion on the Costa Brava. The *really* rich are quite safe from the masses in the very expensive resorts, or on their large yachts or private islands or secluded estates. On the whole it is the middle classes who find that all their old haunts have been overrun.

The narrow selfishness of the Mishan kind of complaint can be exposed by the following illustrative exercise, which consists of enumerating the various groups who will be affected in one way or another by an increased flow of tourists to hitherto secluded foreign resorts.

They are as follows:

(i) Some early pioneers, who are less happy now that their retreats have become popular and crowded.

(ii) Those pioneers who are more happy now that they are not alone. After all, many of the less affluent who continue to visit the same old haunts enjoy them much more since they became crowded. The natives have learnt to speak their language; they can get English newspapers; the plumbing and sanitation in the hotels is better; there is even beer and fish and chips and Bingo, and lots more entertainment. One can even easily meet the same sort of people one mixes with and likes back home.

(iii) Those people who could not go abroad to the Costa del Sol, Majorca, and so on, before, and who had to stay in Blackpool or wherever, but who now choose to go abroad. They presumably prefer it there – otherwise they wouldn't go there – and in that respect, therefore, their welfare has risen.

(iv) Those people who stay behind at Blackpool or wherever, and find it less congested. After all, given the number of people in the world, if it is more congested on the Costa Brava it must be less congested in Blackpool or other resorts which people have abandoned in order to go abroad. Congestion cannot increase everywhere as a result of easier travel.

(v) The local population, who have received enormous boosts in their incomes and standards of life. Instead of being obliged to work for pittances trying to scratch some sort of living out of rocky and infertile soils they run hotels, restaurants, shops, and a hundred-and-one tourist services. They make contact with the outside world (a form of the human contact that economic growth is supposed to destroy).

So out of these five groups who has lost? Only the first group, the middle-class elements that attached a high value to quiet and privacy among different surroundings. All the other groups affected, each of which, anyway, is probably much greater than the first group, have gained. So much for the disinterested, virtuous, moral fibre of those who scorn the vulgarity of progress.

Another revealing criticism of economic growth has taken the form of the argument that since the middle-class intelligentsia can no longer easily find domestic servants or others to do their various jobs round the house or garden they have to do them themselves, thereby reducing the time they have available for reflection and intellectual pursuits, which, it is added (in order, of course, to preserve the high moral tone of the whole argument), is essential for the proper functioning of criticism in a democratic society.[18]

For the fact is that the middle classes do lose by some of the changes associated with economic growth, such as reduced supply of personal services, congestion of certain facilities, and deterioration in an element of the quality of life that is increasingly important to them – namely the physical environment.[19] Furthermore, economic growth has been accompanied by changes in the labour market, including the increase in demand for skilled labour of all kinds and the rising power of organized labour of all kinds. These changes have eroded the hitherto privileged position of the middle classes. They feel increasingly vulnerable to pressures in society that leave them caught between the rising pressures for higher earnings by the trade unions and the resistance to profits squeezes by the capitalists. At the same time their relative economic security and their socio-economic exclusiveness is being eaten away by the economic changes in society and by some of the

accompanying changes in educational systems, and other ways
in which class barriers are being broken down.

Hence, as Passell and Ross have put it,

A less charitable interpretation of upper middle class
criticism of growth is that the elite understands it has more
to lose than gain from the diffusion of the bourgeois
standards throughout the United States ... Nature lovers
grieve for their loss of privacy in national parks as more
people can afford to make the trip. Skiers must endure
endless lift lines and reckless adolescents on busy slopes
where they once schussed in peace. Hit plays sell out
months in advance; opera tickets are unpurchasable;
grand cru Burgundy prices are bid up by noveaux wine
enthusiasts; vacationers must wait hours to pick up mail
at the London American Express. Prosperity means that
nobody wants to clean other people's homes, take care of
other people's children, or grease other people's cars.
Increasingly, service industries are manned by the resent-
ful poor instead of the cheerful daughters of the working
classes waiting to get married ... One of the virtues of a
winter vacation in the Caribbean used to be the uniqueness
of sporting a tan in January. Now this sign of affluence
is shared with a half-million secretaries who can afford a
week at the Montego Bay Holiday Inn.[20]

But the middle classes have always been very keen on
morality. Throughout the last two centuries, morality has
consisted of what happened to be convenient for the purposes
of the powerful middle classes in society, particularly the virtues of thrift and industriousness and respect for property
that were so useful during the industrial revolution.[21] Hence,
it was hardly conceivable that the middle classes would say
that economic growth had been fine so far, but that it had
gone far enough since they felt that they would now stand to
lose as much by further growth, if not more, than they would
gain from it. Such an unashamed avowal of their own narrow
interests would have been completely out of character. Instead,

therefore, the anti-growth crusade has been dressed up in all the trappings of moral righteousness. Economic growth is alleged to be not merely vulgar, coarse, materialist, and soul-destroying, but generally bad for everybody else as well, and the poor are advised not to be fooled into thinking that they, too, will like it when they are richer, for poor people have simply been brainwashed into acquiring lots of artificial needs; and poor countries have allowed the bad habits of richer countries to be thrust upon their simple, happy, primitive societies where, if people didn't exactly live happily ever after, they lived at least to the age of about thirty on the average. By contrast the anti-growth lobby is full of people of great delicacy and aesthetic sensibility, who love nature and the sound of the birds (so these must be protected from DDT, if not from men armed with shotguns who hunt for sport), and beautiful views of the countryside unspoilt by electricity pylons, and so on. But, as Anthony Crosland pointed out many years ago, 'Generally, those enjoying an above average standard of living should be rather chary of admonishing those less fortunate on the perils of material riches.'[22] Similarly, Richard Stone writes: 'The back-to-nature movement, which seems to have a certain vogue among modern youth, is acceptable only to affluent people who have no conception of what it entails. Those who live under primitive conditions look with hungry eyes on what they conceive, rightly in my opinion, to be the marvellous scientific and economic achievements of the West. It is cruelly frivolous to deny them the fruits of these achievements.'[23]

The accusation that environmentalism and the anti-growth movement is an elitist, middle-class concern is often countered by the argument that it is the working classes who suffer most from environmental pollution. For example, the working classes tend to live in the dirtiest parts of towns, or closest to smelly factories or noisy motorways. All this is quite true, and is another example of the probable misallocation of resources on account of the externality character of much environmental pollution. But two points need to be made in reply to this argument.

First, those aspects of the environment that the working classes are most concerned with are generally not the same as those that the more articulate and powerful middle classes tend to make all the fuss about. As Dr Murray, the medical adviser of the Trade Union Congress, said at the T.U.C.'s environmental conference in 1972, his members 'are not burning themselves up about the pollution of beaches and the noise around us. This is a middle class development.' He went on to add that his members complain about pollution when it affects them directly. Indeed, the trade unions have a tradition of concern with the environment in their places of work which is hardly shared by their employers. 'The steaming in the mills, the ghastly conditions in the mines and steel works have been alleviated by union pressures',[24] without much support from those who are now eager to publicize their concern with the quality of life.

One simple example of the way different classes in society are affected by, and react to, different aspects of the same type of pollution is the divergence between the noise conditions inside most factories and the noise conditions that are now deemed to be intolerable by those concerned with the environment in general. The Noise Advisory Council decided in 1971 that 70 decibels is the highest level of noise that should be borne by householders adjacent to motorways, which is all very well and desirable.[25] But a survey of noise conditions in factories showed that 90 decibels all day long was common in many parts of most factories, and a limit of 90 decibels has just been laid down by the Department of Employment in its Code of Practice.[26] Those who are familiar with the logarithmic scale used for measuring decibels will recognize that the noise level apparently accepted as tolerable all day long in factories is incomparably greater than that which is to be accepted in the environment in general.

All these aspects of the working environment, which the trade-union movement has been struggling against for decades, unaided by the vast majority of the middle classes, will still be unsatisfactory long after the current concern with the external environment has gone out of fashion. (Already it is reported that sales of *The Ecologist* have fallen by about 80 per cent over the past year or so.)[27] But the workers will not be able to forget quite so easily the working conditions that most of them see every day.

Secondly, even if it were true that the working classes were equally exposed to the same sort of pollution and environmental problems as seem to worry the middle classes, this does not imply that they would, or should, attach the same weight in their overall pattern of objectives to clearing up such pollution. For what determines the relative importance a person attaches to any particular objective is how far he has succeeded in meeting other objectives. To go back to the Robinson Crusoe illustration in Chapter 1, it may be assumed that if there are two Crusoes on different islands, with exactly the same physiological tastes and appetites and so on, so that each derived exactly the same satisfaction from eating varying amounts of bananas and hence each had the same interest, *other things being equal*, in allocating time to the search for bananas, they would still be advised to allocate their time differently if, on one island, drinking water was in unlimited and readily accessible supply, whereas on the other island it was very difficult to come by. Clearly, in the latter island, Crusoe would be well advised not to spend much time collecting bananas, but to concentrate first on finding water to drink. It would be absurd to tell him that he should spend as much time looking for bananas as does the other Crusoe, on the grounds that he likes them just as much – or even more. In the same way, the workers may live in the smelliest part of the city, but they still attach more importance to better food, clothing, housing, working conditions, and so on, than to the quality of the environment.

There is ample evidence that this is not merely a reasonable assumption to make about the way they *ought* to rank their preferences, but that it is, indeed, the way they do rank their preferences. For example, a survey of reactions to environmental conditions among people living around London airport showed that the middle-class respondents were much more likely to be aware of the pleasant or unpleasant features

of their environment than the working-class respondents.[28]
A sociological study conducted by the United States Public
Health Service in Clarkston, Washington, yielded the same
sort of results. For example, it was found that

> 44 per cent of the local managers, proprietors, and pro-
> fessional people – a group one would expect to have a
> greater frequency of relatively high incomes and wealth –
> were 'aware' of an air pollution problem and were
> seriously 'concerned' about its effect on their health and
> their real properties. However, only 32 per cent of the
> clerical and skilled laborers, and only 19 per cent of the
> semi-skilled and unskilled workers expressed a similar
> awareness and concern.[29]

The growth issue: a middle way

None of the above would matter if the various anti-growth
groups were merely misguided. But the middle classes which
provide much of the steam behind the anti-growth movement
are also powerful. They are articulate, they are the leading
figures in both right-wing and left-wing political parties; they
tend to dominate the media of communication and ideas, they
write most of the books, they give most of the lectures and
talks on the radio and television, and they are able to impose
their values on the classes above them as well as on the classes
below them. Nevertheless, the anti-growth movement would
still not have got very far if it had lacked the one essential
element of success; namely, that there is a grain of truth in it.
In the richer countries of the world there *is* more cause for
misgiving as to the desirability of fast economic growth than
perhaps at any time in the past. Of course, this too has been
said over and over again in the past, and proved to have been
wrong. After all, John Stuart Mill might have been writing
some of the contemporary anti-growth literature when he
wrote, over 120 years ago: 'If the earth must lose that great
portion of its pleasantness which it owes to things that unlimited increase of wealth and population would extirpate from

it, for the mere purpose of enabling it to support a larger but not a better or a happier population, I sincerely hope, for the sake of posterity, that they will be content to be stationary, long before necessity compels them to it.'[30]

The valid reason for greater scepticism today as to the benefits of faster growth is not, however, the danger of some impending shortage of raw materials or accumulation of pollution or any of the other anti-growth arguments which are considered in more detail below. Nor is it that increases in 'needs' merely wipe out the additional welfare that increased output would otherwise confer. Growth does, however, involve costs, both the straight economic costs discussed in Chapter 1 (namely the extra investment and hence sacrifice of current consumption) and possibly some adverse sociological costs – though the evidence here is extremely fragmentary and quite inconclusive. But this does mean that faster growth should not be pursued irrespective of these costs, as is so often recommended in much public discussion of the growth problem.[31] In view of these costs it is arguable that the advanced countries are approaching a situation where more emphasis should be placed on the creation of a civilized society, when 'for the first time since his creation man will be faced with his real, his permanent problem – how to use his freedom from pressing economic cares, how to occupy the leisure which science and compound interest will have won for him, to live wisely and agreeably and well.'[32]

Furthermore, it is likely that there is a less pressing need now to sacrifice the consumption of present generations in order to make future – and hence richer – generations even richer. Not only need we be less concerned with the standards of living of future generations, but the scope for raising income levels through technical progress is also becoming increasingly obvious. Sheer increases in physical capital per head are no longer such a vital ingredient in the growth process in advanced countries.

One of the results of increasing affluence over the last few decades has been the great rise in the demand for education and in the ability of nations to satisfy this demand. This has led to a vast extension of technical skills, scientific knowledge, and habits of mental enquiry and intellectual analysis that are the basis of increasing technical progress. Man's appetite for knowledge – which is largely artificially induced – and man's capacity to acquire and expand the frontiers of his knowledge appear to be inexhaustible. It is this, above all, that will enable growth to continue indefinitely. And it is this unbounded human ability to push forward the frontiers of knowledge that the doomsday school of thought has completely overlooked. At the same time it is this that provides one of the more valid arguments for refusing to make heavy sacrifices of current consumption in the interests of faster growth. For the growth will come anyway through the inevitable accumulation of human capital.

as did malthus

The message of this book, therefore, is one of moderation. Growth is neither an end to be pursued at any cost nor one to be despised and rejected. It is true that extreme positions one way or the other always look more interesting and original than middle-of-the-road ones; rousing battle cries either to step up the growth rate in order to keep up with the Japanese or the French, or to stop the earth at once before it is too late, stimulate the emotions more than an economist's plea to balance the pros and the cons and to seek the optimum solution. In the major part of this book, however, I shall be concerned with criticizing the extreme anti-growth school of thought. This is a largely negative and destructive exercise, but it is essential to get this red herring out of the way in order that we may then pay attention to the more important issues that are touched upon at the end of the book.

3 National Product and the Quality of Life: Some Historical Perspectives

Economic welfare and total welfare

The most widespread myth about the economist's position in the debate about economic growth and welfare, or the 'quality of life', is that economists are all GNP-worshippers. In fact, all economists know that, at best, GNP (gross national product) is simply one component of welfare, namely that part of total welfare which, in the classic phrase of one of the greatest economists of the century, Pigou, 'can be brought directly or indirectly into relation with the measuring rod of money'.[1]

Indeed, in order to describe the relation between economic welfare and total welfare, Pigou went on to point out, fifty years ago, what some people today believe to be a great revelation, namely:

> there is no guarantee that the effects produced on the part of welfare that can be brought into relation with the measuring-rod of money may not be cancelled by effects of a contrary kind brought about in other parts, or aspects, of welfare; and, if this happens, the practical usefulness of our conclusions is wholly destroyed ... The real objection then is, not that economic welfare is a bad index of total welfare, but that an economic cause may affect non-economic welfare in ways that cancel its effect on economic welfare.[2]

Furthermore, in his monumental work *The Economics of Welfare*, Pigou actually used the now fashionable term 'quality of life' in the course of his enumeration of the various ways in which a rise in *economic* welfare (which is more or less what a rise in GNP is supposed to measure) may fail to lead to a corre-

sponding rise in *total* welfare. In particular, Pigou drew attention to the fact that 'non-economic welfare is liable to be
modified by the manner in which income is earned. For the
surroundings of work react upon the quality of life.'[3] He also
discussed the effect on welfare of aesthetic and ethical sensi-
tivities, or the manner in which income is spent, and some of
the other ingredients of welfare which now tend to be trum-
peted by extreme environmentalists as if they constituted final
proof of the irrelevance of national-product measurement for
policy purposes.

The environmentalist criticism of the national-product concept overlooks the fact that this concept, which embraces
countless individual items that contribute to welfare, is the
only substantial part of welfare that has been systematically
and carefully measured. It is also the only such component of
welfare the relation of which to total welfare has been
thoroughly analysed. The same cannot be said of any other
major group of ingredients of welfare. After all, suppose one
had started out by saying, 'Now, let us measure human welfare or happiness in order to see whether it is rising or falling,
and under what conditions it does so, and so on.' Presumably
one would have tried to draw up a list of all the things that,
according to one's value-judgments, contributed to 'human
happiness'. One would then probably have felt obliged to leave
aside ingredients such as people's love of their neighbours,
joy of living, satisfaction from family reunions or from their
leisure activities, pleasure in breathing the clear morning air
or watching birds, and so on, on the grounds that though they
might be the most important things in life (to some people),
no way of measuring them could be found. Then, with luck,
up would speak some bright spark who would point out that,
while not disputing the supremacy of the items listed, it would
be a pity to drop the whole idea of trying to measure how much
welfare has changed just because no quantitive estimate could
be made of these particular components, so why not at least
measure those components which people *did* seem to want and
to find very important, and which *could* be measured, since
they were the subject of transactions in terms of some common

unit, namely money? 'True', he would add, 'this isn't the whole of welfare, by any means, but it would at least seem to be part of it, and possibly an important part judging by the amount of time and trouble people devote to getting more of these things, so we might at least measure that part of welfare which is measurable.'

In a sense, this is more or less what happened. But many decades after the economic statisticians began their extremely difficult work of measuring national product, and many decades after the difference between this concept and that of total welfare had been carefully spelt out by the economic theoreticians, the concept of national product – the only relatively unambiguous measure we have that adds together, in a meaningful way, thousands of components of welfare – has come under fire on account of its inability to do what economists never tried to do with it, namely to measure *total* welfare.*

Nevertheless, although national product must not be equated with total welfare, there is some truth in the view that, on the whole, economists have tended to assume that a rise in *economic* welfare (as measured by a rise in national product) would lead to a rise in total welfare.† In other words, although economists certainly do not *define* economic welfare (or GNP) as meaning the same as total welfare, so that they clearly recognize the possibility of divergence, they have generally assumed that, in practice, the two things will be closely correlated. Even Pigou was prepared to make the assumption, on probabilistic grounds, that what added to economic welfare would, in

* Perhaps, as Walter Heller said, 'What makes people think that GNP has become the economist's Holy Grail is the indispensable role it plays in measuring the economy's output potential and its performance in using that potential. It is highly useful and constantly used by economists (a) as a guide to fiscal and monetary policy for management of aggregate demand, and (b) as a measure of the availability of output to meet changing national priorities.' Professor Walter Heller, 'Coming to Grips with Growth and the Environment', paper presented to Resources for the Future Forum on *Energy, Economic Growth and the Environment*, Washington D.C., April 1971 (mimeographed version, p. 18).

† In fact, the conditions under which a rise in measured national product are believed to reflect a rise in 'economic welfare', narrowly defined, are rather complex, and require, at least, correction for price changes, which raise difficult index-number problems, not to mention questions such as the way income distribution has changed.

general, add to total human welfare. As another distinguished economist pointed out later, 'Such a judgment is not easy to accept. If we really do not know, we do not know – and there is no point in pretending that we have enough information for a probability judgment.'[4]

The main reason why there is no basis for the probabilistic judgment that the growth of national product necessarily increases total welfare is that there can never be objective factual evidence on the relationship between the two concepts – that is, on the way they have changed over the past. For there is little chance of reaching widespread agreement on a measurable definition of *total* welfare. As regards economic welfare, although there is some disagreement in the economics profession as to how accurately this is measured by national-product data, there are at least numerous estimates of national product that represent a large area of agreement as to what the figures mean and the precise nature of the various limitations of them.* But there is no agreement at all as to what constitutes welfare or 'happiness', in any wider sense, so it is not surprising that there are no estimates of it. Furthermore, even if measurements were made of some widely agreed concept of welfare, it would always be open to anybody to dissent from the agreed definition and to say that, in his opinion, welfare constituted something entirely different. There would be no way of proving that he was wrong; the definition of welfare involves a value-judgment, and hence it is not susceptible to empirical verification.

It is partly for this reason that no science can tell us whether modern man is happier than mankind a hundred years ago, or even ten years ago. The concept of happiness is one for which there can be no scientific objective measure. This does not preclude the possibility of experiments to check whether people *believe* they are happier. If people are defined as being happier when they believe they are happier, then the problem would

* Gross national product is defined as equal to the flow of final 'goods and services' in the economy, and it is hardly possible to find a more value-loaded word than 'goods'. There is consequently some disagreement in the profession as to how far some of the items measured are really 'goods' at all. Clearly this must depend on value-judgments, as does the wider concept of total welfare.

be soluble.* But even if it were possible to accept the evidence to the effect that people felt worse off, this does not prove that it is economic growth that has made them feel worse off: perhaps they would have been even unhappier in the absence of economic growth. It is self-contradictory to argue that (i) economic output is not the only thing in life, and (ii) if welfare has fallen it can only be as a result of the economic growth that has taken place! In any case, it is always open to somebody to say that such surveys are no guide to whether people really are happier or not, for people might be deluded into thinking they are happier when they are not really so, and are merely under the influence of government-sponsored brainwashing, or drugs, drinks, television, or some other form of escapism.

Since the concept of happiness, like that of *economic* welfare for that matter, involves value-judgments, there are two main ways in which people may differ in their views as to whether economic growth leads to higher welfare or increased happiness. First, they may agree about what items constitute total welfare (as well as national product), but disagree on how these items have changed over time. Secondly, they may agree about the facts – for instance, the change in national product, in the crime rate, in the expectation of life, in hours of work, and so on – but disagree on the importance of these items in their concept of total welfare. The most that can be done, therefore, is to survey some of the main developments in society to which reference is frequently made – or to which, in my opinion, reference *should* be made – in any discussion of how far welfare has changed, and then leave it to the reader to decide how far, given his particular value-judgments, he shares my view, that, taken by and large, welfare has probably increased over the

* In his article 'Economic Growth: The Need for Scepticism' (*Lloyds Bank Review*, October 1972), E. J. Mishan refers to some evidence to the effect that the percentage of people saying that they were 'very happy', in reply to a survey, had declined over time both in the U.S.A. and in Britain. But he does not report the percentage who replied that they were 'very unhappy' (if this possibility were open to them), which may also have declined, so that we are unable to judge what change took place in the overall degree of reported happiness. Furthermore, such surveys are not easy to interpret since much depends on the sort of prevailing fashions of opinion, which are partly determined by campaigns, such as those waged by Dr Mishan and others, to persuade us that we are really all worse off.

last century, or even the last few decades, together with economic growth. Much of this chapter, therefore, will be devoted largely to surveying some of the empirical evidence that, on my value-judgments, indicate a rise in welfare.[5]

'Welfare' in perspective

POLLUTION AND THE URBAN ENVIRONMENT

One of the reasons for the currently popular view that economic growth has been accompanied by a decline in welfare is the growing recognition of the damage that may be done to the environment in the absence of appropriate policies of environmental protection. People complain about the noise from motorways or jet planes, or the way that some beaches are fouled as a result of inadequate sewage discharges or oil spillages at sea, and so on. But although appropriate policies to control all forms of pollution should be implemented and there is no cause for complacency, a factual survey of the overall pollution position soon dispels the notion that the existence of these blights on our environment implies a fall in overall welfare. In later chapters we shall study the pollution problem in far greater detail, and it must suffice here, in this very general survey of changes in some components of welfare, to try to put the pollution problem into perspective. Many people today clearly do not appreciate what the physical environment was like in the past and how great an improvement in the environment has taken place. For example, when Chateaubriand was taking up his post at the French Embassy in London in 1822 he wrote: 'At Blackheath, a common frequented by highwaymen, I found a newly built village. Soon I saw before me the immense skull-cap of smoke which covers the city of London. Plunging into the gulf of black mist, as if into one of the mouths of Tartarus, and crossing the whole town, whose streets I recognized, I arrived at the Embassy in Portland Place.'[6]

It is fashionable nowadays to complain about the level of carbon monoxide in the air in congested areas, such as around Oxford Street, on account of the motor-car, but in the middle

3

of the last century it was reported:

> The space bounded by Oxford Street, Portland Place,
> New Road, Tottenham Court Road, is one vast cesspool,
> the sewers being so imperfectly constructed that their con-
> tents are almost always stagnant ... Now when the reader
> reflects that thousands of working men are closely con-
> fined, for perhaps 14 or 15 hours out of the 24, in a room
> in which the offensive effluvium of some cesspool is
> mingling with the atmosphere ... he will cease to wonder
> at the amount of disease ... [7]

More generally, the conditions in London in the mid-nineteenth century have been described in all their horrifying detail
in the classic works of Dr Hector Gavin, notably in his *Sanitary
Ramblings* (in which he described the environmental conditions
in every street in Bethnal Green, as 'A Type of the condition
of the Metropolis and Other Large Towns'). Almost any page
of this work contains descriptions such as the following:

> Pleasant Row ... Immediately facing Pleasant Row is a
> ditch, filled with slimy mud and putrefying filth, which
> extends 100 feet. The space between Pleasant Row and the
> central square is beyond description, filthy; dung-heaps
> and putrefying garbage, refuse, and manure, fill up the
> horrid place, which is covered with slimy foetid mud. The
> east end has likewise its horrid filthy foetid gutter reeking
> with pestilential effluvia; the southern alley is likewise
> abominably filthy ... I entered one of these houses on the
> southern side, and found that every individual in a family
> of seven had been attacked with fever ... the privy of this
> house is close to it, and is full and overflowing, covering
> the yard with its putrescent filth ... [8]

It is not surprising that the deaths from typhus alone in
England in the mid-nineteenth century were nearly 20,000 a
year, and that 60,000 deaths a year were attributed to tuberculosis, not to mention high death-rates from numerous other
diseases associated with insanitary and unhealthy living conditions.[9] In this respect conditions in London were by no means

unique. Inquiries carried out by the Health of Towns Association into the sanitary conditions in the other main cities and towns of the country produced a more or less uniform picture, such as: 'Bolton – very bad indeed; Bristol – decidedly bad; the mortality is very great; Hull – some parts as bad as can be conceived; many districts very filthy; with a few exceptions, the town and coast drainage extremely bad; great overcrowding, and want of ventilation generally.'[10] The only places today where such conditions can be found are in the poorest cities of the world, such as Calcutta.

It should not be thought that the conditions described above were special to the nineteenth century in the advanced countries and that, once the worst features of the industrial revolution had been remedied, they began to get worse again. For the continued economic growth of the last few decades has been accompanied by further dramatic improvements in many variables that are usually ignored by those who are determined to conclude that economic growth is harmful. In Chapter 5 we survey some of the quantitative evidence concerning the decline in the pollution of the environment over the last decade or more, in order to put into perspective wild statements such as Mishan's description of ' ... the Britain of 1951 ... before the car and the developer had made hideous our cities and suburbs, before television held people in a semi-bovine state up to six hours a day ... The skies in those innocent days were not rent by shrieking aircraft, nor was the air thick with car fumes. People could stroll along the street and converse without screaming at each other.'[11] Before coming to the detailed evidence concerning the decline in air pollution during the last two decades, it might be mentioned, *en passant*, that Mishan seems to have a very personal recollection of how quiet our major cities were in those idyllic days. In fact, although there are no records of noise levels in earlier days (since it is only as a result of economic growth and greater freedom from more urgent cares that we now bother about these things), most people who remember London fifty or more years ago can recall the continual deafening noise from trams and the clatter of horses' hooves. Many people who remember those 'good old days' will, in fact, affirm that the big cities are now much quieter.*

Dr Mishan does not mention that his halcyon year of 1951 was the year preceding the terrible smog of December 1952, which stimulated the authorities to set up the Beaver Committee, whose report was largely instrumental in producing the legislation that has since resulted in a dramatic improvement in the air that we now breathe in the cities (see Chapter 5, p. 123). Furthermore, when his attention is drawn to this improvement in the air in cities he seems to think that it is of little importance. In 1971, he wrote: 'Through the emission annually of millions of tons of foul gases the automobile's contribution to sickness and death from cancer and from bronchial and other disorders is just beginning to be understood.'[12] (In fact, there is no evidence that cancer is caused by air pollution, as opposed to smoking, though it is true that there is some evidence of a relation between air pollution and bronchial disorders, including emphysema. In any case most of the pollution in Britain does not come from motor-cars but from stationary sources, particularly coal fires in homes and the older industrial plants, neither of which are equipped with tall chimneys.) Air pollution has greatly declined in Britain during the last ten to fifteen years, with beneficial effects on health. Consequently, Dr Mishan seems to have changed his tune entirely and now (1972) writes: 'The British public is beginning to tire of comparing the relative demerits of smog in London 20 years ago and of carbon monoxide and lead poisoning today ... '[13] Those thousands of people who would otherwise have suffered from emphysema might attach slightly more importance to the improvement in the air in our cities than does Dr Mishan.

* Nor should it be thought that the ills of mankind have been caused by our abandonment of nature. So-called 'natural conditions' are conditions in which man can hardly survive at all. As Mr Hessayon put it recently in a comment on this sort of 'back-to-nature' attitude ' ... Des Wilson, writing about Upper Volta in West Africa, described a land where nature is nicely balanced, and where one in every five babies dies and where the life expectancy is thirty-five ... The Irish in 1840 left their potato crop to nature, and a million died of hunger when it was swept away by blight.' D. G. Hessayon, 'Homo sapiens – the species the conservationist forgot', *Chemistry and Industry*, May 20th, 1972.

HEALTH

The problem of pollution, however, is a very complex one, and it will be considered in more detail later in a separate chapter. Here we shall consider one or two of the other components of welfare that are generally overlooked by the anti-growth school of thought. For example, one of the most important components of welfare is health, and there is no doubt that this has steadily improved over the last few decades, quite apart from any health benefits obtained from the reduction in pollution. To some extent this general health improvement is already measured in a rise in the health-expenditure component of the GNP. But the rise in health expenditures included in the GNP will correspond to the *costs* of health care and may considerably underestimate the welfare that will be obtained, since most health expenditures are provided by the State and do not pass through the market mechanism.* For example, when a new vaccine or drug is developed that, at low cost, virtually eliminates diseases such as polio or diphtheria, the resulting increase in human welfare may be out of proportion to the medical expenditures actually incurred. This is one of the ways, well known to economists, in which a rise in GNP will *under-estimate* the rise in welfare, not overestimate it.[14] And it is clear from the data that there have been enormous reductions in the health risks from many of the diseases which still plagued society earlier in this century, long after the industrial revolution had reached a peak and the scourges of typhoid, typhus and cholera had been eliminated from advanced societies.

For example, deaths from respiratory tuberculosis were still running at about 25,000 per annum in England and Wales as recently as the 1930s. But they have now been reduced to about 1,000 per annum.[15] In the U.S.A. annual deaths from tuberculosis have been reduced, over the same period, from a rate of over 50 per 100,000 persons to about 3 per 100,000.[16] Diphtheria is another killer disease which was still widespread in the 1930s but which has been practically eliminated under the

* If health services were provided by the market mechanism there would be a stronger presumption that costs and benefits were reflected in relative prices.

combined impact of medical advances and improved sanitary
conditions. In England and Wales reported deaths from
diphtheria appeared to be rising towards the end of the nineteenth century to a peak of about 8,000 per annum in the
1890s, though this no doubt partly reflects improved diag-
nosis.[17] This figure was cut to about 3,000 per annum in the
inter-war period in England and Wales (it was about 7,000 per
annum in the U.S.A.). In both countries there are now virtually
no deaths from diphtheria. Of course, the above figures relate
only to deaths, the number of cases notified being over ten
times as great. In other words, during the inter-war period
about 50,000 to 60,000 cases of diphtheria were notified every
year, year after year, in England and Wales, mainly of children,
compared with only about a dozen cases per year during the
1960s. The elimination of acute anxiety and strain from hundreds of thousands of families as a result of the virtual eradication of this and other potential killer diseases must mean an
incalculable increase in their welfare. Deaths of infants of less
than one year old have fallen from about 60 per thousand, pre-
war, to 20 per thousand in recent years in England and Wales,
and also in the U.S.A.[18] While it is right that the public should
be alarmed by the possibility that, for example, some children
may be affected by lead in the atmosphere around one or two
industrial premises in Britain, if this is weighed against the
extent to which millions of families have been spared the
terrible anxieties associated with the prevalence of diphtheria,
polio, tuberculosis, whooping cough, scarlet fever, and so on,
it is difficult to conclude that, on any set of value-judgments,
there has not been an astronomic improvement in the general
health of the population during recent years. The anti-growth
lobby is quick to point out a connection between economic
growth and a relatively limited health hazard, such as the lead
hazard mentioned above, but if they were serious they would
presumably want to consider also the relationship between
economic growth and the incomparably greater effect on welfare caused by the virtual eradication of several very widespread
deadly illnesses.

LEISURE AND WORKING CONDITIONS

There are various other important components of welfare that are not reflected in GNP and which have been increasing over time. In the next chapter we discuss some attempts that have been made to adjust GNP estimates for these items. They include the output of public capital, such as schools, hospitals, roads, libraries, parks, and other public buildings or installations. Unlike private capital or the capital equipment of nationalized industries, the 'output' of these forms of the community's capital stock is not included in GNP. But it has certainly been increasing.

The same applies to numerous leisure activities, not to mention housewives' services. Perhaps the most important elements of welfare that are not reflected in GNP are the conditions of work and the degree of leisure enjoyed by the working population. After all, as Mishan himself says, 'Yet who can deny that, like our environment, the sort of work that men do and their attitude toward their work are among the chief components of human welfare.'[19] The problem, of course, is to find quantitative indicators of working conditions. One obvious indicator, which is probably highly correlated with the attention paid to the working environment in general as well as being a very important indicator in its own right, is the number of factory accidents. And it happens that, in spite of a large increase in the industrial work-force in Britain during the course of the century, the number of fatal industrial accidents has fallen steadily to an all-time record low. It is now, at about 800 per annum, half of what it was about twenty years ago and only one-sixth of what it was at the beginning of the century.[20] In the U.S.A., although no further improvement can be identified during the last decade, the previous years had witnessed a similar steady fall in the number of fatal work accidents.[21]

Furthermore, the hours of work have greatly fallen over the course of the century.* Other things being equal this would

---

* See p. 82 for references to calculations by Sametz of long-period changes in working hours and leisure. Other direct estimates are given in Max Kaplan, *Leisure in America* (Wiley, New York and London, 1960), and, for Britain, in

reduce GNP but would raise welfare (quite the contrary of the bias which the critics of growth usually attribute to the GNP figures). For few people would deny that greater leisure-time is one of the most important components of welfare. There is little point in protesting, as does Mishan, at the way that modern society has reduced the degree of communication among human beings when one of the major developments over the last few decades has been to give the majority of the working classes the time and opportunity to see their friends, or people living far afield in foreign countries, and the possibility of spending time with their own families. Fortunately, this particular component of welfare is also one that can be quantified, and attempts to evaluate its contribution to welfare are discussed in more detail in the next chapter.

Faced with quantitative evidence of the improvement in working conditions and leisure, the anti-growth school have to fall back on immeasurable concepts such as the workers' 'self-respect'. Thus Mishan writes:

> Adapting his mode of living to the technology of industry and to the flow of gadgets on the market, the man in the street ... sees himself more and more a bewildered spectator to what goes on about him ... True, his leisure may increase over time and there may be goodies-a-plenty in the supermarkets ... But what of his self-respect? For scientists, technocrats, and professional men there will still be opportunities for distinguishing themselves, though the pace of obsolescence of knowledge is sure to place them, too, under increasing stress ... The plight of the ordinary mortal, however, is seemingly inescapable ... How can he hold his head up when it is plain beyond doubt that as a producer he does not rate; that nobody depends on him for anything; that he is but a drone in a world become a buzzing hive of technology.[22]

---

various sources, of which one of the most recent is M. A. Bienefeld, *Working Hours in British Industry: An economic history* (Weidenfeld and Nicolson, London, 1972).

Dr Mishan should have proclaimed this message during the 1972 British coal strike, or the railwaymen's strike, or the dustmen's or sewage workers' strike. He would have soon been told how much the workers concerned were aware of the dependence of society on their labour.

In any case, the discovery of these psychological aspects of the conditions of work is not new. The concept of 'alienation', which is now an important weapon in the anti-growth armoury, was made famous by Karl Marx over a century ago. Marx pointed out that, under capitalist conditions, work was 'external to the worker, that it is not a part of his nature, that consequently he does not fulfil himself in his work but denies himself, has a feeling of misery, not of well-being, does not develop freely a physical and mental energy, but is physically exhausted and mentally debased'.*

Of course, it is open to anybody to assert that these psychological states are even worse today, and since it is impossible to measure these states it is impossible to disprove such assertions. But, quite apart from casual observation of the conditions inside most places of work today compared with those of thirty or fifty years ago, there are good prima facie reasons for supposing that the morale and self-respect of the worker is higher today than in the past. The continuation of full employment, the growth of union strength, the introduction of

---

* Karl Marx, *Economic and Philosophical Manuscripts of 1844* edited by Dirk Struik, translated by Martin Milligan (Lawrence and Wishart, London, 1970), p. 110. At another point Marx says: 'The crudest methods (and instruments) are coming back: the treadmill of the Roman slaves for instance is the means of production, the means of existence of many English workers ... The machine accommodates itself to the weakness of the human being in order to make the weak human being into a machine.' (op. cit. p. 149). It is arguable that economic growth has greatly helped to eradicate precisely this aspect of early industrial society, which Marx rightly condemned. Automation, for example, has more and more freed people from the most boring, routine, 'treadmill' jobs. As one minister in the 1964–70 Labour Government put it, perhaps with excessive lyricism, 'In the electronic age the machine can be exploited to a degree undreamt of by Henry Ford by greater use of human intelligence and creativity and less of repetitive skills. After two centuries of machine-induced inhibition the wondrous creature – man – comes into his own again. It is as though Constantinople has fallen again, a new Renaissance, a rediscovery of man the individual after the dark age of man the cog.' (Edward Short, *Education in a Changing World* [Pitman, London, 1971], p. 18.)

3*

legislation such as that preventing unfair dismissal, or the provision of redundancy pay and severance allowances, have all made the employee less dependent on the vagaries of any particular employer or the fortunes of any particular firm. Furthermore, if a man fell out of work through sickness or some other reason fifty years ago there was little for his family to do except starve or scrape by on workhouse charity. This constant source of anxiety for millions of people has now been greatly reduced (thanks to unemployment benefits, free health services, and the like) though unfortunately it has not yet been completely removed.

In the years before all these lifelines had been rigged up, and particularly when unemployment was running at far higher rates than have been known since the war, most working people accepted that their lot was a very bad one, they did not expect it to improve, and only prayed that it would not get any worse on the following day. Those who were lucky enough to have jobs usually worked in conditions which were far noisier, dirtier and more insanitary than is the case today, and were under constant fear of losing those jobs. To maintain that the conditions today are more conducive to mental anxiety on account of a faster pace of technical progress exhibits either a complete ignorance of what life was like for real working people in the not too distant past or a complete lack of imagination of what such conditions must have meant to the average working man.

INCREASED INCOMES AND APPRECIATION OF THE 'QUALITY OF LIFE'

Confronted with tangible evidence of developments which must surely have tended to increase the assurance and self-respect of the average worker, the anti-growth men fall further back on even more nebulous assertions such as that: 'economic growth has brought about, and depends upon, extreme specialization of knowledge and tasks that tend to dull the spirit, to narrow one's sympathies and to cut one off from the largeness of life … once subsistence levels are passed, men's more enduring satisfactions are to be found in love, trust, friendships and, in a civilized society, are augmented by their perceptions of nature, and of beauty, art and music.'[23]

Quite apart from the fact that people's notions of what constitutes a 'subsistence level' are not fixed but rise over time,* what reason is there to believe that the opportunities for love, trust, friendships, and the appreciation of beauty, art and music are declining as a result of economic growth? Indeed, there are obvious prima facie reasons for assuming the contrary. For example, the fact that the struggle for material survival is less acute, so that life is less a form of jungle warfare, is just as likely to eliminate some of the friction in human relationships as to add to it.

Those who attack some of the most unpleasant features of modern society seem to have no conception of the poverty, squalor, misery and ignorance that was the lot of the mass of the population in the recent past. It is true that there are still enormous pockets of poverty and squalor, and it is no doubt true that a more equal distribution of income would help to eliminate this. But the fact remains that, in the U.S.A. for example,

Between 1959 and 1969, the number of persons below the poverty line fell from 39 million to 24 million, from 22·4% to 12·2% of a rising population. The improvement came from a 3% increase in productivity per year, a drop

* The relativity of the notion of subsistence and the way this has risen over time can be clearly seen from the following extract from Ricardo's *Principles of Political Economy and Taxation*, published in 1817, where he wrote: 'It is not to be understood that the natural price of labour, estimated even in food and necessaries, is absolutely fixed and constant. It varies at different times in the same country, and very materially differs in different countries. It essentially depends on the habits and customs of the people. An English labourer would consider his wages under their natural rate, and too scanty to support a family, if they enabled him to purchase no other food than potatoes, and to live in no better habitation than a mud cabin; yet these moderate demands of nature are often deemed sufficient in countries where "man's life is cheap", and his wants easily satisfied. Many of the conveniences now enjoyed in an English cottage, would have been thought luxuries at an earlier period of our history.' *The Works and Correspondence of David Ricardo*, edited by Piero Sraffa (Cambridge University Press, 1951), pp. 96–97.

in unemployment from 6% to 4%, shifts of the poor from lower to higher income occupations and regions, and an extraordinary growth in government cash transfers, from $26 billion in 1960 to over $50 billion in 1970. Every one of these factors is in some way the direct outgrowth of, or associated with, or facilitated by, per capita economic growth.[24]

It is hard to believe that the 15 million people who have been removed from below the poverty line according to these estimates have less opportunity now for 'the appreciation of beauty, art and music'. Indeed, it is much more likely that the greatly increased concern with environmental protection indicates more a decline in acquisitiveness and obsession with material goods than a worsening of the environment, particularly since, as we show in detail in a later chapter, the environment has been getting better, not worse. As one person has bluntly put it, 'The sole reason we can now feel concerned about the quality of life instead of worrying where the next meal is coming from is that through our great industries we have, as a society, built up immense material wealth.'* For example, it would not have been possible, in Britain, to have enforced the Clean Air legislation of the 1950s and 1960s, which involved the switch from heavily polluting coal-fired domestic heating to smokeless fuels, in the days when miners could hardly support a family even when employed, and large numbers of them were in fact unemployed. Similarly, a recent

* Philip Sadler, 'Industry must answer back' (*Financial Times*, April 6th, 1972). In terms of the individual, the point has been well put by Thomas Crocker, in the following way: ' ... if I must choose between two otherwise equally satisfactory home sites, I will select that site which is not downwind from a smoky factory. However, if the choice is one of starving in an idyllic setting or having wholesome food and adequate shelter while living near the smoky factory in which I earn the money to buy this food and build this shelter, I will choose to live near the factory. Thus, over some set of ordering of my wants I will always select that set of alternatives which best satisfied my basic so-called biological needs; but after some positive degree of satisfaction of these needs has been achieved ... I will then reorder my wants so that cleaner air receives higher priority than does additional food, clothing and shelter.' – *Natural Resources Journal*, Vol. 8, April 1968, p. 241.

Gallup poll in the U.S.A. showed that three-quarters of the adult population were willing to pay additional taxes to improve the environment:[25] it is doubtful if the same response would have been obtained among the population of Calcutta, where 50 per cent of the families live in one room.

Furthermore, quite apart from the effect of higher incomes on the extent to which people will attach priority to the quality of life, and hence the extent to which the authorities can be expected to devote resources to the preservation of the environment, many of the tangible developments mentioned above, such as the increase in leisure opportunities, the speed of international travel, and so on, must surely have made it easier for the ordinary person to extend his knowledge of the world and his familiarity with its artistic and other wonders. It may well be perfectly feasible for a small elite to make their way slowly to Delphi or Florence overland, but for the average American secretary or Lancashire textile-worker, with only two weeks' paid holiday, it is quite out of the question.

In the same way, one should not overlook the liberating effects of many of the gadgets of modern civilization that are so much despised by the anti-growth school of thought. Even the humble washing-machine may not mean much to the middle classes who previously relied on domestic servants, but it means a great deal to the working-class wives who are thereby relieved of one of the chains of drudgery that bound them to their homes. The motor-car, too, that arch-villain in the anti-growth demonology, has enabled the ordinary man and woman to make an acquaintance with the countryside and with foreign countries that hitherto has been very much the private preserve of the wealthier classes. Of course, as Michael Lipton has pointed out, now that the roads are no longer reserved to the wealthier classes and tend to become occasionally congested by the slower-moving and badly maintained cars of the poorer members of society, the former complain.

To summarize this section, therefore, there is no doubt that GNP is not a good measure of *total* welfare, which it is *not* designed to measure, and it may not even be a very good measure of changes in *economic* welfare, which it *is* designed to measure.* Many components of welfare are not reflected in GNP at all, and some of these may have been getting worse over the years as a concomitant of economic growth and the absence of appropriate policies concerning the way the fruits of economic growth are used and distributed. For example, it is probably true that, over the last fifty years, there has been an increase in the concentrations of nitrogen oxides and certain other pollutants in the air, a rise in the nuisance from aircraft noise, a spread of various pesticides and insecticides which *may* be harmful (though they have not yet been proved to be harmful to human beings), an extension of derelict land, and a rise in the number of cases of psychiatric disorders that are reported or diagnosed (which is not the same thing as a rise in the real incidence of psychiatric disorders, of course, since there has also been a tremendous rise, over the years, in the number of psychiatrists, and in public awareness of mental illness and the possibilities of treatment).

It is right to remind the general public what is well known to economists, namely that GNP is not identical with welfare. But if one's aim is, as Mishan claims, 'only to bring into the arena of debate considerations that do not enter into the glib half-truths uttered by growth-men, and cannot be resolved by scientific methods of investigation', why bring into the arena only the *reductions* in welfare that are not reflected in GNP? For GNP also fails to record, or to measure adequately, many components of welfare that are probably increasing. Among the most important of these are those just discussed, notably the enormous improvements in the overall health of the population, the generally vast improvement in the sanitary and hygienic conditions of towns in most advanced countries (not to mention the welfare obtained from other forms of social

* The technical economic literature is full of reasons why changes in GNP are not accurate indicators of changes in welfare, ranging from index-number problems, through failure of relative prices to reflect marginal social costs accurately, to absence of any income-distribution content or the impossibility of identifying any aggregate community-indifference curve or social-welfare function. The technical literature is also full of reasons why GNP does not yet accurately serve its main function in economic policy, namely as a measure of the short-term changes in productive activity and pressure of demand in the economy.

capital), the substantial improvement in working conditions and the general status and legal protection afforded to employees, the greater security and protection of the old, the sick and the unemployed, the reduction in hours of work and the increase in holidays, the great reduction in domestic drudgery for the housewife, and the increased freedom to discover new horizons and new lands. If our ambition is merely to remind the public and the politicians that GNP is not everything in life and to ensure that other aspects of economic welfare or of total welfare are taken into account in the interests of a more balanced debate, objectivity would require us to list the benefits that are excluded from GNP as well as the costs. In the next chapter we shall consider attempts that have recently been made to quantify some of these adjustments to the GNP estimates.

In the course of doing this we shall also see that the attempt to go from GNP to some wider concept of welfare raises difficult philosophical questions, such as the relation between welfare and changes in 'needs'. This happens also to be one of the popular criticisms of economic growth – i.e., that much of the measured increase in output is merely a response to rising 'needs', so that the gap between needs and satisfactions has not been narrowed. This is the 'consumer-society' critique of economic growth, which is often put in terms of the artificiality of the new needs that are constantly emerging. The same argument often crops up in connection with the development of the backward countries of the world, which are often alleged to be victims of the 'revolution of rising expectations' as if there were something necessarily evil about hope. In the next chapter it is argued that these criticisms of the welfare implications of rising consumption are much less powerful than they might appear to be at first sight.

4 GNP, 'Needs', and Welfare

A 'welfare-orientated' measure of GNP

Although, as explained above, few economists believe that changes in GNP indicate equal changes in total welfare, the basic conventions that have been adopted by the statisticians of most countries for purposes of GNP-measurement are still founded on some notion of what measure of *economic* activity can best represent the contribution of that activity to welfare. Nevertheless, it is accepted that the postulated link between welfare and GNP as conventionally measured is subject to various qualifications.

First, some fundamentally arbitrary value-judgments have to be made about what economic activities give rise to '*final* goods and services'. For example, there has long been much dispute in the economics profession as to the validity of including in GNP items such as expenditures on defence, or law and order.* Some economists have argued that these expenditures do not reflect desirable 'goods', but are merely 'regrettable necessities' that have to be incurred in order that modern industrial society can operate, and so should not be counted as positive components of welfare. Similarly it has been argued that commuters' transport expenditures should not be included in GNP since these are part of the urbanization costs of economic growth, not positive final benefits enjoyed by the population.

Secondly, many items which might be generally agreed to form part of economic welfare have been excluded from the estimates on account of practical estimation difficulties. For example, it might be accepted that GNP should include housewives' services and the services obtained from consumer durables. But, at the same time, it would probably be agreed that objective estimates of these items are difficult to find. For

---

* See my discussions of some of the different views on this in Chapter 2 of my *Introduction to National Income Analysis* (Weidenfeld and Nicolson, London, 1972 edition).

they do not all pass through the market, and so their prices and values are not reflected in any objective market transactions.

Thirdly, it is recognized that, at best, economic welfare is only a part of total welfare, and, as Arthur Okun recently put it:

> It is hard to understand how anyone could seriously believe that GNP could be converted into a meaningful indicator of total social welfare. Obviously, any number of things could make the Nation better off without raising its real GNP as measured today: we might start the list with peace, equality of opportunity, the elimination of injustice and violence, greater brotherhood among Americans of different racial and ethnic backgrounds, better understanding between parents and children and between husbands and wives, and we could go on endlessly. To suggest that GNP could become *the* indicator of social welfare is to imply that an appropriate price tag could be put on changes in all of these social factors from one year to the next … it is … asking the national income statistician to play the role of a philosopher-king, quantifying and evaluating all changes in the human scene. And it is absurd to suggest that, if the national income statistician can't do that job, the figure for GNP is not interesting.[1]

Of the three types of gap between GNP and welfare enumerated above, few economists would dream of trying to bridge the third, but many would welcome attempts to narrow the first two, and some attempts to do so have been made.* One of the earliest of such attempts, by Sametz (see footnote to

---

* In fact the distinction between the three classes of criticism of the GNP measures is not as sharp as suggested above. In his authoritative and masterly survey of this question in 'Welfare Measurement and the GNP' (*Survey of Current Business*, January 1971), Ed Denison points out that it is not possible to draw a clear distinction between some of the items which are left out for practical reasons and, say, aspects of the environment such as the freedom to go where we like without fear of being attacked, or to attend a lecture without disruption, or to have congenial neighbours, or to be discriminated against, which are included in the sort of items listed by Okun above. It may merely be easier to measure, say, the effect of a deterioration in the physical environment in terms of increased air pollution and its effect on house values or on health, than a deterioration in the

table 4.1, below), highlighted the enormous importance, in relation to changes in conventional measures of GNP, of the increase in the value of leisure-time over the last century. His estimates of national product adjusted for leisure (as well as for other items, such as the costs of urban civilization and the inadequate allowance for improvements in the 'quality' of some goods) suggest that the rise in the adjusted measure of (net) national product over the last century has been very much higher than the rise in the conventional unadjusted series, as shown below.

TABLE 4.1

Sametz estimates of U.S.A. National Product adjusted for leisure, costs of urban civilization, and other items: 1869–1966
(billion dollars at constant prices, and indices)

	(1) GNP	(2) Leisure	(3) Total GNP plus leisure	(4) Index of Col. (1)	(5) Index of Col. (3)
1869–78	9·4	1·2	10·6	100	100
1929	97·0	60·0	157·0	1,033	1,481
1966	315·0	240·0	555·0	3,250	5,235

Source: A. W. Sametz, 'Production of goods and services: the measurement of economic growth', in E. B. Sheldon and W. E. Moore (editors) *Indicators of Social Change: Concepts and Measurement* (Russell Sage Foundation, New York, 1968), p. 83, Table 2.

Contrary to the assertions of those who constantly complain that, on account of various omissions, the growth of conventionally measured GNP overstates the 'true' rise in welfare, the above figures show that one of the omissions from GNP,

---

other aspects of the environment, but the distinction is one of degree, not of principle, and hence cannot be sharply drawn. An unpublished paper ('Economic Growth and Social Development') by Mervyn King, of the Cambridge Department of Economics, however, has taken several indicators of non-monetary components of welfare, such as infant mortality and the like, and has shown that a statistically meaningful composite index of these is correlated with growth rates of GNP.

namely leisure, has shown a spectacular rise over the last century, and has hence made an enormous contribution to the rise in economic welfare of the U.S.A. Exactly how important the rise in leisure has been, and how it compares with some of the other adjustments that might be required in order to approach a more welfare-oriented measure of national product is, of course, a matter about which there will be much debate for some time to come. For there are numerous difficulties involved in making these estimates, and, as Sametz would be the first to point out, the above estimates were of a rough, pioneering character (though even this required much ingenious calculation). They have been followed by some more sophisticated and comprehensive estimates of a welfare-oriented measure of national product that were prepared by William Nordhaus and James Tobin.[2]

Nordhaus and Tobin set out to adjust the conventional measure of national product for both the favourable (plus) items that are excluded (such as leisure, or non-marketed services) and the unfavourable items that are excluded, such as the costs of urbanization. They also took account of some of the items that are included in national product but that, in the opinion of the authors, ought not to be included in any measure of welfare. These comprised items such as 'defensive' expenditures of the kind 'that are evidently not directly sources of utility (satisfaction) themselves but are regrettably necessary inputs to activities that may yield utility. Some government purchases are of this nature – for example, police services, sanitation services, road maintenance, national defence.'[3]

The outcome of their adjustments is that the rate of growth of what they call 'Measureable Economic Welfare' (MEW) over the period 1929 to 1965 has been slower than the growth of net national product (NNP) as conventionally measured. But unless it be thought that this proves that all these 'bads' that had been omitted from GNP have now been shown to be very important it should be pointed out at once that quite the opposite conclusion emerges from the Nordhaus and Tobin estimates. The reason why the *growth rate* of MEW has been slower than the *growth rate* of NNP is that the value of desirable leisure and non-market activities that had also been excluded from conventional GNP is so high that if they, too, are brought into the picture the starting level of MEW (in 1929) is very much higher than the starting level of the conventional NNP. As a result, although in *absolute* terms the 'goods' that have to be added to NNP to derive the MEW measure have been rising much more than the 'bads' that have to be subtracted, the *proportionate* rise in the total is smaller after both adjustments have been made. This can best be seen from the following table.

TABLE 4.2

Nordhaus and Tobin estimates of Measure of Economic Welfare for the U.S.A.: summary table
(billions of dollars, 1958 prices and indices)

	1929	1965	1965 as index 1929
Net National Product			
(Conventional definitions)	183·6	563·1	306·5
of which 'regrettable necessities'	−17·0	−94·1	
leisure	339·5	626·9	
non-market activities	85·7	295·4	
disamenities	−12·5	−34·6	
services of public and private capital	29·7	78·9	
other adjustments	−65·4	−194·5	
'sustainable measure of economic welfare'	543·6	1241·1	228·5

Source: Nordhaus and Tobin, op. cit. Table 2 (mimeographed edition, p. 21).

As can be seen from the above figures, the conventional measure of net national product in 1929 was only $183·6 billion (at 1958 prices) whereas the value of leisure ($340 billion) plus the value of non-market activities ($85·7 billion) amounted to about $425 billion, which is very much greater than the negative adjustments that had to be made of $30 billion for the regrettable necessities and disamenities such as defence or the costs of urbanization. Hence, the total initial measure of economic welfare in 1929, after making both kinds of adjustment, was

$543·6 billion. As a result, even though the absolute increase in the favourable items, notably leisure and non-market activities, has been very much larger than the absolute increase in the unfavourable items since 1929, the *proportionate* rise in what was initially a much larger total has been less. The following diagram summarizes these relationships.

Changes in National Product and 'Measurable Economic Welfare', U.S.A. 1929 to 1965 ('000 million U.S. dollars at 1958 prices)

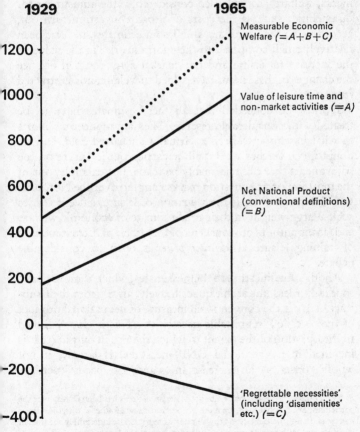

Source: Nordhaus and Tobin, see Table 4.2

In other words, it is true that the growth rate of 'measured economic welfare' according to these estimates, is slower than the growth of GNP as conventionally measured, but the absolute rise in the 'good' items that are normally excluded from GNP has exceeded the absolute rise in the 'bad' items (both those that are included and those that are excluded from GNP) by over $318 billion over the period concerned. This is a very large sum; it equals over half total U.S.A. net national product in the mid 1960s. Hence, after making all these adjustments, welfare has still risen considerably; the adjustment for disamenities such as the costs of urban congestion turn out, according to the Nordhaus and Tobin estimates, to have been relatively small compared to the enormous rise in the value of the increase in leisure and non-market activities. On balance the changes in these items have added to welfare, not subtracted from it.*

It must be conceded that all these estimates have to be treated with considerable reserve. They are pioneering efforts in what has hitherto been a virtually uncharted field, and no doubt much further work will be carried out in future on the adjustments that can reasonably be made. For example, one of the most important question marks hanging over the Nordhaus and Tobin estimates is the valuation of leisure, since it carries such a large weight in their total estimate of economic welfare and, as the authors obviously recognize, their particular method of valuing leisure at *constant prices* is open to considerable debate.

Another qualification to their estimates, which is more philosophical, if less important quantitatively, arises from their subtraction from the conventional measure of net national product of the so-called 'regrettable necessities'. This is closely linked to the question of the extent to which the rise in output (that is included in conventional GNP measures) is largely, if not wholly, offset by an increase in 'wants' or 'needs' (perhaps

---

* Of course, the *proportionate* rate in the negative items has been faster, over the particular period concerned, than the proportionate rate in the favourable adjustments, so that if these relative growth rates were to persist indefinitely the former would eventually catch up with and then overtake the latter.

artificially stimulated) and so cannot be interpreted as reflecting any genuine *net* rise in welfare. This has been a major theme of the anti-growth school, and it raises some basic philosophical issues, so it is dealt with separately and is the subject of the next section of this chapter.

'Needs', 'satisfactions', and welfare

As indicated above, Nordhaus and Tobin subtract from the conventional measure of national product an estimate of what they call 'regrettable necessities', of which a major item is defence expenditure. They argue: ' ... we see no direct effect of defence expenditures on household economic welfare. No reasonable country (or household) buys "national defence" for its own sake. If there were no war or risk of war, there would be no need for defence expenditures and no one would be the worse without them.'[4] But the same sort of reasoning applies to almost any component of GNP. Nobody would want hospital accident wards, or even home first-aid kits, for their own sake. They are only required because of the risk of accidents. Motor-car seat-belts are required, not for their own sake, but to prevent injury in accidents. It is not possible to draw logical distinctions of the Nordhaus/Tobin kind between the purposes served by various goods. If they are wanted they are wanted, and that is the end of the matter. If there were no winters, there would be no need for winter woollies or heating expenditure; if one never had toothache there would be no need to visit the dentist. For very poor people, even food, after all, is merely required in order to offset the pain of otherwise being hungry and dying of starvation. Surely it is not to be argued that in such cases the food in question (or other similar basic essentials) should *not* be included in GNP and that we should include only the more frivolous inessentials. If so, this runs quite counter to another popular view to the effect that much of the growth of GNP as measured is misleading because it includes so many of the items that are not really necessary. In other words, some people argue that we should exclude from a welfare-oriented measure of GNP the goods that we do not really need. And others – including, apparently, Nordhaus and Tobin – argue that we should exclude the goods that we do really need since these are just regrettable necessities.

In fact, Nordhaus and Tobin recognize the logical difficulties to which their procedure leads when they write: 'Maybe all our wants are just regrettable necessities; maybe productive activity does no better than satisfy the wants which it generates; maybe our net welfare is tautologically zero.'[5] Unfortunately, they then proceed to suggest that this objection is not a serious one; but it is, and it applies as much to the inclusion in GNP of ordinary consumers' expenditure on consumer durables and clothes or more exotic foods, and so on, as to the 'regrettable necessities' that they wish to deduct from GNP in order to move towards a yardstick for measuring welfare.

It seems to have been generally accepted in the economics literature that no useful distinction can be made between the two alternative ways of increasing utility, namely, reducing needs or increasing the extent to which they are satisfied. One of the first systematic expositions of the theory of utility in economics was Jevons' *The Theory of Political Economy*, first published in 1871, where he wrote: 'It will be readily conceded that pain is the opposite of pleasure; so that to decrease pain is to increase pleasure,'* or, as put earlier by the poet Dryden, 'For all the happiness mankind can gain Is not in pleasure but in rest from pain.'† But there is no logical conflict between this and the view that man is somehow 'better off' or 'happier' if an increase in the goods and services he consumes or acquires is

---

* Jevons also quoted Bentham (in *Introduction to the Principles of Morals and Legislation*) approvingly as stating that 'By utility is meant that property in any object, whereby it tends to produce benefit, advantage, pleasure, good, or happiness ... or (what comes again to the same thing) to prevent the happening of mischief, pain, evil, or unhappiness to the party whose interest is considered.' W. S. Jevons, *The Theory of Political Economy* (London, 1871).

† Plato, in *The Republic* (Book IX), argues convincingly that pleasures do not require the previous experience of some 'pain' (and vice versa), as in the example he gives of the pleasure of smelling a perfume. Countless other examples are easily imagined.

merely a response to an increase in his needs. There are no objective scientific grounds for assuming, as does Mishan for example, that 'only as given wants remain constant and productive activity serves to narrow the margin of discontent between appetites and their gratification are we justified in talking of an increase in welfare'.[6] And whether the increase in his needs is artificially induced or not is also irrelevant; moreover it is impossible to make any sharp distinction between artificially induced needs and other 'natural' needs.

The relationships between changes in needs, satisfactions, and happiness give rise to various complications, which seem to be of three main kinds. First, as a matter of positive fact, given the generally accepted interpretation of the word 'happiness', it may well be that people are happier when they experience an increase in certain needs, even if these cannot be entirely satisfied. Secondly, as a matter of value-judgment, one might well hold that, irrespective of whether an increase in needs made people 'happier' or not, it raised human welfare rather than reduced it. For example, one might approve of the needs in question – they might include an awakened need to do something about improving the environment – or one might think that man's spiritual superiority over animals lay in the multiplicity and diversity of his needs. Thirdly, the artificiality or otherwise of the needs is a red herring which, as is argued below, has no bearing on the basic issues.

As regards the first point, if, for example, I have a 'need' to listen to music, but do not have the time or the money to go to as many concerts as I would like, I will be unable to fully satisfy my need. But I would not accept that, on account of this gap between my needs and their satisfactions, I am 'worse off' than if I did not have this need. I would still maintain that, even though I cannot completely satisfy it, as a result of this particular need I lead a fuller and richer life.

Of course, it may be that a person who feels a need to listen to music and who is then completely deprived of opportunities to do so might suffer greatly. This is a risk that has to be accepted as part of living. To reduce this risk by reducing man's needs is to avoid some of the risks of life by living a little less intensely. As a contemporary philosopher, Anthony Kenny, has put it:

> The greater a person's education and sensitivity, the greater his capacity for the 'higher' pleasures and therefore for a richer life; yet increase in education and sensitivity brings with it increase in the number of desires, and a corresponding lesser likelihood of their satisfaction. Instruction and emancipation in one way favour happiness, and in another way militate against it. To increase a person's chances of happiness, in the sense of fullness of life, is *eo ipso* to decrease his chances of happiness, in the sense of satisfaction of desire.[8]

Or as it says in the Bible, 'for in much wisdom is much vexation, and the more a man knows the more he has to suffer'.* Kenny also argues that it may well be that an individual feels positively 'happier' when he experiences an increase in desires that he cannot fully satisfy. He reminds us of Bertrand Russell's assertion that 'to be without some of the things you want is an indispensable part of happiness',[8] a proposition that many people might well accept. As regards the second point, it is necessary to distinguish between the objective factual question of how far people feel 'happier' (given some agreement as to how happiness is to be defined) when they have more needs, and the question of how one defines 'good' or 'bad' in relation to changes in peoples' needs. For example, even if we were to accept that, other things being equal, a rise in needs made people feel unhappier, it is still open to anybody to say that people are 'better off' and that welfare has risen, given his particular concept of what constitutes human welfare.

My point is that what constitutes being 'better off' is a value-judgment that can quite well take the form of believing that what distinguishes man from animals is precisely the multiplicity and diversity of his needs, so that, without excluding the right to pass moral judgments on some of these needs, the more needs man has the 'better' he is a man. Or, in the words of the

* The words of the son of David, King in Jerusalem, *Ecclesiastes*, 1.18.

French sociologist Henri Lefebvre, 'Plus l'être humain a des besoins, plus il existe'.[9] The irony of the current attack on the way that the capitalist system creates additional needs is that part of Marx's original attack on the soul-destroying nature of capitalism was that capitalism destroyed man's basic needs. Nowadays, the doctrine among extreme left-wing critics of economic growth is that growth does not add to welfare since it is merely the response to an increase in needs. In other words, economic development makes man worse off!

Of course, the gap between man's needs and his satisfactions can be narrowed by reducing his needs to the level of, say, the domestic dog, which are confined to a square meal (uncooked) per day, daily walks, and a moderate display of affection by his owners. Some people may argue that this is the road to happiness, and, if combined with a dedication of one's life and thoughts to spiritual matters, is also the road to salvation. It is quite open to others to maintain that man fulfils his nature more by acquiring more 'needs', and that this is desirable, and that in Nietzsche's words, 'to attack the passions at their roots, means to attack life at its roots'.[10]

As mentioned above, it is often argued that whether an increase in needs implies more or less welfare depends on whether the needs are artificially induced. Now one may approve of some needs and disapprove of others: there is no logical compulsion to generalize about the relation between welfare and 'needs' per se, irrespective of the nature of the needs. One may believe that an increased need to worship God or to listen to music is morally 'good', or that, as a matter of objective fact, it makes people happier; and that an increased need for drugs or drink or women is morally 'bad', or makes people unhappy. But it is difficult to see how the artificiality of the need or desires in question determines whether it is classified as 'good' or 'bad' and hence to be welcomed or rejected. After all, in the above example of my desire to listen to certain kinds of music, I was certainly not born with it.

As Anthony Crosland has pointed out, it is impossible to draw a sharp dividing line between those of our needs that are innate and natural and those that have been artificially developed as a result of many factors, including our whole social environment.* Furthermore, even if it were possible to draw a dividing line between artificial and natural needs, what is so moral about natural needs and so immoral, or undesirable, about artificial needs? Would some peoples' artificially induced 'need' to listen to music or to acquire knowledge be less desirable a component of welfare than some other peoples' instinctive, natural and primitive instinct to rape women? There is obviously no way of settling disputes about what needs are good or bad and how far some needs add to welfare or subtract from it. The rival views on this subject are not rival propositions about the way the world behaves; they are simply rival definitions of 'good' and 'bad', 'better' and 'worse'. Some people define 'better' in such a way that it means increasing the number of needs (possibly of specified kinds) as well as the number of satisfactions. Others define it to mean a decrease in the number of needs, so that the less the needs the 'better off' man is. Others define it solely in terms of the gap between the needs and the satisfactions, so that if this remains constant as a result of a rise in needs offset by a rise in satisfaction man is no better off or worse off. Others define it as positively related to the amount of satisfactions, irrespective of the amount of needs.

Thus, with both needs and satisfactions rising, but the latter rising less than the former, one school of thought could say that welfare has risen on account of the rise in needs, another could say that it has fallen for the very same reason, a

---

* Crosland took issue with Galbraith over this 'artificial needs' objection to increased private consumption a long time ago. As he said, 'If we were speaking merely of longer tail-fins on longer cars, or titivating fripperies and novelties, then well and good. But there is surely more to it than that. Almost all wants above the basic minimum of essential food, clothing and shelter are in some way artificially stimulated: are they therefore to be considered as of no significance? The demand for greater variety and higher standards of food, clothing and housing is induced not by innate need – the savage does not have it – but by the conventional expectations of the society; is it therefore to be considered as not worth satisfying? In most countries a proportion of the population feels little want for education, and the want has to be not merely stimulated but actually enforced by compulsory state education; are we then to say that the provision of education is not urgent?' – The Conservative Enemy (Jonathan Cape, London, 1962) p. 99.

third could say that welfare has fallen because the gap between needs and satisfactions had risen, and a fourth could say that welfare has risen because satisfactions have risen. Of course, more complex definitions of welfare or happiness could also be devised, notably a definition which made an increase in welfare dependent both on the change in *needs* and the gap between them and satisfactions.

To summarize, therefore, it appears that the argument that welfare does not rise with increased output because 'needs' also increase is a gross over-simplification of the problem. The effect of changes in both needs and satisfactions on the extent to which people *feel* happier is a matter of objective fact (if very difficult, in practice, to ascertain). But the question of whether, irrespective of their own impressions, they are to be regarded as being 'better off', in some fundamental sense, as a result of changes in both needs and satisfactions, is, as pointed out above, a matter of value-judgment, and is not so simple an issue as it might seem at first sight.* In particular, if the facts show that certain 'needs', such as those for environmental protection, have increased over time as much as expenditures to meet them, it does not necessarily follow that welfare has failed to rise. Nor does the conclusion one draws from the same facts necessarily depend on whether the increase in needs is in any sense artificially induced. The same facts can be interpreted in different ways according to one's value-judgments as to what constitutes happiness. And value-judgments which allow happiness to rise as a result of an increase in certain needs, or as a result of a rise in satisfactions that has been matched by a rise in needs, are by no means inconceivable or unreasonable.

* Whether or not 'needs' are increasing faster than satisfactions is, however, a factual question, and I know of no evidence to support the assertion that, for example, 'As production increases, and with it the standard of living measured in terms of per capita GNP, the gap between the actual condition of life of the average individual and his horizon of satisfaction appears to be increasing.' – *Science Growth and Society*, Report of the O.E.C.D. Secretary-General's Ad Hoc Group on New Concepts of Science Policy (Paris, 1971), p. 26.

The treatment of environmental protection expenditures in national-product estimates

It should now be clearer why it is possible to take very different views on practical statistical questions such as how to adjust the measurement of GNP to allow for expenditures on 'regrettable necessities', or 'defensive expenditures', as they are also called. For example, should a welfare-oriented measure of GNP include or exclude expenditures to preserve or improve the environment when the 'need' for such expenditures has risen? And does this depend on whether the rise in environmental needs is the result of the growth of output and its associated pollution, so that, even after incurring the environmental-protection expenditures, the environment is no better than it was back in the days when there was less pollution? This is the same sort of issue as the older issue in national accounting theology about whether to include, in GNP, the increasing expenditures on law and order that are merely the response to the increase in crime and violence that, in turn, may be attributed to the evils of industrial society and its growth. In both cases the argument is that the increase in the expenditures ('satisfaction') is merely the response to an increase in 'need', so that society is no better off as a result. But this argument is open to the same objections as the argument that much of the rise in private consumers' expenditure is merely the response to an increase in needs (many of which are artificially induced by one means or another, including advertising or the desire to emulate one's neighbour).

In the case of the 'defensive' expenditures incurred to improve or protect the environment, it may appear at first sight that they should certainly be included in any measure of economic welfare on the grounds that they do, in fact, make the environment better than it would otherwise be. In a detailed study of this and related issues Juster argues that much depends on whether the environment has, or has not, deteriorated over the time-period in question (since this can be interpreted as representing the change in the net flow of services from the environment).[11] If the environment has deteriorated over the period in spite of the rise in expenditures to protect it, he concludes that welfare has not risen over the period in question (other things being equal, of course). But this conclusion is not logically inescapable. For decisions as to which types of increased need add to the fullness of life and which do not are value-judgments. And an increase in the 'need' for environmental protection is not *necessarily* classed as subtracting from welfare. This *may* be the case when the need has arisen as a result of a deterioration in the environment; but suppose it has arisen because of a mass publicity campaign in favour of a cleaner environment? If people were indifferent to the environment before but are now unhappy about derelict land and smoky cities as a result of the activities of the environmentalist lobby, are they better off or worse off if this leads to *some* extra defensive expenditure, but not enough to make them quite as satisfied with the environment as they had been to begin with? Surely, the increase in expenditures on environmental protection in recent years is a mixture of various sources of increased 'need' for this particular form of 'defensive' expenditure (including simply the fact that our basic needs for food, shelter, and so on, have been increasingly satisfied). Hence, in so far as our value-judgments attach positive welfare to a greater desire to have a clean environment, other things being equal, we might want to include some of these expenditures in a welfare-oriented measure of GNP, but exclude others.

Welfare and 'keeping up with the Joneses'

An issue related to the one just discussed is Mishan's assertion that 'what matters more to a person in a high consumption society is not his absolute real income, his command over material goods, but his position in the income structure of society ... the more truth there is in this relative income hypothesis – and one can hardly deny the increasing emphasis on status and income position in the affluent society – the more futile as a means of increasing social welfare is the official policy of economic growth'.[12] Leaving aside the fact that one *can* easily deny that economic growth has been accompanied by increasing emphasis on status and income position,[13] it should be recognized that the relative income hypothesis is a double-edged weapon in the hands of those who are concerned about the pollution of the environment. For if a person's welfare is entirely a matter of his *relative* position, then extra pollution is of no importance to society as a whole. For *either* we all become equally more exposed to pollution, *or* it is unevenly distributed, in which case although some people suffer from being *more* affected than others, those who suffer *less* presumably gain from a rise in *their* relative position.[14]

But, of course, few people would suggest that welfare depended solely on one's relative income. Most people would probably accept that welfare depended on both (i) one's relative position, and (ii) the absolute amount of goods and services that one enjoys. But in that case growth in the latter must add to welfare. In other words, there are two possibilities: either welfare depends *only* on one's relative position, or it depends both on this *and* on the absolute amount of goods and services one enjoys. If welfare depends on both, then the increased output of goods and services cannot be written off as if they did not contribute to welfare. And if welfare depends only on one's relative position, then there is not merely no point in growing, there is no point even in staying where we are. In the latter case, why not let GNP fall and pollution rise? As long as everybody becomes worse off together it will make no difference to welfare – or, if some people get poorer more quickly than others, the fall in their welfare will be offset by a rise in the welfare of those whose *relative* position has become better. In short, the 'relative income hypothesis' – as the 'keeping up with the Joneses' doctrine is known in economics jargon – has very little force as an anti-growth argument in general, and, in particular, if pushed too far it could constitute an argument for complete indifference to the increase in overall pollution.

'Needs' and welfare in developing countries

The whole of the above discussion has been about the pros and cons of further economic growth for advanced countries, where it is at least understandable that important sections of the community should question how much priority should be given to further increases in the output of goods and services rather than to what John Stuart Mill called the art of living as distinct from the art of getting on.[15] But for the vast majority of the world's population it does not require much imagination or knowledge of their terrible poverty to rule out the question of whether further economic growth is desirable for them.

Nevertheless, it is often argued that the developing countries should not make the same mistakes as were made by the now advanced countries and pursue economic growth in spite of its adverse social or environmental effects, and that they should not fall victims to the trap of 'rising expectations'. Furthermore, it is often heard that if the developing countries sought to achieve standards of living comparable to those now enjoyed by the advanced countries there would simply not be enough resources to go round.

One conclusion that might appear to follow from these pessimistic doctrines is that, since the rich countries of the world can hardly be expected to reduce their levels of material prosperity, the poor countries must not be encouraged to believe that they too can aspire to such levels of prosperity. They must, hence, accustom themselves to the idea that they should give priority to environmental preservation rather than economic growth. Of course, it is bad luck for them that the point at which economic growth has to stop should just have arrived about the year 1970, when some countries had achieved a certain affluence but before the rest of the world had had an opportunity to do likewise.

This view, not surprisingly, is rejected by the developing countries. The so-called 'Founex Report', drawn up by a group of experts[16] convened by UNO to prepare a report on Development and the Environment for the 1972 UNO Stockholm Conference on the Human Environment, pointed out that although

4

The developing countries would clearly wish to avoid, as far as is feasible, the mistakes and distortions that have characterised the patterns of development of the industrialised countries ... the major environmental problems of developing countries are essentially of a different kind: they are predominantly problems that reflect the poverty and very lack of development of their societies. They are problems, in other words, of both rural and urban poverty. In both the towns and in the countryside, not merely the 'quality of life' but life itself is endangered by poor water, housing, sanitation and nutrition, by sickness and disease.

In other words, in these countries there is no conflict between growth and the 'quality of life'; growth is essential in order to preserve life and to remedy some of the worst features of the environment from which these countries suffer.

Further, even if there were a conflict between growth and the environment, there is no reason why poor countries should choose between them in the same way as rich countries. The 'trade-off' between the two is likely to be very different in countries where economic output is very much smaller than in more affluent countries. Rational choice depends not only on one's basic preferences between goods and services of the conventional kind, on the one hand, and environmental quality, on the other hand; it depends also on how much of each one has.

Poorer people will naturally have a greater incentive to give priority to more goods and services than to the environment in general. In the same way, poor countries, in which a large proportion of the population may be constantly preoccupied with the problem of obtaining enough to eat for the next twenty-four hours, would be foolish to make heavy sacrifices of economic progress in the interests even of their own environment, let alone that of the world in general. A man who is not sure how to provide the next meal for his family is hardly likely to worry much about the problems of posterity. In fact, the notion that the developing nations would be well advised to benefit by the lessons of the advanced countries, and be chary of putting economic growth before the preservation of the environment, displays an appalling degree of insensitivity to the real problems of these countries.

Furthermore, the technical relationships between economic output and environmental pollution imply less pollution damage per unit of output in many developing countries than in the more advanced countries. For a key feature of the pollution problem, from the economic point of view, is that it is very much a localized phenomenon. Up to a point, the dilution and absorptive capacity of the biosphere is so great that the damage done by most forms of pollution varies by several orders of magnitude according to exactly where it is done. For example, it is well known that the damage done, say, by some effluent entering a river will depend very much on the precise flow of water in the river, the distance between the discharge and the utilization point, air conditions, and many other parameters which vary from place to place. The same applies to many kinds of air pollution. Thus, if, for example, a factory emits some pollutant into the air near a crowded and populous area, the damage done, in terms of its effects on humans (directly or indirectly), may be considerable. But if the same factory is situated in a remote part of the country the damage done will be negligible. It is true that an effluent entering into some remote stream might harm the fish in it, but if the fish were never to be the object of human satisfaction, this would be of no practical consequence.*

In poorer countries there is little doubt that the production of many goods could be carried out with less harmful effects than in the advanced Western world, where the population density in and around the centres of production is generally very great. In such cases, the poorer countries have a double interest in selecting from the possible growth/environment combinations one that gives higher priority to growth than would be the choice of the advanced countries. They have a more urgent need than advanced countries for increased economic output, and, in addition, greater scope for producing certain forms of output at relatively low pollution cost.

* See also the discussion of the definition of pollution on p. 107.

Finally, it should not be thought that the developed countries should grow more slowly in order to leave resources available for the growth of the developing countries, as the latter made perfectly clear at the 1972 UNO conference mentioned above. Growth of the former is essential to provide the expanding markets for the products of the latter. Nothing would do more harm today to the exports of the primary producers, for example, than a prolonged stagnation in the industrialized countries of the world.

For various reasons, therefore, the concern for the developing countries that takes the form of advising them not to make the mistake of pursuing the vain illusion of raising welfare by means of economic growth, particularly when this might even damage their environment, is a concern that the developing countries can do without. Of all the forms of bad advice on development that the poorer countries have had to put up with over the last twenty years or more, this is about the worst.

The political and social costs of slow growth

Finally, even if none of the above arguments were valid and it could be demonstrated that economic growth does not lead to any rise in welfare in the advanced countries, it would still not follow that attempts should be made to bring growth to a halt. For, in the absence of some transformation in human attitudes the like of which has never been seen in spite of constant admonition by powerful and inspiring religions over thousands of years, human nature has not yet abandoned the goal of increases in the goods and services that are enjoyed. To some people this goal is a denial of holiness; to others it is a testament of the infinite variety of the human spirit. Only an altogether unparalleled optimism can lead one to believe that the vast mass of the population will voluntarily accept an abandonment of the goal of economic growth, at least for the foreseeable future. This means that if growth were to be abandoned as an objective of policy, democracy too would have to be abandoned. Whatever the 'costs of growth' in terms of the quality of the environment – and, as we shall continue to argue in later chapters, these costs are probably negligible – the costs of deliberate non-growth, in terms of the political and social transformation that would be required in society, are astronomical.*

* See also further discussion of this point in Chapter 8, p. 247.

5 Economic Growth and Pollution

The increasing importance of pollution

One of the reasons why national product is an imperfect measure of economic welfare is that it fails to take full account of what are known as 'externalities', or 'spillover' effects. Of these, the most flagrantly obvious is pollution. If an individual suffers from smoke or smells or noise generated in the course of productive activities his welfare is reduced but GNP is unaffected. Of course, some pollution hits firms, as well as private individuals, and this will reduce GNP.* (This would be the case, for example, when firms are obliged to incur higher costs, such as costs of painting their premises, or treating metals for corrosion caused largely by the sulphur dioxide in the atmosphere, or treating their fabrics to protect them from damage done by air pollution of various kinds.) Nevertheless the first type of pollution damage – i.e. that to private individuals – is not accounted for in measured GNP. And one of the reasons why pollution has come to occupy a central place in the growth debate is that it is thought to be one of the major instances of a growing gap between the national income and welfare. It is also thought that pollution must necessarily increase with economic growth and that, in the long run, this means that growth would have to be brought to a halt if the human race is not to be poisoned or asphyxiated.

Although it is argued, at various points in this book, that concern with environmental pollution is excessive, there is no doubt that there is a genuine pollution problem, that it must be taken seriously, and that appropriate policies must be adopted to deal with it. In order to take pollution seriously, instead of frivolously and irresponsibly, it is necessary to put

* See also Chapter 7 below for further discussion of effect on GNP of pollution and of pollution abatement expenditures.

pollution into perspective, and to analyse more carefully the sense in which there is a pollution 'problem' and the extent to which growing pollution must really constitute an inescapable constraint on growth. This will be the subject of this chapter. The following chapters will then consider in more detail the principles of pollution-control policy and the costs of eliminating excessive pollution.

There are two good reasons for thinking that society should attach more importance to preserving the environment than has been the case in the more distant past. First, there appears to be a natural hierarchy of human wants, and as societies become richer and satisfy their more basic needs, such as for food, clothing and shelter, the need for a better environment or an improved 'quality of life' in the widest sense becomes increasingly important. This is a natural process and is not to be disparaged, but it should be observed, *en passant*, that it means that the wealthier members of the community are likely to be those whose basic needs are the first to be satisfied and who are likely, therefore, to gain most from a shift in the use of society's resources towards preservation of the environment. This is one of the reasons why concern with the environment can easily become excessive, for there is a presumption that it may not be in the interests of the community as a whole to devote as many resources to preserving the environment as some of the more vocal and articulate sections of the population would like.

The second reason for taking the pollution problem seriously is that the rate at which many pollutants have been entering the environment has increased to the point where it can no longer be taken for granted that the environment has an unlimited capacity to absorb them harmlessly. In other words, environmental resources such as clean air or water, or usable land, are not in unlimited supply.

'The Pollution Problem' as a resource-allocation problem

These two reasons for increasing public concern with the environment provide the clue to understanding in what sense there is a real 'pollution problem' or an 'environmental problem'. For the problem is simply that, because of the rising public demand for the preservation, or improvement, of environmental resources (land, air, water, and so on), too many of these resources are being 'used up'. To pollute the air or the water is, of course, the same thing as using up some of the resources of clean air or water. When there were unlimited supplies of clean air or water in the sense that the volume of pollution was too small to have any significant effect on the environment, a steady rise in the public's demand for clean air and water created no problems. Conversely, it would not matter so much if the environment were increasingly polluted as long as access to clean air and water and so on remained relatively unimportant ingredients of human welfare. In other words, there is an 'environmental problem' because, given the changing pattern of social needs, too much of our environmental resources are being 'used up', or, which amounts to the same thing, not enough resources are devoted to preserving the environment. In short, the pollution 'problem' is simply a *resource-allocation* problem.

But the demand for a better environment is not the only demand that rises rapidly as economies grow. So why is there not a similar problem with respect to other needs and demands that increase rapidly as society becomes richer? After all, as societies become richer, people also want many other things that they had previously not regarded as urgent or important, such as various items of hardware, like high-fidelity equipment or motor-cars. But although most people would probably prefer to have more hi-fi equipment than they actually possess, few people maintain that economic growth has given rise to a hi-fi 'problem' in the sense that not enough resources are allocated to the provision of hi-fi equipment.

The reason is, of course, that, subject to certain reservations that have long been recognized in economics, the market mechanism will tend to ensure that the rising demand for hi-fi equipment is matched by an increase in supply, even if this involves a redistribution of resources away from other uses. This market mechanism fails to ensure, however, that society's demand for a clean environment is automatically satisfied. This is largely because there are not enough clearly defined property rights in the environment, in the sense that not merely do people not own clean air, clean water, 'quiet', and so on; they cannot easily extract a payment from anybody who wants to use it up by polluting it, either. Hence the costs of pollution are not usually borne by those that are responsible for the pollution and are borne, instead, by the victims. This means that there is no automatic incentive for polluters to reduce their pollution to the point where the benefits to them of being able to pollute the environment just match the costs to society of this pollution.

It is a failure to recognize that the pollution problem is one of resource misallocation at any point of time, and not one that arises solely on account of economic growth, that has been the source of considerable confusion in the public debate about growth versus the environment.[1] For even if there were no growth, and even if national product were declining, there would still be a danger, in the absence of appropriate policies, that pollution would be excessive and that insufficient resources would be devoted to the preservation of the environment. Growth has merely made us more conscious of this particular form of resource misallocation for the two reasons given above. In fact, in a sense, this is the advantage of growth in the context of the environmental-pollution problem, for it is now much more probable that societies will give due attention to this form of resource misallocation and introduce the measures needed to reduce pollution to the proper amount. What is the 'proper amount' must be deferred to the next chapter, but meanwhile the point to be established is that pollution is more likely to be reduced in a growing environment than in one that is not growing.

This is particularly true in developing countries, which is where some of the worst pollution in the world is usually found. In very poor countries pollution is commonly of the kind that was found in nineteenth-century Britain or other Western nations, particularly pollution of water on account of poor sanitation arrangements and absence of appropriate

4*

sewers and the like.[2] This is often accompanied by excessive urban densities, together with high unemployment, causing environmental degradation of many kinds.[3] There is no doubt that economic growth is the only way that the poorest two-thirds of the world's population can eliminate the pollution and environmental degradation that always go hand-in-hand with poverty.

But even in advanced countries, economic growth is also probably the only means by which pollution can be kept down to socially desirable levels. Rising incomes mean that the public are more willing to see resources devoted to environmental protection; and a climate of economic growth, which implies technological progress and the introduction of new machines and new techniques of production, is one in which it is far easier for firms to introduce equipment embodying tougher anti-pollution characteristics.[4]

The concept of pollution

Of course, many people are shocked at the notion that all that is required is to reduce pollution to the socially 'optimum' level, and that the pollution problem is basically just a problem of resource misallocation. For many of the 'eco-doomsters' – and indeed, some scientists who are not even eco-doomsters – take the view that all physical pollution is 'bad', and that the 'optimum' level of pollution is zero. For example, Professor Richard Scorer, who is an outstanding authority on the scientific and technical aspects of air pollution, writes: 'An excess of speed has no bad effect whatever as such whereas an emission of pollution is always objectionable ... '[5] Similarly, one of the top British officials concerned with water pollution writes: 'Water can be said to be polluted when, because of man's actions in causing the addition of matter or heat to water, the physical, chemical or biological characteristics of the water are changed.'[6]

These two statements are not of course exactly the same. The second is defining pollution in physical terms, and the first is saying that physical pollution is always undesirable, but they come to the same thing given that the word 'pollution' carries a pejorative connotation in common parlance. Now there is no way of demonstrating that a definition of pollution in physical terms is 'wrong'. All that one can do is to show that it is unhelpful or misleading. And both the above definitions are misleading, for both imply that physical changes in the environment are always harmful, which is patently absurd. Clearly the term 'pollution' should only be used when it is intended to imply that some harm is being done, not merely that some physical change is taking place. As one eminent scientist puts it, 'A pollutant is a substance in the wrong place in a concentration which is harmful'.[7] Furthermore, pollution does not depend solely on man's actions, and much pollution arises from natural phenomena (often on a scale far greater than any man-made changes).

Indeed, many of the man-made physical changes in the environment are extremely beneficial to mankind, and sometimes to the animal world as well. Leaving aside obviously beneficial man-made changes in the physical environment, such as land reclamation, irrigation, and so on, there are also activities that produce what would normally be defined as 'pollutants' but that often have beneficial effects in unexpected ways. For example, even such a body as the Clyde Fishermen's Association has conceded that the warm water discharged from Hunterston power station had a very favourable effect on the growth rate of fish and shellfish in the area and that, as a result, their members have been catching much bigger prawns. In fact, a commercial operation to breed prawns in the warmer seas around the Hinkley Point nuclear power station in Somerset is now being set up.[8] A certain amount of air pollution has also been shown to have some beneficial effects on account of its fertilizing properties. In heavily industrialized areas it has been suggested that ammonium sulphate particles can be formed, and if they are washed out, or deposited dry on agricultural land, they add to its fertility.[9] Similarly, some atmospheric sulphur dioxide (SO_2) is a source of badly needed fertilizer in certain parts of the world, as has been shown in a survey by the Grassland Research Institute at Hurley, Berks.[10]

As a matter of fact, almost all the pollutants commonly discussed are harmful only in very large doses, and are often beneficial, or even essential, in certain amounts.[11] Even arsenic, which is toxic by itself, counteracts the toxicity of selenium, and has been added to poultry and cattle feed in areas where animal feeds are naturally high in selenium. And perhaps most metals in trace amounts are essential to life, although they will become toxic when they rise above certain low levels.[12] The same applies to many other products. For example, the carcinogenic chemical 3,4-benzpyrene exists in sizeable concentrations in cabbage, lettuce, spinach, leeks, and tea. Would those who are prepared to eliminate pollutants altogether ban the consumption of these products, not to mention the cyanide in cherries, plums, and peas, the oxalic acid in rhubarb, and the solanine in potatoes?[13]

Man as the measure of all things

Thus it is much more useful to think of pollution as existing only in so far as harm is done to human beings somehow or other, directly or indirectly. In a sense, pollution is like many peoples' conception of sin, according to which an isolated individual on a desert island would be unable to commit any sin (more's the pity). (I should add that my ex-colleague on the Royal Commission on Environmental Pollution, the Dean of Windsor, who had previously been Bishop of Norwich, disagreed with me over this matter.) Since economics is a social science, economists are interested in phenomena only in so far as they affect human beings; and this applies to pollution as much as to anything else. It is a basic proposition of economics that commodities cannot contribute directly to the welfare of the community as a whole, except via their contribution to the utility or welfare of individual members of that community. Thus we are not interested in animal or vegetable life for its own sake, but only in so far as it provides benefits to humans.

As regards water pollution, for example, we are interested only in mankind, not fishkind.

Furthermore, economists do not see the problem of pollution as one of *eliminating* it, but of finding the 'optimum' amount of pollution, allowing for the costs, as well as the benefits, of pollution abatement. To many people, by contrast, the problems of pollution are purely technical problems: i.e. how does one eliminate it? Not, how much *should* one reduce it? To listen to some scientists on the question of water-pollution, for example, one gets the firm impression that they regard the proper objective of policy as being to eliminate pollution entirely, and the costs side of the story enters into it only in so far as it means that they have difficulty in achieving this objective. But even if the funds were to be made available I, for one, have no wish to spend thousands of millions of pounds on what would be, in effect, the conversion of all our rivers into beautiful open-air swimming-pools for fish. I live in a town where there are not even adequate swimming-pool facilities for humans.

Of course, the existence of fish life and other animal and vegetable life may contribute to human welfare, and in so far as they do they should be valued accordingly. But that is a far cry from the simple eco-doomster position according to which priority must always be given to nature. For example, it is well known that lighthouse beams attract migrating birds, many of whom are dazzled and then killed when they hit the lantern or other parts of the lighthouse structure. Nobody would suggest that the lighthouse should be closed down or ocean traffic brought to a halt.

The claims of the natural environment have been effectively put into their proper place by Ozorio de Almeida as follows:

Perhaps the best way to put the environment issue in proper perspective is to ask straight away the basic question: according to whose criteria is the environment to be considered healthy, adequate, pleasant, desirable? If the subject were an anaconda, and if the anaconda had a mind capable of value-judgments, it would probably suggest that the world should be a swampy forest; a dromedary would wish it to be a desert. But what should it be for the human race? Certainly not all desert or all swamp. A first assumption of this study will be that environment is supposed to serve human rather than reptilian, ruminant, pachydermic, or any other interests. There is no doubt that human needs themselves may best be served by a degree of contact with certain types of domesticated or wild animals and plants. Within those limits or degrees, the environmental conditions necessary for them must be preserved. But it is to be understood that the final standards for judging the adequacy of any environmental conditions must be specifically limited by human needs and interests, both in the present and in the foreseeable future. In short, the environment under consideration will have to be considered from a 'subjective' stand-point, and the 'subject' will have to be 'man'. 'Man', moreover, must be understood to be 'homo sapiens' at his most advanced stage of civilization, in a habitat representing adequate conditions of personal security and full satisfaction of his basic needs for food and protection against the weather and any kind of elemental disaster. It is for this 'subject' that environment must be preserved or restored.

It may be useful at this stage to clarify a certain misunderstanding that has permeated the whole debate on environmental protection and restoration, even in relatively sophisticated circles – namely that we have to keep or protect environment or ecological 'equilibrium'. In relation to this, we run up against very serious problems. The problem to be solved in fact is not achieving an 'ecological balance', but, on the contrary, obtaining the most efficient forms of 'long-term ecological imbalance'. The problem is not to exterminate mankind now, in the name of ecological equilibrium, but to prolong our ability to use natural resources for as long as possible.[14]

In the same way, horror stories about the imminent disappearance of certain species, such as the peregrine falcon in

North America, need to be put into perspective. Quite apart from the fact that the major threat to this, and other species, has not been pollution but the failure of the authorities to enforce the game laws adequately, one should ask how much sleep do people actually lose today over the disappearance of say, the Dinosaur? In fact innumerable species have disappeared over the course of time, and, it should be noted, not as a result of man's depradations; they disappeared long before man began to have any impact on the environment, during those halcyon days when the so-called 'ecological balance' had not yet been disturbed by mankind. It is no longer possible to see a live dinosaur, but I doubt whether this results in much loss of human welfare. Nor do I think that the human race suffers greatly from its inability to see a live web-footed Beckermanipus.

In any case, the notion that modern economic growth or inadequate respect for the environment is a major cause of the disappearance of certain species bears little relation to the facts. It is all very well for Professor Scorer to lament the threat to tigers and to complain that it is much more serious if they become extinct than if we lose great works of art, which, according to him can be recreated, but in the first place, nobody has ever been eaten by a work of art (i.e. the ability to recreate something is an absurd criterion by which to value it; it must have an independent value); secondly, great works of art cannot be recreated either; and, thirdly, and most important, it is nature, not man – even hunting man – which has caused the disappearance of most extinct species.[15] As the editor-in-chief of the *Bulletin of Atomic Scientists* has written:

Many rationally unjustifiable things have been written in recent years – some by very reputable scientists – about the sacredness of natural ecological systems, their inherent stability and the danger of human interference with them. But the history of life on earth is full of ecological catastrophes in which man has played no role at all. Thousands upon thousands of species have become extinct in the course of evolution; the whole animal worlds of the age of the giant lizards has disappeared from the earth. The once fruitful Sahara has become a desert. All this resulted from natural processes; changes in climate caused by relocation of sea currents, other geologic upheavals, or the spread of new pathogenic micro-organisms ... Man now threatens the survival of the wolf, polar bear, rhinoceros and Bengal tiger; but a greater number of species would have disappeared by natural processes if man did not contribute – consciously or unconsciously – to their preservation.[16]

A balanced use of the environment

To the economist, optimal policy consists of weighing up the loss of human welfare caused by environmental damage (including reduction in wild life) against the gain to human welfare arising out of mankind's use of the environment. In practice, of course, as is shown in later chapters, it is impossible to put accurate figures on the two sides of the balance sheet, but it is vitally important to accept the principle in order to keep things in true perspective. Thus, for example, it would be quite wrong to spend vast sums of money to clean up some remote salmon river in the north of Scotland, or to prevent damage to some oyster bed. After all oysters and salmon fishing make a negligible contribution to the welfare of the average person.

Thus, before we come to look at the factual evidence about the rise in pollution and its alleged relationship to economic growth, it must be recognized, as Walter Heller points out very clearly, that:

> the most vexing difference between ecologists and economists may not be in their conflicting interpretations of the evidence but in their divergent modes of thinking ... What the economist regards as rational is to seek, not total or maximum, cleansing of the environment – prohibitions tend to be prohibitively expensive – but an optimum arising out of a careful matching of the 'bads' that we overcome and the 'goods' that we forgo in the process.[17]

The proposition that there is some balance to be struck between the costs and benefits of using the environment and that it would be foolish to try to eliminate pollution entirely does not imply, however, that pollution could not possibly rise to the point where the damage it did was very great indeed and where society might be forced to pay a very high price, including even a deliberate reduction in the growth rate, in order to bring pollution down to tolerable levels. This is a question of fact, not of principle. I have suggested above that, in practice, economic growth does not necessarily lead to a worsening of the environment and that the opposite may be the case under most conditions. This proposition runs directly counter, of course, to one of the basic assumptions fed into the computerized predictions of the recent report by Meadows and Associates, *The Limits to Growth*.[18]

Pollution hysteria

This study, sponsored by the Club of Rome, purported to show that economic growth should be brought to a halt now, because otherwise it would lead to some global catastrophe owing to the fact that, within the next century, growth would come up against one or other (or all) of three basic constraints. These were (i) pollution; (ii) supply of raw materials; and (iii) the balance between population and food supplies. This study purported to demonstrate that, as economic growth proceeds, pollution inevitably rises, raw materials become exhausted, and food supplies are unable to keep up with the expanding population, so that, in the long run – i.e. in about 100 years or so depending on the precise assumptions made – the growth process comes to a catastrophic halt, and standards of living collapse. It is argued that, in view of these results, it would be preferable to bring growth to a halt now.

These results are accompanied by a smattering of disconnected facts and figures and impressive computer feed-outs and diagrams which give an impression of scientific objectivity and precision but which do not seem to be explicitly used in the estimation of the assumptions on which the whole calculation is based. In the words of *The Economist* (March 11th, 1972) 'The report represents the highwater mark of an old-fashioned nonsense, because the ... team has pumped into its computer so many dear, dead assumptions'; or, in the words of another review article, ' "The Limits to Growth" in our view, is an empty and misleading work. Its imposing apparatus of computer technology and systems jargon conceals a kind of intellectual Rube Goldberg device – one which takes arbitrary assumptions, shakes them up and comes out with arbitrary conclusions that have the ring of science.'[19]

Unfortunately, the ordinary man in the street does not realize that all that a computer does is work out very quickly the implications of the assumptions and instructions that are fed into it. As Sir Eric Ashby, Chairman of the Royal Commission on Environmental Pollution from 1970 to 1973, said, 'If you feed doom-laden assumptions into computers it is not surprising that they predict doom' (*The Spectator*, May 27th, 1972). And, as various scientific authorities have pointed out, the pollution assumptions fed into the computer in this particular case were nonsensical.

Professor Mellanby, who is one of the world's foremost authorities on the scientific characteristics of pollution, wrote of the Club of Rome study: 'The authors continue to insist that pollution is a new, and exponentially increasing problem, forgetting that *real* damaging pollution has decreased in recent years in most developed countries, and that the increasing pressure to control pollution means that at least one of the curves [in their study] is manifest nonsense.'[20] Similarly, Sir Eric Ashby wrote: 'There is a further difficulty about deciding policies in the abatement of pollution; that is that the dangers lie in the future and we have to anticipate them without being able to predict them. It is here that the public have been mischievously misled by some people who profess to be able to predict doom a century or so ahead.'[21]

Furthermore, many people who have never heard of the Club of Rome study are seriously worried about the effects of pollution and the extent to which it constitutes a constraint on further economic growth. Hence, it is necessary to dwell on the pollution threat at some length. Of course, there *is* a pollution problem, and in view of the inevitable scientific ignorance of the ultimate effects on mankind of the many pollutants entering the environment (particularly of the newer synthetic variety) it would be absurd not to take reasonable precautions and exercise surveillance, and to implement policies to reduce pollution to optimum amounts. But public hysteria about pollution is (a) counter-productive, for when the public realizes how often they have been scared unnecessarily they will no longer take seriously those organizations engaged in practical pollution control and research; and (b) likely, meanwhile, to be positively harmful in various direct ways. As a recent *Nature* editorial put it, 'The truth is that the public confusion which has been created in the past few years by warnings of catastrophe is a serious impediment to the rational conduct of society.'[22] In a climate of panic, decisions are taken which are likely to harm sections of the community; in certain cases on a relatively small scale, in other cases, possibly on a catastrophic scale.

Some ecological groups have been organizing activities by schoolchildren to monitor the pollution in their local rivers. In the U.S.A. this has reached the point where Christmas presents now include pollution-monitoring kits for children, and in Britain, too, projects to arrange for schoolchildren to help monitor water-pollution have been sponsored.[23] There have been no cases of fatal illness from water-pollution in Britain for over fifty years; but every year over a hundred children are drowned from playing in or near water! How many more will drown as a result of this kind of activity? A sane and balanced attitude to the solution of urgent problems would include, instead, a campaign to ensure that more children are taught to swim at an early age.

A far more serious example of the risks of exaggerating the dangers of pollution is the pressure, which in many countries has been successful, to ban the use of DDT. We all know that there are several poisons readily available which, if taken in excess, as many of them commonly are, can be fatal. Aspirin, tobacco, alcohol, and various other dangerous products fall into this category. One of the least dangerous by far is DDT, and which has hardly ever killed anybody although hundreds of thousands of people have been employed in spraying it for about thirty years. At the same time it has saved millions of lives in the countries where its use has helped to eradicate malaria, not to mention the contribution it makes to conserving agricultural crops in countries where this can make all the difference between staying alive or dying of starvation.

Nevertheless, under pressure from conservationist groups, who assert that DDT is wiping out certain forms of bird-life (though, according to various authorities, such as Lord Todd, failure to enforce game laws is a far more significant factor in their decline),[24] various countries have banned DDT. In Ceylon, where malaria had been almost eradicated, the banning of DDT in response to the conservationists' campaign led to a rapid rise in the malaria death-rate. In Sweden DDT had to be quickly reintroduced when insects started to destroy forests.[25] And similar effects on pests in New England were soon noticed as DDT use began to be curtailed. Yet Mr William Ruckelshaus, the Administrator of the U.S.A.'s Environmental Protection Agency, decided, in June 1972, that 'the long-range risks of continued use of DDT for use on cotton and most other crops is unacceptable and outweighs any benefits', and he consequently imposed an almost total ban on its use in the U.S.A., as from the end of 1972.

This decision has still not been justified by any agreement among scientists as to the danger of DDT. For although the scientific advisory committee appointed by Mr Ruckelshaus to investigate the matter recommended that its use should be phased out, its findings as regards the imminence of any danger to human health were completely ambiguous.[26] The Committee concluded merely that the present use of DDT 'does not present an imminent hazard to human health, in terms of bodily functions and safety', but that its continued use is 'an imminent hazard to human welfare in terms of maintaining healthy desirable flora and fauna in man's environment'. In short, the case against DDT is not that it directly, or even indirectly, affects human health – like the innumerable other tolerated poisons, such as tobacco, alcohol, and so on, which *do* harm humans. It is entirely in terms of the damage to certain parts of the physical environment, although the benefits it confers on other parts of the physical environment, and the vast contribution it makes to human health in the eradication of malaria, should have been weighed in the balance.

Of course, it may not matter so much to rich countries, like the U.S.A., where the malaria danger is relatively low to begin with and where cotton textiles can easily be replaced by synthetics. Where DDT matters most is to the poor countries, for

> the people who require cheap food, communities with limited production, and the people who are too poor to leave malarious areas or protect themselves with drugs. To these people there are great short-period advantages in using DDT ... The disadvantages are in the minds of a more leisured section of the middle class of the economically advanced countries. This group is much concerned about conservation of the countryside, which they can enjoy provided not too many other people are there as well.[27]

The fact that there is no scientific evidence that DDT has any harmful effect on human beings (as attested by numerous eminent scientists, including even the scientific body that advised Mr Ruckelshaus to ban it in the U.S.A., and the Nobel Prize winner Dr Norman Borlaug) has not prevented the environmentalists from putting about scare stories, such as that mother's milk contains DDT. (Of course it does, but in small harmless doses, unlike the caffeine, nicotine or alcohol which is also contained in many mothers' milk.)[28] Professor Mellanby has pointed out that the danger of developing lung cancer from sitting next to a smoker in a bus is at least 200 times as great as that of developing cancer from the average concentration of DDT in a human being in Britain.[29]

The DDT story is simply one of the most dramatic cases of the real damage that can be done by the hysterical approach to pollution. There will no doubt be many others, quite apart from the eventual backlash effect when the public wakes up to the way the eco-doomsters jump from one scare story to another as they each, in turn, become refuted in the light of more sober scientific evidence. One of the most recent instances of damage done by excessive concern over pollution has been the energy crisis in the U.S.A. in the winter 1972/1973. Many factors were responsible for the fuel shortage during this period, but among these were the opposition by environmentalists to the construction of an oil pipeline from Alaska and to the construction of some new nuclear power stations during the previous few years.

Again, there is no evidence of any harmful effects on human health from these projects, but there is a strong likelihood that thousands of people were exposed to risks of dying from pneumonia or similar illnesses as a result of the shut-down of heating systems in many parts of the eastern seaboard of the U.S.A. during the winter of 1972/1973.

There are many reasons why, in the face of conflicting scientific evidence, the extreme environmentalists have been able to enforce policies that, on balance, certainly harm human welfare, taking everything into consideration. One of the reasons is, of course, that pollution is a relatively new scientific problem. Hence, scientists are, understandably, at the beginning of much of their research into the purely scientific aspects of pollution, and tend to differ about the likely effects on health of many pollutants, in the same way that economists (and all other scientists for that matter) tend to differ about the problems that are at the frontiers of their subject. But another reason is that the general public is easily impressed by figures which, from a scientific point of view, are meaningless, such as figures of the millions of tons of pollutants that enter the atmosphere or the oceans. These may sound terrifying, but they are often completely insignificant in relation to the absorptive capacity of the environment in question, or the amount of pollutants already entering the environment from natural causes.

For example, it has been estimated that if the whole of the annual production of the world's mercury mines were to be dumped straight into the sea it would take between 2,500 years and 10,000 years before the sea's natural concentration of mercury was doubled.[30] The general public does not realize how insignificant many of the apparently massive figures of pollutant production are in relation either to natural occurrences or to the size and absorptive capacity of the natural environment. As Petr Beckmann has put it:

A single hurricane releases the energy of a hundred thousand hydrogen bombs. The billions of tons of water lifted from the oceans and raining down again, the billions of tons of air circulated round the globe boggle the mind. The cloud formations in the atmosphere are visible from the moon; the plume of smoke emerging from the stacks of an industrial plant cannot even be discerned from a jet plane. Half of all the carbon dioxide emitted into the air is absorbed by the oceans … Such are the gigantic self-cleaning capacities of nature; even the hundreds of cubic kilometers of ash spewed into the atmosphere by the largest volcanic eruptions on record have been cleaned up by these capacities within years. Can man's puny little carbon-dioxide production compete with such gigantic processes as volcanic activity?[31]

Dr Mishan terrifies his readers by telling them that there are now about 10 million tons of pollutants in the atmosphere. In fact, it has been estimated that swamps and other natural sources emit as much as 1,600 million tons per year of methane gas into the atmosphere without it doing any harm. Even cattle, which emit methane in large amounts, are estimated to contribute several millions of tons of it every year into the atmosphere. And there are innumerable other examples, which dwarf Mishan's puny figure of 10 million tons of man-made pollutants. For example, about 170 million tons of a certain form of hydrocarbon are emitted every year from forests and other vegetation.[32] In none of these cases is any harm done, apparently, because the absorptive capacity of the environment is incomparably greater than the layman realizes.

For example, it is true that about 200 to 300 million tons of carbon monoxide are put into the air every year; mainly from motor-cars and trucks, i.e. not by natural processes. At this rate the concentration of it in the atmosphere should have doubled over the last five years, in the same way that the concentration of carbon dioxide is rising. But, as a matter of fact, the average concentration of carbon monoxide has not changed over twenty years. Of course, carbon-monoxide concentrations may become very high in some streets at certain times of the day and be very low only 100 yards away; in such cases there is less a world environmental problem than a local industrial hygiene problem, which could be solved by re-routing traffic or re-siting factories rather than by stopping economic growth. For the world as a whole it appears that there is some mechanism, not fully understood yet by scientists, which keeps the carbon monoxide in check. Some scientists think that it is eaten up by certain bacteria in the soil; others think that it is depleted in chemical sinks through reaction with atmospheric materials. Furthermore, there is now, apparently, reason to believe that carbon monoxide produced by natural processes far exceeds that generated by man-made combustion (as has long been known to be the case with sulphur dioxide, a major form of air pollutant, which is produced naturally by volcanoes and rotting vegetation). Finally, there is also some evidence that humans are unaffected by higher concentrations of carbon monoxide than had previously been thought to be the case.[33] At a recent scientific symposium in London, in April 1971, Professor Kurti, the Professor of Physics at Oxford University, reported some work carried out by Professor Elliott Montrol, in the U.S.A., to the effect that a car emits only six grammes of pollutant a mile whereas a horse, over the same distance, emits about 600 grammes of solid pollutant and 300 grammes of liquid pollutant.[34]

Another hazard over which there has been much scientific disagreement is that of the danger from lead in the atmosphere. Professor Bryce-Smith, of the University of Reading, has been one of the leaders of the campaign to introduce much more stringent controls on emissions of lead into the atmosphere.

Now, with the lead issue, as with any other pollutant for that matter, there is no cause for complacency. Lead poisoning is a particularly nasty way of dying, and there is no doubt at all that lead is toxic above levels which are sometimes reached in human beings (though not anything like as frequently as in the past when 'acute poisoning from lead, arsenic, phosphorous and many other substances was an accepted risk from industrial employment').[35] Hence, there is no doubt that extreme vigilance is required. Nevertheless, most qualified scientific opinion appears to take the view that lead in the atmosphere is far less hazardous than is maintained by Bryce-Smith and by those in the U.S.A. who have persuaded the administration to impose strict controls on the amounts of lead permitted in gasoline. This is certainly the view of the Chief Medical Officer of Health in Britain, and of the overwhelming majority of the scientists who contributed to a conference on the subject held by the British Occupational Hygiene Society, and others.[36] The general scientific view is that the lead absorbed these days by humans is mainly from old, flaking paint; lead pipes in old houses (through which the water passes); cooking utensils and crockery. Children are much more likely to be affected by sucking old lead paint on toys or other objects than by breathing lead in the atmosphere.

But it is possible to continue for ever listing the various scare stories of the 'Everybody knows' kind, which are invariably discredited by reputable scientists in due course.

For example, not long after the American Food and Drug Administration warned the public not to eat swordfish on account of its mercury content it was found that some swordfish and tuna which had been dead for a hundred years contained just as much mercury as freshly caught fish of the same species.[37]

One of the favourite arguments of the extreme environmentalists is that pollution should be stopped now, even at the price of economic growth, because of the possible irreversibility of the resulting damage. Reference is then usually made to Lake Erie, which had been rumoured to have become irremediably dead and devoid of all fish-life as a result of the 'eutrophication' (overgrowth of plants on account of too much nutrient in the water, largely from the phosphates in detergents). But there have been reports of dramatic increases in the fish catch in this lake recently, and in 1972 it had its highest fish catch on record. There is even growing doubt among the scientists as to the effects of phosphates in detergents (some scientists now suspect that eutrophication of water is caused by nitrates, not phosphates after all). Nevertheless, with the aid of the anti-phosphates scare all sorts of substitutes for the standard detergents were successfully marketed in the U.S.A. for some time before the American authorities were obliged to publicize the fact that these substitutes were often harmful to the users in various ways. One of the harmful effects was that they destroyed the fireproof qualities of many clothes in which they were washed, thereby greatly increasing the risk of accidents to children from fires.[38]

Of course, understanding of the environmental impact of many pollutants is in a rudimentary state. One of the difficulties faced by any science at an early stage in its enquiry is the difficulty of finding adequate data. This is especially true of pollution. Accurate measurement of many pollutants is simply not possible except at enormous expense. For example, measures of sulphur-dioxide concentrations in the air are greatly influenced by factors such as whether the measurements are taken on a windy day, or in proximity to a tall building, trees, hills, and so on. It has been estimated that in order to measure the mean daily sulphur-dioxide concentration in an area with 90 per cent accuracy it would be necessary to have four recording stations per square mile.[39] Nevertheless, as the rest of this chapter shows, there are quite enough data to refute the gloomy predictions about an inevitable increase in pollution if economic growth is allowed to continue.

Recent trends in pollution

It is now necessary to question the assumptions that pollution must rise with economic growth to such a level that, even if mankind is not first struck down by starvation or the exhaustion of raw materials, it would be nearly killed off by the pollution of the environment. This prediction is based on propositions such as that 'The few kinds of pollution that actually have been measured over time seem to be increasing exponentially'.[40] This echoes the sort of completely inaccurate and sweeping generalizations about pollution that have been circulated by some scientists who ought to know better, such as Professor Commoner, who writes: 'A rather striking picture does emerge from the data that are available; most pollution problems made their first appearance, or became very much worse, in the years following World War II.'[41] Professor Mellanby's comment on this proposition was: 'This is really a most incredible statement. Anyone who is familar with London, Sheffield or Pittsburgh knows that one real and damaging form of air pollution has been eliminated from many of our cities and industrial areas. Many rivers and lakes are still seriously polluted, but in almost every case there has been an improvement in the last 10 or 20 years.'[42]

The few kinds of pollution that have been measured have been decreasing for some time in Britain, and their rise has been checked in the U.S.A. during the last few years. In Britain the dramatic reduction in air pollution is well documented. The total smoke produced in Britain fell from 2·3 million tons in 1953 to 0·9 million in 1968; the total quantity of sulphur oxides emitted in the air in Britain has been falling since 1962, and there has been a sharper fall in ground-level concentrations of sulphur oxides.[43] Over the decade 1961 average smoke concentrations in urban areas in Britain fell by 60 per cent, and SO_2 (sulphur dioxide) concentrations fell by 30 per cent, despite increasing population and industrial output.[44] And these are averages of *all* urban areas, so they include those towns that have not yet taken advantage of the powers conferred on them under the Clean Air Acts to introduce smokeless zones. Hence, the reduction in air pollution in some major cities, such as London and Sheffield, has been much greater than the above figures indicate. In these cities the fall in smoke per unit of industrial output has been of the order of

85 per cent over the ten-year period in question.[45] Over this same period the average hours of winter sunshine in London have doubled; in 1958 average visibility was one mile; now on an average winter day in London visibility is up to four miles, and in summer it is twelve to twenty miles.

There has also been a fall in the pollution of rivers in Britain, though this has been less dramatic than in the case of air pollution. But this is merely because, on account of other pressing needs in the public sector, such as housing, schools, roads, and hospitals, the necessary authorizations for the very heavy expenditures involved in reducing water pollution have only been granted during the latter part of the 1960s. Nevertheless, the latest survey of rivers in Britain shows that the percentage of 'grossly polluted' rivers has fallen from 6·4 per cent in 1958 to 3·7 per cent in 1972 (in terms of mileage) and that the mileage of completely unpolluted rivers has risen slightly from 72·9 per cent in 1958 to 77·4 per cent in 1972.[46] In certain cases the improvement in river conditions has rapidly led to a sharp increase in fish-life. For example, in 1958 there were no fish in the River Thames from about fifteen miles upstream of central London to a point twenty-five miles downstream. In 1972 fifty-five different species of fish were found in the river, including roach, pike and smelt (a member of the salmon family and a sea fish), not to mention haddock, herring, plaice and sole.[47] Following the return of the fish there has been a sharp rise in the population of different bird species in the London area, particularly the water-birds. Thousands of duck and wading birds, mostly migrating from their breeding grounds in Russia and Northern Europe, are now spending their winter vacation on the upper reaches of the Thames estuary, where, until a few years ago, one could only see swans and gulls living on sewage pickings.[48]

It is true that the reductions in pollution in other countries have not been so dramatic yet as has been the case in Britain, particularly as regards air pollution. But this is not because Britain is favoured by some exceptional technical circumstances which enable this country alone to achieve such great reductions in pollution. It is simply because anti-pollution legislation has been introduced in the other countries later than in the U.K. But the point established so far is that the statement that all measured pollution has been rising exponentially is simply untrue.*

But even in the U.S.A., where tough anti-pollution legislation has only been introduced during the last few years, there was already some reduction in measured pollution in the 1950s and 1960s, as a result of various autonomous changes associated more with economic growth than with legislation. For example, smoke concentrations in urban areas declined slightly between 1957 and 1970, largely on account of the dispersion of industrial plant and the movement of population out of central cities. But there has already been a decline also in carbon-monoxide emissions, which is partly due to the installation of anti-pollution devices in motor-cars from 1968.[49] Much greater reductions in this and other forms of pollution from all sources will, of course, take place over this decade as a result of the policies now being introduced in the U.S.A. and in many other countries.

Recent anti-pollution policies

Reference has already been made to the improvements that have already taken place in the environment in Britain, largely as a result of policies that have been in operation or have been greatly strengthened during the last twenty years or so. This applies chiefly to air pollution, where the Clean Air Acts of 1956 and 1968 have provided local authorities with the powers and incentives to almost eliminate smoke pollution from their areas. And this improvement is by no means at an end. By 1980

* At a public meeting to discuss *The Limits to Growth* at the U.S. Embassy in London, April 13th, 1972, Meadows answered the point about the London air by claiming that the Clean Air Acts had merely shifted our smoke on to somebody else, and that Sweden was now suffering from the air pollution that we had got rid of. But, of course, the Swedes complain about SO_2 from our higher factory chimneys, not about our smoke, and nobody here has claimed that we have cut SO_2 emissions by anything like the same amount.

it is expected that virtually all smoke will be eliminated from London air on account of the extension to the whole of the Greater London area of smoke control orders which, in 1969, still only covered 67 per cent of premises in this area. Similar extensions of the area covered by these orders can now be anticipated in the rest of the country. For more and more areas now follow the example set by the other authorities, stimulated perhaps by public and governmental pressure and the increasing awareness amongst their inhabitants of the gap between their amenity standards and those of the towns where the powers have already been used in full. As a result there has been marked acceleration in the extension of smoke control orders recently. During the first six months of 1972 the areas covered by these new orders increased by more than the area covered by new orders in the whole year 1971. In the same six months' period the number of premises covered by the orders rose by 226,297, which represented a 60 per cent increase over 1971.[50]

The legislation of the last fifteen years or so has not been the only factor behind the fall in air pollution in Britain. Other factors have helped, notably rising incomes, which have made possible the installation of central heating or more modern heating appliances that cause far less pollution than the conventional British coal fire. Also, as the Royal Commission on Environmental Pollution pointed out in its First Report, these factors have been further reinforced by the increasing use in Britain of natural gas (which does not create any SO_2 pollution at all) and nuclear energy.

The latter, together with a generally increased use of electric space-heating in homes, enables such pollution as is produced to be emitted from power-stations remote from urban concentrations, where it can be rapidly dispersed (as in the case of conventional power-stations) or carefully regulated and screened (as with nuclear power-stations).[51] But these changes in the industrial origin of air pollution in Britain are also backed up by policies designed to ensure that power-stations, or other air-polluting plants, such as oil refineries, are remote from centres of population, and are designed to minimize pollution anyway. For example, the air pollutants can only be emitted at much higher escape velocities, in very high chimneys, so that their impact on the environment is often virtually zero (given the relatively short duration of SO_2 and the rapid dispersion of smoke in the upper atmosphere). Strict attention has also been paid to reducing their water-polluting effect – for example by the use of closed-circuit water-cooling techniques in modern power-stations.

The air-pollution policies in Britain are not confined to the regulation of smoke and SO_2, although these are the main pollutants and are also very good indicators of the presence of various other minor pollutants produced as a result of the incomplete combustion of fossil fuels. For example, diesel-engined trucks are well known to be frequent sources of smoke emissions, particularly when they are travelling slowly. Regulations to further control the smoke emissions from such vehicles were introduced in June 1972, and as from October 1972, tougher power-to-weight ratios for such trucks were laid down in order to reduce the pollution resulting from their inability to accelerate and to climb hills rapidly.[52] Regulations have also been introduced to halve the lead content in petrol by the end of 1975 – i.e. from over 0·8 grammes per litre in 1972 to 0·45 grammes per litre by the end of 1975.[53] This is nothing like as drastic a cut in lead in petrol as is envisaged in U.S.A. legislation, but the chief motive behind the American requirements on lead is that lead in petrol damages the catalytic converters that will have to be installed in American motor-cars in order to reduce their emissions of other pollutants (notably the carbon monoxide, unburnt hydrocarbons and nitrogen oxides), not in the interests of cutting lead pollution in the atmosphere *per se*.

As regards water pollution in the U.K., the main constraint here, as indicated above, has been the restriction on the amount that local authorities have been allowed to spend – or encouraged to spend – on sewage treatment and the amount of financial assistance that they could count on obtaining from central government funds. But for some years now it has been the declared policy of successive governments to make up the backlog.* The amounts to be spent on river improvement over the next few years appear to be sufficient to enable a substantial improvement to be made in the condition of most British rivers and estuaries by 1980. For example, the percentage of rivers that will still be 'grossly polluted' should have fallen from 4 per cent in 1970 to 1 per cent in 1980, and the percentage of rivers free of pollution should have risen from about 75 per cent in 1970 to 81 per cent in 1980.[54]

Policies to reduce air pollution and water pollution of the most common kinds by no means exhaust the extension of anti-pollution policies in Britain. Action is also being increasingly taken to control the dumping of toxic wastes, to reduce litter, and to control noise.†

In the U.S.A. a host of very stringent new anti-pollution

* Various statements by Mr Peter Walker concerning the announced target expenditures on the water-cleansing programme may give the impression that the Conservative Government is much more environment-conscious than the Labour Government had been. This is far from the case, however, since the currently quoted figure of £1,300 million expenditure on rivers etc., over the next five years, represents the effect of rising prices on a programme largely laid down by Mr Crosland in the Labour Government. Furthermore, not all this amount is destined to reduce water pollution; and much of it represents the increased expenditure required to provide water services to meet the rising demand for water, and which would be needed irrespective of any pollution of the rivers. (See various statements by Peter Walker, and by Mr Eldon Griffiths, the Under-Secretary to Mr Walker at the Department of the Environment, such as Mr Walker's statement at the opening of a water-pollution control works at Tewkesbury, September 11th, 1972, and various statements by Mr Griffiths, including his reply to a Parliamentary Question, on July 5th, 1972). Of the £1,300 million figure that is constantly referred to in connection with the present government's expenditure plans to improve the rivers, only about £600 million of this corresponds to improved sewage (see, for instance, the British submission to 1972 UNO Stockholm Conference, p. 30, and see the speech by Mr Eldon Griffiths at Birmingham, July 12th, 1972).

† For example, the increase in litter fines from £10 to £100, the Deposit of Poisonous Waste Act, 1972, and the acceptance by the government of tighter restrictions on noise, as proposed by the Noise Advisory Council. Passenger vehicles coming into service after October 1st, 1973 and other vehicles after October 1974, will be required to keep below lower decibel levels than has been the case in the past, and improved arrangements have been made to limit neighbourhood noise from stationary sources. See Department of the Environment Circular 16/73, *Planning and Noise*; various reports by the Noise Advisory Council; and *Code of Practice for reducing the exposure of employed persons to Noise* (H.M.S.O., London, 1972); and reply to a parliamentary question by Mr Peter Walker, June 29th, 1971.

policies has been introduced during the last few years. In the earlier legislation, such as the Clean Air Act of 1963, the emphasis was on Federal support and subsidies for local initiatives, but in the Air Quality Act of 1967 the first major shift was seen in the direction of the Federal establishment of the criteria and standards that should be applied. This was further greatly tightened up in 1970 Clean Air Act Amendments, which established the procedure by which national air-ambient standards would be set and enforced. Under this Act violations of air-quality implementation plans were prohibited and became liable to criminal penalties. This Act also shifted to local authorities the burden of proof that a level of pollution that had been deemed as hazardous by the Environmental Protection Agency (E.P.A.) Administrator was clearly not hazardous. This Act, and its subsequent amendments, provide for the E.P.A. to adjudicate on the acceptibility of plans drawn up in various States and other legislative areas to improve their air-quality standards. These plans have to be detailed and include not only satisfactory targets as regards air quality with respect to six main air-pollutants, but also proposals for enforcement action, control strategy, compliance schedules, methods of surveillance, and so on.[55]

There is little doubt that the current anti-pollution programme in the U.S.A. will achieve a dramatic reduction in air pollution in American cities. It is envisaged that by 1977 emissions from stationary sources of SO_2 will be reduced by about 85 to 90 per cent, of hydrocarbons by 80 per cent, and of nitrogen oxides by 90 per cent.

The reduction in emissions of pollutants from motor-cars will be of the same order of magnitude, but there has been much dispute as to whether it is feasible in the time-scale permitted.[56] This is a matter which is still subject to enquiry and judicial investigation, but the issue is not whether such improvements can be achieved by the end of this decade or not; the whole argument is about whether they can be achieved by 1976.* Hence, there is no doubt that the main targets of the

* In April 1973, the deadline for compliance with the motor-car regulations was postponed by one year.

5

American anti-pollution policies will be reached by the end of this decade, long, long before the Club of Rome predicted that we would all be asphyxiated.*

Most other major industrial nations have also been very active in the introduction of anti-pollution policies during the last few years, and in several countries, notably Japan, Sweden and Germany, considerable amounts are, apparently, to be spent on pollution abatement. For example, a Japanese ten-year plan to reduce pollution has been drawn up, which will be supervised by a newly created Environment Agency, and which is expected to cost about £3,500 million over the ten-year period from 1971.[57]

As might have been expected, given its record in social matters and its vulnerability to pollution, Sweden was one of the first countries to set up a government agency to tackle pollution back in 1967, and to introduce comprehensive measures, including heavy government subsidies, to curb pollution. Germany, too, seems to be taking the subject very seriously judging, for example, by the moves made to force industry to pay for cleaning up its pollution, the severity of the legal penalties being introduced for breaches of the regulations (ten years in prison or very heavy fines in some cases), and the heavy expenditure programmes in certain areas, such as the plan to build 5,000 new sewage works during the next few years. It is expected that the River Rhine, which is notorious for its pollution, will be entirely free of organic pollution by the end of the 1970s. There has even been some conflict between the European Economic Community and the German government as a result of a new law in Germany designed to achieve a very drastic reduction in the lead content in petrol, which the E.E.C. Commission thought went too far and could lead to the increased use of other ingredients in petrol which would be worse (and might also create new barriers to trade).[58]

* The Clean Air Acts are not the only element in American anti-pollution policy. The National Environmental Policy Act (N.E.P.A.), which became law on January 1st, 1970, also provided for a machinery that would extend environmental protection to other media, including a massive clean-up programme for American rivers, controls on the disposal of toxic substances, measures to reduce pollution from aircraft, and so on.

Taking these various countries together, it can be seen that there is a second reason for rejecting predictions that economic growth must eventually be halted on account of the inevitable increase in pollution. This is that, even if it were true that all pollutants had been increasing in the past, this could not provide the basis for any sweeping predictions about the future, given that governments have only relatively recently begun to adopt tough anti-pollution policies in the main industrial countries.*

It is a characteristic weakness of shoddy scientific method to make predictions into the future on the basis of relationships that may have existed in one policy context, but which will clearly be completely different in a transformed policy context. The eco-doomsters' predictions seem to assume that the public just sits back tamely, allowing itself to be increasingly asphyxiated by fumes or poisoned by dangerous substances in the water, without reacting in any way by obliging their political representatives to introduce more stringent pollution-control policies. It is difficult to understand how the eco-doomsters can reconcile this image of a completely apathetic, fatalistic public with the public that they hope will rise up and force governments to bring economic growth to a halt and to combat their age-old aspirations for higher standards of living.

Of course the eco-doomsters will say that even if there is a concerted attempt to reduce pollution there are technical limitations on the extent to which this can be done. But, as seen above, even before the pressures to reduce pollution became as intense as they have been during recent years, great strides were made in the elimination of the main pollutants wherever the authorities took action. Furthermore, pollution-removal technology is still in a rudimentary stage, on account of the absence of incentives, until recently, to put much effort into the search for anti-pollution devices. With the growing pressure on industry and public authorities to cut pollution there is likely to be a very rapid technological process in the pollution-abatement industry.

* This does not apply to trans-national pollution, such as the polluting of the air over southern Scandinavia by factories in Western Europe, for obvious reasons.

Technical progress in pollution abatement

In *The Limits to Growth*, it is postulated that the most 'optimistic' assumption that can be made about pollution abatement is that the ratio of pollution to output can be reduced *over the next hundred years* to one-quarter of its present level.[59] Such figures of 'total' pollution are strictly speaking meaningless, but, in so far as ratios can be calculated for individual forms of pollution in relation to specific indicators of output, it has already been shown above that far greater reductions in air pollution than this have already been achieved in Britain over the space of about fifteen years, and that the current targets for reductions in air pollution in the U.S.A. imply that, in spite of rising output, air pollution will be reduced to about one-tenth of its present level in the space of only about seven or eight years.

These figures alone show how wildly wrong assumptions about pollution in the doomsday literature have been. But these reductions in pollution are just beginning. Similar developments are taking place in other and less widely known fields of production which hold out the promise that equally dramatic progress will be made in reducing other forms of pollution. For example, in the chemical industry, pollution per ton of product in many lines of production has already been cut to one-fifth or one-tenth of the earlier levels. Even greater progress has been made in many branches of the oil-refining industry, where as a result of massive reductions in the amount of water used per unit of throughput and in the amount of pollution per unit of water used, the overall effluent discharged per unit of output has been cut, in many cases, to about 1 per cent of earlier levels.[60]

Other major water-pollutant processes, notably pulp, paper, and chlorine production, have already achieved substantial reductions in the amount of pollution per unit of output.*

---

* For example, discharges of B.O.D. (biochemical oxygen demand), which is an important form of pollution from the Swedish pulp and paper mills, have fallen by 65 per cent over the past ten years in spite of a 70 per cent rise in output (Bulletin of the *Swedish Water and Air Pollution Research Laboratory*, Vol. 2, No. 1, 1973).

Indeed, in chlorine production in Sweden, pollution has been almost eliminated in the new KemaNord plant at Stenungsfund, partly with the aid of closed-circuit water-circulation systems. Again, in Sweden considerable progress is being made in the reduction of mercury pollution, which is important in the pulp and paper industries. Another example of technical progress in water pollution is the use in various harbours (Montreal, Los Angeles and Nagoya harbour in Japan) of the system of regenerating bodies of 'dead' water by means of aeration through plastic pipes set into the bed of the harbour.[61]

Under pressure to reduce pollution, progress is also being reported in many other fields. For example, recent aircraft engines, particularly the RB211, which is used to power the Lockheed Tri-Star planes, are much quieter than the earlier generation of engines, and this is, again, just the beginning. Now that a high premium is placed on quiet engines, the manufacturers are working on the problem; they did not need to do so before. As a result progress is being made towards a completely new generation of engines (for example, those using thrust-control devices such as a variable-pitched fan) that will further reduce aircraft engine noise.[62]

Another problem that is likely to be beaten within a relatively short time is that of plastic-waste disposal. Various promising lines of attack are being pursued, including high-temperature pyrolysis (i.e. materials are burnt at very high temperatures, leaving barely any deposit, in constructions that are rather like giant laboratory test-tubes), self-destructive plastics of the kind being developed by Professor Gerald Scott in Britain, and an alternative dry-distillation technique introduced by the Sanyo Electric Company in Japan.

Many of these are well beyond the experimental phase. For example, the Goodyear tyre company opened the world's first smokeless tyre-incinerator in Britain in 1972; many American chemical companies are already selling plastic that will decompose in time after the articles made from it have been discarded; and other techniques are also widely in operation. Of course, it is not necessarily desirable that all plastics be destroyed. The processes under investigation include techniques to recycle the plastics for re-use; others include better arrangements to ensure that they are collected and used for land-fill purposes. In fact, for this purpose plastics have advantages, namely that they do not decompose and hence do not settle, so that the surface constructions that may be built on these afterwards (for example, sports fields, industrial estates, and so on) are more solidly based, and the sub-structure does not release odours, gases or liquids to pollute the surrounding areas, which is always a possibility with the conventional land-fills comprising garbage and the like.[63]

The threat of radioactivity has been seriously worrying many people, and it is true that a greater use of nuclear energy will help to avoid an energy crisis. The eco-doomsters here fall back on the uncertainty argument, namely that it is not enough to bury radioactive waste at the bottom of the oceans or elsewhere, however stringent the precautions, since one never knows how it may be disturbed and released some day in the distant future. As Professor Beckmann says, commenting on a British report to the effect that 'We are committing future generations to a problem that we do not know how to handle', this sort of statement might equally well refer to burial of the dead in cemeteries.[64] In fact, Alvin Weinberg, the Director of the Oak Ridge National Laboratory (the U.S.A. nuclear research organization) has stated:

It is perfectly possible to reduce the radioactive effluents from a properly working nuclear power-station to essentially zero; to 1 or 2 per cent of the natural background radiation that we receive all the time. We didn't do this, because we didn't think it was worth doing. But now we think it is worth doing; the international standard for radioactive emissions has recently been cut approximately a hundredfold. So we set our minds to doing it – and we *are* doing it.[65]

Of course, there will always be *some* risk; life is full of risks, some minor and some of catastrophic size; but merely to say that there is some risk doesn't help much in deciding what to do about it. As Beckmann points out, the latest techniques to store radioactive wastes involve so little risk that the probability of accidents is much smaller than the probability of similar damage from, say, a fire. For 'a five-year-old child can set a city ablaze, but it cannot, with reasonable probability, throw a pound of radioactive wastes into a city's water supply'.[66]

Of course, there is always *some* risk of almost any catastrophe one cares to think about. Almost every day I run the risk of being run over by a car or hit on the head by a golf ball; but the costs of avoiding such risks, including staying indoors all day (only to run the risk of being caught in a fire, or dying earlier as a result of lack of exercise) seem to me to be greater than the risks involved in going outside. Life is full of risks, and rational, prudent behaviour consists of weighing up the costs of insuring against the risks in question. The fallacy in the crude eco-doomsters' risk argument, in other words, is that it overlooks the costs of avoiding the risks. If we can reduce or eliminate even the minutest risk of radioactive harm or of being subtly poisoned by some yet undiscovered metal or organo-chlorine accumulated in fish, at no cost at all, then, of course we should do it. But if the cost is to stop economic growth, then I for one am prepared to run the risks involved.

6 Pollution Policy and the Price Mechanism

Pollution and the firm

We have seen that a pollution 'problem' exists because pollution is essentially an 'external diseconomy', which means that the harmful effects of pollution – i.e. the costs it imposes on the community – do not enter into the calculations of the producer responsible. This, in turn, is largely because either (i) the environment which is polluted, such as the air or the water, is not clearly anybody's 'property', so that the polluter does not have to pay the owner for using it up, or, (ii) the environment is somebody's property, as is the case with many common-law rights to clean air or water, but these property rights are difficult or expensive to protect as far as most individuals are concerned, and payment cannot usually be extracted from polluters. In either case, polluters will not have the same incentive to 'economize' on their pollution as they have in respect of things they have to pay for, such as labour, capital or raw materials. The economic problem, therefore, is to find the best way of inducing polluters to economize in pollution up to the point where a further reduction in pollution would cost society more than the resulting benefits.

In order to understand more fully the reasons why the absence of property rights in the environment leads to a 'pollution problem', and the pros and cons of alternative policies to remedy the situation, it would be desirable to set out the full economic analysis of the problem in terms of the standard tools of economic theory. But most readers probably do not wish to embark on a crash course on these concepts for the purposes of better appreciating the subsequent steps in the argument. Consequently we shall try to present the main features of the analysis in a fairly rough and ready manner.

There are two main ways in which one can look at the role of pollution in the productive activity of the firm. For the activity of polluting consists of producing some pollutant, such as smoke, which adulterates some part of the environment, such as clean air. Hence, pollution can be analysed either in terms of *the pollutant* – for example the smoke or the effluent or the noise – that is produced as a by-product of some activity, or in terms of *the clean environment* that is destroyed, or 'used up' by the pollutant. The latter approach consists of regarding the clean environment that is used up as a result of pollution like any other input into a firm's productive process, like labour, or capital, or raw materials. For when a firm pollutes the environment it is, in effect, using up some of the existing supply of clean air or pure water. The former approach, which is perhaps more conventional in economic theory, consists of looking at the pollutant itself as an undesirable by-product of the productive activity that gives rise to it. Thus, for example, air pollution associated with steel production can be looked at either in terms of the smoke produced as a by-product of the steel, or in terms of the clean air 'used up' to produce steel, together with the iron, labour, fuel, and so on.

If pollution is regarded as an undesirable product, it differs from ordinary products in that it carries no price. Normal products carry prices. These prices are related to the benefits the products confer on the purchasers, and they also provide an incentive to producers to produce the products as long as the returns they get from doing so exceed the costs. Since pollution is harmful, it is probably intuitively obvious that, by analogy with the positive prices for ordinary products, pollution should carry a negative price. This would both correspond to the *negative* benefit it confers on people and would also constitute the required *disincentive* to producers to supply this undesirable product. In other words, we would have the exact counterpart of the prices for 'goods', which correspond to the benefits to the consumers and which provide incentives for their production. One is simply the converse, or the mirror image of the other; in the same way that ordinary products are regarded as 'goods', pollution is a 'bad'. What is meant by a negative price? Well, a positive price means that the more the

5*

firm sells the more it receives. So a negative price should mean that the more the firm sells the more it pays. A tax on a product is one form of negative price, since the more of the product that is 'sold' the more tax has to be paid. In so far as a pollutant does not carry any negative price there is (i) no relation between its price and the damage it confers on people, and (ii) no disincentive to producers to produce this undesirable by-product. Hence, an excessive amount of it is certain to be produced.

The same conclusion is reached if pollution is looked at from the second point of view suggested above, namely as a free input of the environment into the productive process. In this case the polluter is seen as having no incentive to economize in his use of the free factor of production, the environment (or 'the facility to pollute'). If a steel producer, for example, finds a way of making steel that economizes in his use of fuel or labour or capital equipment, but which produces more smoke (i.e. greater input of clean air), he will tend to adopt it, since he saves money by using less of the normal inputs and it costs him no more to increase his use of the environment. Similarly, if the firm finds it cheaper to switch to the distribution of milk in plastic containers instead of in glass bottles, he will do so whether or not the production and disposal of plastic containers imposes higher total costs on society, including pollution costs, than do glass bottles. It is true, of course, that technological innovation in some industries has reduced the amount of pollution per unit of output; for example, the switch from coal to other sources of fuel over the last decade in Britain, which has been partly the result of technological progress, has helped to reduce air pollution in British cities. But this benefit to the environment has been fortuitous, and one cannot rely on technological change being of a kind that will reduce pollution, in the absence of the appropriate incentives.

It should not be thought that it is only private industry that, in its concern for profits, tends to push pollution beyond the socially optimal point. Much pollution is produced by public authorities for the very same reason as given above for firms, namely the 'externality' character of pollution. For example, many sewage works in Britain are inadequate, partly because the benefits from better installations – namely cleaner effluent and hence cleaner rivers – would be enjoyed by communities living further downstream. Hence, the benefits are often 'external' to the particular local authority that would have to pay for the improved sewage works. This is why, in general, 'there are no votes in sewage'. One of the motives for the recently proposed re-organization of river and water services in Britain into much larger 'Regional Water Authorities' is that this particular weakness of the system should thereby be remedied.

Nor is it true – as is often maintained by sections of the extreme political left – that pollution is unique to capitalist countries on account of their subservience to the profit motive.[1] For many years now the authorities of the Soviet bloc have been increasingly concerned with very serious pollution, and have been obliged to take increasingly strict measures to fight it.*

If a polluter is induced, by some means or other, to reduce pollution, he will incur costs in doing so. He will usually have to replace some of his use of the environment by making greater use of other factors of production, such as labour or capital (for example a taller chimney or a water-purification plant). In effect he will be obliged to adopt a different technique of production than the one he would choose when the environment was free. Since these other factors of production carry a price (for example the wage, in the case of labour), his costs of production must rise when he uses more of them in order to cut pollution. The more he reduces pollution, the more it will cost him. Furthermore, in general, the more pollution is reduced the more difficult technically, and hence the more expensive, it becomes to reduce pollution by *a further unit*. (In economics jargon, the more pollution is abated the higher, in general, are the ['marginal'] costs of abatement – i.e. the costs of reducing pollution by a further unit.)

The costs that matter to society are the real resources that the polluter has to use in order to economize on his hitherto free use of the environment (or, which comes to the same thing, to

* See discussion on pp. 44–6 of pollution in the Soviet bloc.

cut his output of the undesirable pollutant by-product). For these resources can no longer be used by society for other purposes. In other words, one way or another, firms reduce pollution by substituting other factors of production for it. (It is because of this *substitutability* aspect of the reduction in pollution that it is sometimes easier to look at pollution in this way – i.e. as an input into the productive process, rather than as an undesirable by-product.) Since, in order to make less use of the environment firms have to make more use of other factors of production, the latter are no longer available to society for other purposes, such as the production of food, clothing, consumer durables, machines, motor-cars, medical supplies, houses, and so on. Thus these costs of pollution abatement are also costs to society, and the more pollution is cut the more society must sacrifice the other things that it could have obtained with the resources in question. The problem, therefore, is how far society should sacrifice other goods in order to reduce pollution. To answer this we have to examine the benefits from pollution abatement.

The benefits of pollution abatement

The benefits of reducing pollution simply equal the damage that the pollution had been doing. In Chapter 7 we examine some of the facts about the costs of reducing pollution and the benefits to be derived therefrom (i.e. the damage done by pollution). Here we are concerned only with the principles. The damage done by pollution may take many forms, such as damage to health, loss of amenity, industrial change (such as corrosion of metals or deterioration of dyes), damage to crops or wild-life, and so on. It is by no means confined to economic damage in the sense of damage to industrial or other output. As far as the economist is concerned, any loss of human welfare resulting from pollution should be included in the social damage from pollution abatement. Nor need this damage be confined to the present or the immediate future; the economist would include the benefits to be reaped in the long term.

Like the costs of pollution abatement, the benefits of abatement are not likely to vary in exact proportion to the amount by which pollution is abated. At very high levels of pollution a given reduction in pollution may bring substantial benefits, but when pollution has already been reduced to relatively low levels the gain to welfare from further reductions in pollution may be relatively very small. This would be the case, for example, if there is only a small amount of polluted effluent in a river, which merely makes the water look less than perfectly pure and clear. A slight reduction in pollution at such low levels will probably make a negligible difference to welfare, so there would be little point in spending large sums for this purpose. At the other extreme, if pollution is very high, a small reduction in pollution may make a great difference to the level of dissolved oxygen in the water and hence determine whether fish can easily survive in it and, generally, whether it has an acceptable appearance and smell. At this level of pollution it would be worth spending a good deal to cut pollution by a marginal amount.

'Optimum' pollution

In general, therefore, the more pollution is cut, (a) the more it will cost society to reduce pollution by a further unit, and (b) the less will society gain from cutting out a further unit of pollution. And clearly, it makes no sense for society to push pollution abatement beyond the point where the costs of doing so are greater than the benefits society will reap from doing so. 'Optimum' pollution is the level of pollution at which this point has been reached, i.e., the level at which the social costs of reducing pollution by a further unit just equal the social benefits of doing so, and where a further reduction in pollution would then cost more than the further benefits to be obtained from doing so.*

* The final part of this definition assumes that abatement costs do rise, and benefits fall, as pollution is reduced to successively lower levels, as suggested in the preceding text.

In defining optimum pollution in this way the economist is not expressing any particular value-judgment about what is included in the costs and the benefits. Anybody is free to define these as he likes. The only value-judgment implicit in the above definition of optimum pollution, therefore, is that society should maximize its welfare. Unless one dissents from that it is difficult to dissent from this definition of optimum pollution. In particular, it is not true that this definition of optimum pollution necessarily leads to an undesirably high level of pollution on the grounds that many of the costs of pollution are 'external' costs. The above definition does not exclude these costs, but there is no reason to believe that some special extra weight should be attached to them. External costs are no more costly to society, pound for pound, than any other costs, including the costs of abatement (which, as indicated above, merely reflect, if indirectly, the value that society puts on the goods and services that could be produced with the resources involved). It is merely an accident of the legal and institutional organization of society that some costs are 'external' to the person responsible.

For example, under the proposed reorganization of the water services in Britain, the sewage authorities and the river authorities will be combined in much larger administrative units, so that the costs of pollution caused by inadequate sewage, which had hitherto been external to the sewage authorities, will now become internal to the new larger organizations. But this cannot change the costs of the pollution to society, or the costs of sewage. Similarly, the fact that air-line operators do not have to pay to soundproof the homes of people who live near airports is merely the result of particular legal and institutional arrangements and does not mean that the costs to society of any soundproofing required would be any different. Nor would the costs of a given amount of sound-proofing change if the law were amended in such a way that the airlines had to bear them, so that these costs would no longer be 'external' to them and would enter into their calculations of how much noise their aircraft should make. Of course, such a change in the institutional arrangements, whereby what had

hitherto been an 'external' cost as far as the airlines were concerned is transformed into an internal cost, might induce them
to spend more money on quieter engines and hence reduce
soundproofing needs. But this is irrelevant to the point being
made here, namely that the actual resource cost to society of a
given piece of soundproofing – say, double-glazing a certain
window in a certain manner – does not depend on who is
legally responsible for bearing the cost.

There are, however, many qualifications that can legitimately be made concerning the application of the optimization
criterion set out above (though it should be added that these
qualifications are an integral part of the body of economic
theory, not omissions from the theory). First, in practice, it is
very difficult to measure the costs and benefits of pollution.
These difficulties lie first of all in our fundamental ignorance of
the technical scientific relationships between, on the one hand,
changes in physical levels of pollution and, on the other hand,
physical variables, such as the incidence of bronchitis, the speed
of metal corrosion, the loss of fish life, and so on. They are not
primarily caused by the inability of economists to attach monetary values to these factors, though it must be acknowledged
that, even if the precise physical data were to be provided by
the scientists and technologists, it would then be very difficult
to attach price-tags to them. Some of the implications of these
difficulties for policy will be considered later in this chapter.
All that needs to be said at this point is that they have no bearing on the principle of trying to maximize social welfare by
equating the marginal costs of pollution abatement with the
marginal benefits.

Secondly, the significance attached to estimates of the costs
and benefits of pollution abatement is not entirely free from
value-judgments. For the relevant prices and costs that enter
into the estimates reflect the existing social and institutional
arrangements of society in many ways. For example, the manner
in which income is distributed as between labour and capital,
or the socially conventional view as to the appropriate rate of
profit, will affect the relative prices of goods embodying different proportions of labour and capital. Relative costs and

prices will also be affected by the degree of monopoly tolerated in society. The effect of this sort of consideration on the costs of pollution can, perhaps, be illustrated by an extreme example. Suppose that immigrants into Britain were only allowed to work in laundries. The price of laundry services would then be much lower than if the laundry industry were in the hands of a tight white Anglo-Saxon monopoly. The valuation of the damage done by smoke from a factory chimney to, say, a workman's shirts would be much less, since it would not cost him so much to have them laundered.

Hence, the damage done by pollution would be valued *by the market* more cheaply than if the price of laundry services were kept higher under a different legal and institutional framework.

Optimum pollution and income distribution

Another, and somewhat related qualification to the optimum criterion set out above concerns income distribution. For pollution affects the distribution of welfare in society. As well as reducing *total* social welfare (in the absence of corrective measures) pollution also affects its *distribution*. In so far as pollution costs are not borne by those who cause pollution, or by the purchasers of their products, but by people who happen to be victims of the pollution, some of the total welfare of society is being redistributed away from the victims of pollution in favour of the other groups in the community. Manufacturers (or their shareholders) who can pollute free of charge make bigger profits than if they were obliged to cover the full social costs of their production, including the external costs generated by their pollution. And the purchasers of the goods and services concerned buy them at lower prices than if the prices covered the full social costs. Hence, the manufacturers and consumers of the particular products concerned gain at the expense of the victims of the pollution.

Of course, such redistributive effects may not always make the distribution of economic welfare less equal than it would have been otherwise. Sometimes the polluters will be relatively poor people and the victims may be richer, as may be the case where a poor community cannot afford better sewage, so that the rich owners of yachts moored downstream suffer from the untreated effluent flowing into the river. Because of the effect of any change in resource allocation on the distribution of income or welfare, the effects on income distribution of any policy to treat pollution should be taken into account as long as income distribution is accepted as part of social welfare. Of course, it is always open to somebody to make the value-judgment that he is simply not interested in income distribution.

Few people would explicitly make this value-judgment. A more acceptable reason for ignoring the distributional consequences of pollution policy would be that if the incomes are thought to be distributed too unequally, this should be dealt with anyway by measures designed to redistribute them directly, rather than by measures designed to deal with resource allocation. For, it can be argued, if resources are allocated 'optimally', so that total economic welfare is maximized, it will always be possible to distribute this welfare in such a way that some people are better off, without anybody being worse off than if resources are not allocated optimally. In simple terms, with a bigger cake it must be possible for some people to have bigger slices without anybody necessarily having a smaller slice. Hence, it would be argued, it is best to allocate resources optimally, since this will produce the biggest possible cake, and then, if we don't like the way it is shared out, we can always change it by some redistributive taxes and subsidies, taking care that these themselves do not misallocate resources.*

There is much force in this argument, and it is probably true that income-distribution considerations are at the root of most of the policies that deliberately misallocate resources in the economy. For example, agricultural prices are often supported at artificially high levels in order to distribute income in favour

---

* It is for this reason that economists tend to favour 'lump sum' taxes and subsidies, i.e. taxes and subsidies that are not proportional to any variable, such as the amount of one's income or the prices of goods, since it is the latter that tend to distort resource allocation one way or another.

of farmers; tariffs are levied on certain imports in order to protect those engaged in the production of the goods concerned;
rents are controlled in order to distribute income in favour of
the occupants; nationalized industries are subsidized in order to
distribute income in favour of the consumers or the employees
concerned, and so on. One wonders how much better off everybody could be if all these particular resource-misallocation
measures – almost all defended, in the end, on income-distribution grounds – were scrapped, and other measures
adopted to redistribute income directly.

On the other hand, the limitations on the above optimization
criterion such as those already mentioned, or the assumptions
that would have to be made about the degree of resource misallocation in the rest of the economy, are considerable. Furthermore, it is not at all easy to devise direct methods that really
have no adverse effect on resource allocation, and that really,
in the end, have as much effect on income distribution as
expected. By contrast, a simple tax or subsidy on some product
may have a relatively clear and pronounced effect on income
distribution compared with its possible adverse effect on
resource allocation.

These are complicated questions, and they have been the
subject of much sophisticated discussion in the literature of
what is known as 'welfare' economics. Most economists would
probably agree that the main contribution they can make is to
remind the policy-maker of all the relevant effects of any
policy, and to attempt to rank these effects – such as the
damage done by pollution, the way it affects different groups in
society, and the way measures to reduce it would affect these
groups. Most economists would also probably accept that 'If
he succeeds in this task it will almost certainly become more
widely appreciated that tinkering with the price mechanism is
one of the more feasible and generally satisfactory ways of
securing whatever distribution of wealth is desired.'[2]

In saying all this, therefore, we are not saying that the
economic principles for optimum pollution are irrelevant. On
the contrary, we are saying that they are not all that simple, and
that the relevant economic theory has by no means neglected

many valid reservations that have to be made to any simple rule. This is very different from abandoning any attempt at a rational policy for pollution, which usually leads to the adoption of some absurd rule of thumb which is not only grossly over-simplified but which bears no relation to any starting principle of what it is that we are trying to optimize anyway. The optimization criterion given above is, at least, derived from the objective of maximizing total welfare.

The reasons why this rule may not always achieve this objective are well known in economic theory, as are also the adjustments that have to be made, in principle, in order that the rule remains consistent with the original objective.

It is surely preferable to operate in this context than in one which does not even seek to promote the highest possible social welfare. In fact, when alternative rules are suggested it usually turns out that the rule proposed is simply designed – if quite unconsciously – to promote the special interests of a small group in the community at the expense of the community as a whole. This may be socially desirable and accept-able, for one of the functions of society is to protect legitimate minority interests. But such policies should reflect the con-scious and deliberate decisions of society, and should emerge from a rational analysis of the alternatives, not from an obscurantist rejection of any attempt to derive criteria, in a logical manner, from generally agreed objectives.

Price incentives for pollution abatement

We have seen that the optimum level of pollution is where the social costs of a further unit of pollution abatement equal the social benefits of this abatement. We have also seen that firms will not normally have any incentive to abate pollution at all, so that pollution will be pushed well beyond the optimum point. What is required is that the firm or the producer should have the same sort of incentive to economize on the use of the environment as he has to economize on other inputs into his productive process. One such incentive would be to make the producer bear the costs of his pollution. In this way his costs of production would reflect the true full social costs of his productive activity.

It will perhaps be intuitively obvious that, subject to certain assumptions, a producer will have an incentive to reduce pollution to the socially optimum amount provided he pays a pollution charge or tax that equals the cost to society of the pollution – i.e., a charge equal to the damage done to society at the point of optimum pollution. For firms will reduce pollution up to the point where the costs of their doing so are less than the tax they would otherwise pay. They will not reduce pollution beyond the point where it would cost them more to do so than to pay the tax. If, therefore, the tax is set to equal the (marginal) social benefits of abatement at the optimum level of pollution, firms will reduce pollution up to the point where their costs of doing so are also equal to these (marginal) social benefits of pollution abatement. And, as we have seen above, this is the socially optimum amount of pollution: for it is the point at which the costs of a further unit of abatement are equal to the benefits. This merely corresponds to the more common-sense general proposition that, subject again to some well-known reservations, if producers have to pay the social cost of an input (in this case the clean environment) they will tend to use it only up to the socially optimum amount.

So far the sort of incentive to firms to reduce pollution that we have discussed has consisted of some kind of tax (or charge) per unit of pollution that they create. But, in fact, in order to provide the producer with the incentive to economize in his use of the environment, it does not matter much whether this incentive consists of a tax that he has to pay for every unit of extra pollution that he causes or a subsidy for every unit by which he reduces his pollution. The incentive to him to reduce pollution is exactly the same in both cases. A tax is merely the most obvious form of incentive to a producer to economize in the use of the input concerned. It also bears most resemblance to the payment that he would have to make if the environment were 'owned' by, say, private individuals and he had to settle some price with them in order to compensate for his use of their clean air or clean water. But the subsidy method would produce the same results as long as it is a subsidy *per unit* reduction in the firm's pollution, in exactly the same way as the pollution charge should be a charge *per unit* of pollution that the firm still causes.

For what matters, in principle, in deciding how to allocate resources are what the economist calls 'opportunity costs'. These represent the costs of what the firm concerned gives up, or sacrifices, by allocating resources in one way rather than another or by making one decision rather than another. And the opportunity cost to a firm of creating an additional unit of pollution is either the tax he pays on it or the subsidy he forgoes as a result of not eliminating it.

But a word of caution is necessary about the equivalence of taxes and subsidies; this is that the subsidy method is an undesirable long-term method. For it is a satisfactory substitute for a pollution charge only if it is related to the amount by which pollution is reduced below some initial level. If it were to be paid indiscriminately to firms for not polluting the environment it would be open to potential polluters to work a sort of 'protection racket' – i.e., to set up business in some highly polluting activity in order to claim the subsidy for shutting down their polluting activity. It would then become rather like the story of the American farmers who are paid not to produce certain crops and who decide to increase their income by increasing the amount of the crops that they will not produce! To avert this situation, which could result in pollution rising instead of falling, it is essential that the abatement subsidy be related to the initial levels of pollution in question, and that they should not be applied to the avoidance of new pollution. But since the case for using the subsidy rather than the charge method would be on equity and income-distribution grounds – i.e., to reduce pollution without inflicting a loss of income on the polluters – the subsidy should, in general, be applied only to existing pollution.[3]

One misunderstanding about the tax-versus-subsidy issue needs to be cleared up at this point. This is the fear that the subsidy method leads to more pollution than the tax method since it reduces the costs of the polluting activity instead of raising them, as with the pollution tax. At first sight it may certainly seem that the subsidy does reduce the costs of the polluting activity in question (steel-making might be a case in point). But, in fact, this is not the case as long as it is a subsidy per unit by which pollution is reduced and not, say, a subsidy on pollution-removal machinery. For in so far as there is the same price incentive to reduce pollution, firms will have to use more of other inputs in place of their use of the environment, in exactly the same way as if the incentive had been provided by a pollution tax. Since these other inputs have prices, the firms' outlay on them must rise irrespective of the reason why the firm is induced to use more of them. Furthermore, as pointed out above, the cost of the environment input (i.e. pollution) to the firm is exactly the same with either method – in one case it is the tax and in the other case it is the subsidy forgone – so that the total costs of production, comprising the costs of the conventional inputs (labour, capital, etc.) plus the cost to the firm of its use of the environment, have risen in exactly the same way whichever method is used.

In fact, pollution charges or abatement subsidies (generally known by the pejorative term 'bribes') are by no means the only two forms of 'tinkering' with the price mechanism that will tend to provide the same incentive to the firm to reduce pollution to the optimum amount. Other forms of providing the polluter with precisely the same 'opportunity cost' of pollution – for this is essentially what one must try to do – include the imposition of a system by which the victims of the pollution pay the polluters according to the value to them of the reduction in pollution, or a system by which the polluters are obliged to pay the victims according to the damage done by their pollution. Both these methods, subject to some assumptions, should lead to exactly the same result in terms of the incentive they give to polluters to reduce their pollution. Whether the cost to them of an extra unit of pollution takes the form of a tax on it, or the subsidy forgone, or the payment they must make in compensation to the victims, or the payment they forgo from the victims for each unit by which they fail to reduce pollution, is all the same thing as far as the *opportunity cost* of pollution is concerned, and hence should have the same effect on the degree to which pollution is reduced.

But all these different methods have different effects on income distribution. For example, with the tax method the proceeds should, in principle, be used to reduce other taxes (or increase government expenditures), for otherwise the pressure of demand in the economy would fall. This method, therefore, tends to benefit taxpayers (or the recipients of the other government expenditures) at the expense of the producers and consumers of the products concerned. Thus, as argued already, the income-distribution effects of any mechanism must always be examined.

For example, imagine an economy in which slavery was tolerated and widely used. From the point of view of the optimum allocation of resources in the economy the optimum use of slave labour would be that at which the product of an extra unit of the labour just equalled the extent to which the slaves disliked that extra unit of work. This optimum could be achieved by making slave-owners pay a tax per hour of slave labour, like the tax on pollution. Slave-owners would then economize in their use of it and would reduce their use of slave labour to the point where the addition made to output by a further unit of labour just equalled the tax, which would also be the socially optimum point. From the resource-allocation point of view this would be fine. But the slaves might not like it. They might prefer a price mechanism in which the price to be paid for their labour was not a tax paid to the state but a wage paid to them. Resource allocation would be the same (subject to the usual static assumptions), but the distribution of income would probably be very different indeed.

Yet another system of providing an incentive to arrive at the socially optimum level of pollution is the system of 'pollution rights' that has been expounded by J. H. Dales, and which has certain attractions.[4] This is the system under which the authorities decide what they think is the desirable level of pollution (as they have to do under *any* system) and they then issue, on the market, 'rights' to this amount of pollution, allowing the equilibrium price that these rights fetch to be settled on the market. For firms that need to pollute as part of their productive process will bid for these rights. Possession of a pollution 'right' entitles a firm to carry out the specified amount of pollution, which is the same as limiting his obligation to reduce pollution. Firms that can reduce pollution cheaply will not want to buy as many such rights as firms that would find it very costly to do so. Market imperfections apart, the price at which the rights will settle will be the same as the optimum tax (or subsidy).

One of the advantages of the pollution-rights method, as Abba Lerner has pointed out,[5] is that it is a way of using the price mechanism in a situation where uncertainty as to the exact damage done by the pollutant is combined with a fear that this damage could rise sharply if the optimum amount were exceeded. In such cases, the authorities want to feel assured that pollution does not exceed some fixed quantitative upper limit. They may not wish to run the risk of overestimating the extent to which a pollution charge would induce firms to abate pollution, or they may want to guard against the likelihood that conditions could change rapidly or that pollution would fluctuate around the optimum if the charge were kept constant. In such cases the authorities could simply operate on the amount of pollution which they thought optimal, rather than its price. They would issue pollution rights to this amount. Of course, they might miscalculate the costs of abatement to firms, so that the price at which the permitted quantity rights settle would differ from the one which they would have adopted if they had used the tax method instead of the rights method. But they would still be safe in the sense that pollution would not exceed the desired amount, and the allocative advantages of the price mechanism would still apply.

The advantages of pollution charges

The 'allocative advantage' of pollution charges is essentially that if all firms are subject to a uniform charge per unit of damage done by their pollution the firms that can reduce pollution most cheaply will do so more than those that face relatively high or steeply rising costs of pollution abatement.[6] In other words, more of any given amount of pollution abatement will be made by firms that can do it most cheaply, and hence use least resources for this purpose and hence least deprive society of the use of these resources for other purposes. It is like using the price mechanism to ensure that shirts are produced as economically as possible, since the price mechanism will tend to ensure that most shirts will be produced by the firms that can produce them most economically.

The imposition of direct controls on pollution corresponds to the use of production quotas or 'norms' according to which different firms are given production targets in the form of direct quantitative regulations. This is generally unlikely to ensure that goods are produced by the firms best able to do so and by the most economical methods. With certain exceptions, it is not the type of economic-policy instrument used in Western countries. The use of direct regulations for the control of pollution amounts precisely to such a system of production quotas and norms.

The same forces which tend to make the price mechanism a cheaper means of producing most goods apply to the abatement of pollution. If a uniform pollution charge is imposed at any particular stretch of river or estuary all polluters will tend to abate their pollution up to the point where it would cost them more to abate further than the charge they pay per unit of pollution.* In other words, at the margin, the cost of pollution abatement is equal in all firms, since it is equal to the charge

---

* In principle, a uniform charge does not mean that it does not vary according to the damage done by different physical units of pollution. A uniform charge means uniform in terms of the charge per unit of damage done. For example, a uniform charge per unit of pollutant applied to different firms along a stretch of river, which took no account of the major variations in the damage done by a given amount of that pollutant according to their precise location on the river, would be sub-optimal. Failure to allow for the fact that a 'uniform' charge is uniform in this sense, not in terms of unadjusted physical units (though, in practice, this will often be the best proxy variable) appears to be responsible for the arguments deployed by J. L. Stein in 'Micro-Economic Aspects of Public Policy', *American Economic Review*, September 1971.

made to all firms. Contrast this with the use of some direct control, such as a regulation to the effect that all firms must reduce their pollution by a uniform percentage, or to some uniform amount. This will obviously involve very high marginal costs of pollution abatement for some firms and low marginal costs for others. Clearly, the same total amount of pollution abatement can be obtained if some of the abatement is switched from the former firms, where it is costly, to the latter, where it is cheap; and savings of this kind can be made by switching up to the point where the marginal costs of further abatement are equal for all firms. This is the situation to which the pollution-charge system tends to lead.

The individual firm will also have an incentive, under a price-mechanism scheme such as a pollution charge, to find the cheapest way to reduce its pollution, whereas many kinds of direct regulation take the form of laying down precise instructions as to the steps that firms must take to reduce their pollution, such as increasing the height of their chimneys or changing to some alternative productive technique. With a pollution charge, some firms will find it cheaper to change their raw-material input, others may carry out more re-cycling, others may institute more effluent-treatment plant inside the firm, others may change location, and so on.

Furthermore, firms will have a continuing incentive to experiment and to seek new and more economical methods of reducing pollution, for the more they do so the more they save on pollution charges, in the same way as the more they find ways of reducing labour per unit of output the more they save on wages.[7] By contrast, if they are given directions to reduce pollution by a certain amount, and possibly also by specified means, they have little further incentive to go beyond this and to reduce pollution even more than the regulations require. Whatever the system of direct control, firms have little or no incentive to do better than the control limit given to them. For this is invariably a maximum pollution limit which they must not exceed; but they win no prizes for falling short of it. With the tax system, however, the more they reduce pollution the less tax they pay. It is not enough to say that the regulations can be tightened up from time to time in the light of technical progress that may be made in pollution-abatement techniques, for the whole point of the charges method is that it provides a continuous and permanent incentive to find improvements in such techniques. Technical progress in reducing pollution will hence be far greater with a pollution charge than with direct regulation. Consequently, the level of pollution will tend to be lower under a pollution-charge system than with the direct-regulation system.

For various reasons, therefore, pollution charges (or some other price-mechanism system) will enable society to reduce pollution more cheaply than direct regulation. Firms will be better placed to find the cheapest method of reducing pollution, pollution reduction will be concentrated on the firms that can reduce it most cheaply, and technical progress in pollution abatement will be continually stimulated. And if pollution charges enable society to reduce pollution more cheaply, it follows that either a given amount of abatement can be achieved at less sacrifice of other goods and services or that, for the same cost, pollution can be further reduced.

The lower cost of pollution abatement under the pollution-charge method is not, however, the only advantage of this method over that of direct controls.* Another advantage is that direct controls tend to be uneven in their application according to how popular the anti-pollution fashion happens to be. At a time when the environmental issue is front-page news and any case of an excess of some pollutant entering the environment hits the headlines, some of the various authorities responsible for pollution control may exercise greater vigilance. But a few years later, when it is education, or the health service, or housing, or public transport, or crime, or drugs, or something else that happens to be the prime concern, environmental protection may not be enforced with quite the same enthusiasm.

This is in no way a criticism of the local authorities or other bodies to whom responsibility for environmental protection has

* The following few paragraphs owe much to the points made by W. J. Baumol in his 1972 Wicksell Lectures, *Environmental Protection, International Spillovers and Trade* (Almqvist and Wicksell, Stockholm, 1971).

been delegated. But the resources and funds put at their disposal is obviously a function of how far their political masters, whether they be locally or centrally elected, think that pollution is a hot issue. Furthermore, the importance attached to protecting the environment, which may often appear to be at the expense of other local interests, such as employment in some polluting industry, may lead to local or regional variations in the enthusiasm with which anti-pollution policies are pursued.

Finally, the enforcement of direct controls is often a difficult and time-consuming process, requiring, for example, the accumulation of sufficient evidence to satisfy a court of law that a certain polluter has exceeded the limits laid down, and even then the fine imposed is often derisory. In fact, direct regulation is also a form of pollution tax, in the sense that a small fine may be imposed if breaches of the regulations are identified and proved to the satisfaction of the courts. But the incidence of this form of tax is often uncertain, subject to delays, and usually too small anyway.*

By contrast, no such vagaries apply to the operation of a tax. Once a tax is instituted a proper machinery has to be set up (and it is invariably set up) to ensure that the required data – however rough and ready they may have to be in many cases – are provided as frequently as required, taking account of feasibility and so on. The collection of the tax is then a routine matter that is unaffected by changes in the winds of fashion or local pressures. Tax collectors collect their taxes year in, year out, and in the same way from one part of the country to another. In fact, a system requiring regular returns of liability to a pollution charge would be one way of increasing our information about pollution, hence making it easier to determine optimum pollution levels. Furthermore, it would probably stimulate technical improvements in monitoring techniques, such as those that have already recently been made in response, no doubt, to the emerging interest in pollution control.[8]

* For example, in Britain over the whole period 1967 to 1971 inclusive, there were eight convictions for air pollution as a result of prosecutions by the Alkali Inspectorate, and the average fine imposed was £3 (reply by Mr Eldon Griffiths to Parliamentary Question, May 3rd, 1972).

Pollution charges versus direct control*

In view of these two apparent major advantages of the pollution-charge system over direct regulation, one may ask why the
opposition to it is so widespread. Yet one of the most hotly dis-
puted issues of pollution policy today concerns not the choice
between alternative forms of 'tinkering with the price
mechanism' but between *any* such method on the one hand,
and some form of direct regulation of pollution, on the other
hand. Various reasons have been advanced for preferring
direct controls to some price-mechanism instrument to check
pollution, and the more common ones will be dealt with in
detail below. It should be conceded at the outset, however, that
one's preference as between some price-mechanism scheme and
direct regulation may reflect one's preference as between the
price mechanism and direct regulation as a general system for
achieving the desired allocation of resources in the economy,
subject to some fairly clearly defined exceptions. In other
words, a preference for direct regulation of pollution is rather
like a preference for direct regulation as a means of obtaining
the desired allocation of labour, or the desired production of
shirts. For a pollution charge does not constitute some completely novel or revolutionary scheme, it is simply a time-
honoured price mechanism. In fact, in the past it has been the
'revolutionary' regimes that have tended to replace the price
mechanism by direct regulation, and many of the people now
opposed to some sort of pollution charge would probably be
surprised to discover what ideological camp they are really in.

Nor do pollution charges constitute some novel, untried
method dreamt up by ivory-tower economic theoreticians. For
example, in Britain some form of financial disincentive to
pollute already exists, up to a point, in the charges for the treatment of 'trade' (that is, non-domestic) effluent discharged to
municipal sewers. The Public Health (Drainage of Trade
Premises) Act 1937 and the Public Health Act 1961 provide

* This whole section follows very closely the discussion of this issue in the
Minority Report by the present writer and Lord Zuckerman contained in the
Third Report of the Royal Commission on Environmental Pollution (H.M.S.O.,
London, 1972).

drainage authorities with adequate authority to control the discharges into their sewerage systems and to 'charge for the reception of the trade effluent into the sewer regard being had to the nature and composition and to the volume and rate of the discharge of the trade effluent so discharged ... ' (Public Health Act 1961). A large number of local authorities do, in fact, charge for trade effluent according to formulae which take account of some indicators of pollution (notably the B.O.D.* and the amount of suspended solids in the effluent). Furthermore, various bodies and individuals concerned with the practical application of charges have confirmed the feasibility and effectiveness of a charges scheme. For example, the Institute of Water Pollution Control stated many years ago:

> One of the most effective methods of reducing the load caused by trade effluents is to make a charge for their treatment which is based on a sliding scale in accordance with their volume and strength. In this way an incentive can be given to the trader to reduce his discharge of waste from his factory, by re-using water, by making minor modifications in manufacturing processes, by recovering by-products or by some other means. Some remarkable results have been achieved in this way with profit to the trader, and with great advantage to sewage works operation, and with considerable resulting contribution to the national economy.[9]

There has also been a move towards the use of pollution charges in the U.S.A., beginning with the imposition of a charge on sulphur oxide emissions announced in the Presidential Message to Congress on February 8th, 1972. As explained in the Presidential message to Congress, this charge, which is to operate as from 1976, 'is an application of the principle that the costs of pollution should be included in the price of the product. Combined with our existing regulatory

* 'B.O.D.' – or biochemical oxygen demand – is one measure of the oxygen, in the water, that is used up by the matter contained in it. The higher the B.O.D., therefore, the less oxygen available to support fish-life.

authority, it would constitute a strong economic incentive to achieve the sulphur oxides standards necessary to protect health, and then further to reduce emissions to levels which protect welfare and aesthetics'. Other moves in the direction of taxing pollution or similar externalities are under consideration, such as the American Administration's proposal to tax lead additives in gasoline,[10] and the Japanese government's consideration of a congestion tax on firms in congested areas.[11] And recently, the notion of taxing pollution received support even from the International Chamber of Commerce at its meeting in Goteborg in 1972.[12]

In the U.S.A., unlike Britain, the environmentalists seem to have woken up, for one reason or another, to the idea that a pollution tax or charge is more likely to meet their aims than direct regulation. It has been reported that

> ... over the past year organized environmental groups have gradually come to see a pollution tax as a strong incentive to institute abatement measures. They also cite the fact that most industrialists have declared their opposition to the measure as proof that it would force them to take the painful steps to reduce their sulphur emissions. A measure of the environmentalists' interest in the concept is the fact that in August last year a number of groups joined to form a 'Coalition to Tax Pollution' and set up an office on Capitol Hill.*

Numerous detailed arguments against pollution charges have been put forward from time to time, and it would take

---

* 'Pollution Tax', *Nature*, Vol. 235, February 18th, 1972. A similar report was contained in *The Guardian*, July 14th, 1971. The environmentalists are still far from understanding the problem fully, however, judging by their objection to the differentiation in the proposed U.S.A. sulphur-oxide tax on the grounds that this will tend to lead to a transfer of pollution from highly congested areas where it does a lot of harm to other areas where it will do little harm, and hence where the tax will be low or negligible. But such a transfer is, of course, desirable, in the light of the principles set out above to the effect that pollution *per se* is not important; what matters is the damage it does, and such a transfer clearly reduces the overall damage. Would the environmentalists complain, for example, if it could all be shot out into space at no cost, so that nobody was harmed by it at all?

too much time to cover them all here. But the following seem to be a fair sample.

(i) The first, and in a sense the most serious objection, is that polluters will, in fact, find it *more* expensive to reduce pollution by a given amount, since, in addition to the *real* costs of abatement that they will incur in order to reduce pollution (i.e. the extra labour, capital, and raw materials they have to substitute for the environment), they will also have to pay the pollution tax on their residual pollution. By contrast, it would be argued, if they are obliged to reduce pollution by direct regulation they incur only the real costs of abatement. If the latter are higher, on account of the failure of direct controls to allocate abatement among polluters in line with their relative costs of abatement, this would be offset by the extra burden on polluters embodied in the pollution tax which they have to pay in addition to their abatement costs.

The fallacy in this argument, however, is that we want to know which method will be cheapest for the economy as a whole, other things being equal, notably the overall level of demand and employment in the economy. For we are interested in the effects of resource re-allocation, not in the effect of reducing the amount of resources used as well. Of course, if the authorities deflate the economy by raising some taxes that are not neutralized by compensating tax reductions elsewhere (or compensating increases in public expenditures) then total output and employment will be reduced, so that the economy as a whole could be worse off than if some other method had been used. But in this case the costs of the pollution abatement consists of both the real resources used to abate pollution in the firms concerned *and* the fall in output and employment as a result of the unintended and unnecessary deflationary effect of the higher tax receipts of the public sector as a whole. But this would no longer be a comparison of the relative costs of the alternative methods of pollution abatement, other things being equal, notably the overall level of demand and employment. Clearly, in order to make the correct comparison, it is necessary to assume that the authorities neutralize the demand impact of their pollution-tax receipts by either tax cuts elsewhere or increases in public expenditure elsewhere. In that case, the only cost of the pollution abatement is the total cost of real resources used by the firms concerned to reduce pollution; we must exclude the pollution charges that are also paid since these, or rather their effects, must be assumed to be offset by neutralizing changes in the government budget.*

Indeed, if the compensating action by the authorities takes the form of tax reductions, there may be a yet further gain in efficiency in the economy. For most taxes lead to a misallocation of resources. A pollution charge is an exception; it corrects a resource misallocation caused by the externality aspect of pollution. If the revenue from pollution charges enables the state to reduce other taxes it will tend to reduce the resource misallocation that is caused by these other taxes and hence make a further contribution to the optimum allocation of resources. This constitutes yet a further way in which pollution charges have a cost advantage over direct regulation.

(ii) A second objection to pollution charges is that the theory, as advanced above, is based on the unrealistic assumption that firms are ruthless profit-maximizers, making careful calculations of the optimal degree to which they should reduce pollution in response to the charge. But the case for pollution charges no more rests on this unrealistic assumption than does the case for, say, the use of the price mechanism to allocate labour or capital investment between firms. Of course firms are not at all like this, and most firms do not make the theoretically ideal calculations of their investment needs, for example, but even those who are opposed to pollution charges would not argue, on this account, that firms' investment projects should be determined by direct regulation. Hence, the above argument no more depends on a very simple view of the way that firms operate than would arguments in favour of using the price mechanism rather than direct regulation to allocate labour and capital and raw materials between different firms according to some quantitative plan.

* From the point of view of the economy, taxes are transfer payments, not resource costs.

6

(iii) A third and related objection to pollution charges is that they can have no effect since the polluters will merely pass them on in higher prices. But producers normally try to cover *all* their costs in their prices – otherwise they would soon go out of business – and one does not say that they are indifferent to how much labour or capital they use.* Firms will still try to employ each factor of production up to the point where further use would not add to their revenues more than they add to their costs. In general, it is the more profitable firms that carry out this process more efficiently. To assume that by paying a 'licence to pollute' firms have no incentive to economize on pollution is like assuming that firms do not economize in their use of other factors of production.

If this were true the whole allocation of resources in the economy would be completely haphazard. It should not be forgotten that a pollution charge would not be like a radio licence, which once paid, entitles the licence-holder to an unlimited amount of listening. A pollution charge would be related to the amount of pollution; the more one pollutes the more one pays. In any case, as the 1971 Annual Report of the President's Council of Economic Advisers pointed out, ' ... every system of rules for use of the environment, other than outright and total prohibition of certain uses, involves granting someone the right or "licence" for some polluting'.

(iv) It is often maintained that a charge scheme is unworkable because we do not have the data needed to decide on the appropriate charge in all cases. For example, we do not have the data required to make full allowance for variations in the conditions (such as state of river flow, air temperature, tidal conditions) that determine the amount of damage done by effluent at any point in an estuary. This is true, but the same

* Similarly it is absurd to argue, as did the representative of the Confederation of British Industry (Mr Biggs) at a conference on the environment in May 1972, that it would be easy for companies in a monopoly position to pay the tax rather than cut pollution. It is no more easy for them do to this than to pay more wages instead of economizing in their labour force. The C.B.I. does not argue that monopolistic firms should be directed as to how much labour they use, rather than just pay a wage, on the grounds that they will simply pass on the wages in higher prices.

lack of data means that one does not know the correct amount of pollution abatement to be imposed by direct regulation either. In principle, the data required to identify the correct objective as regards pollution abatement are independent of the methods that might then be used to achieve this objective. For these data are the same in both cases: they consist of the costs of abatement and the damage done to society by the pollution, and are hence the same whatever policy instruments are to be used for abatement purposes. For example, a person might not know whether he will have more sunshine on his holiday if he takes it in Scotland or in Brighton; and he may also have a choice of going to either place by rail or by car. It would be irrational for him to say 'since I am not sure which place is best, I shall go by car'. It is not by going by car that he will increase his chances of guessing correctly where he will find the most sunshine. The two issues – the correct objective and the means of achieving it – are quite separate in this case, as they are also in connection with pollution abatement. (In fact, for the administrative reasons set out above, it is likely that these data would be built up more rapidly if some authority were responsible for regularly levying charges based on the amount of pollution done than if pollution control were left to direct regulation.)

(v) It is claimed that charges are impracticable because data are not available to permit an accurate calculation of the amount of pollution that should be taxed. For example, it may be that monitoring difficulties preclude the observation of the pollution which is to be charged. This is true, but, again, precisely the same problems apply to the surveillance and implementation of direct controls. The imposition of direct control implies that whatever is controlled can be measured – otherwise it is pointless to institute the control, since it would be impossible to check whether it is respected. And whatever can be measured can also be taxed. For example, if a firm is instructed not to put more than 1 ounce of some heavy metal per day in the river it is unlikely that the check, in so far as there is one, on the amount of the metal contained in its effluent indicates only whether the amount discharged is above or below 1 ounce. A more informative, if not precise, figure would usually be obtained, such as that the amount was 2·8 ounces or 0·7 ounces. The extra information would be virtually free in most cases, and would be adequate for a charging scheme as long as it was recognized from the outset that the charging scheme would be no more precise than the direct control.

Even where it is not practicable to measure how much pollutant is in the effluent and it is necessary, if any control at all is to be exercised, to lay down consent conditions in terms of, say, the raw material or the productive process used, this will usually still be related to some quantifiable flow, or characteristic of the raw material or productive process which could then be used as the basis for a charge. For example, suppose it were thought desirable to reduce the amount of some heavy metal flowing into an estuary, but it was impossible to measure the metal concerned at the sort of low concentrations that might be relevant. Direct control, if any, might then take the form of a restriction, in certain productive processes, on the use of some raw material believed to be responsible for the pollution in question. But if the amount of this raw material used can be measured for purposes of ensuring that the direct control is respected, the measurements can be used as a basis for the pollution charge.

Similarly, if a minimum height of a chimney has been stipulated it must be possible to obtain a measure of the chimney height in order to check that the regulation is being obeyed. It would cost no more to use the measure for purposes of a tax that varied (downwards) according to the height of the chimney. In some cases, of course, verification difficulties may mean that the calculation of the charge will be inaccurate, but in such cases the check on the observance of direct controls will be equally unreliable. In other cases, the costs of operating a charging system might be excessive in relation to the damage done by the pollution, and it might then be thought not worth while to impose the charge. But in such cases it would probably be equally undesirable to attempt to monitor how far the direct regulations are respected.

The whole argument may perhaps be illustrated by considering an apparently absurd and trivial case, namely the offensive
smell of fried onions from some restaurant. Suppose it were
decided that this must be reduced, but that it was impossible to
measure smell,* so that clearly it would also be impossible to
tax it. But in that case it would be equally impossible to limit
the amount of smell by direct regulation. For there would be
no point in the Inspector saying that the smell from the
restaurant was too strong that day, since the owner could
hotly deny it and there would be no objective means of settling
the dispute. One could ask a lot of people to come and have a
sniff, but they would not know exactly what standard of smell
the Inspector had in mind. In such a situation direct control
might take the form of imposing some quantitative limit on
how many fried onions the restaurant was allowed to use per
day, assuming that the Inspector had some means of controlling
this – i.e. of measuring the quantity of onions used every day.
But if this assumption is made it is obviously equally feasible to
tax the use of fried onions. Again, one returns to the basic
point, namely that *whatever can be controlled must be measurable; if
if isn't measurable it is an illusion to believe that it is being controlled.
And if it is measurable it can be taxed.*

(vi) It is often believed that the great advantage of direct
regulation is that the regulating authority knows exactly
whether or not the abatement target will be achieved, whereas
with a charge system they will not know in advance how far
firms will respond to the charge and hence how far pollution
will be reduced to the optimum amount. This is very much like
arguing that the great advantage of direct regulation of clothing
output in centrally planned economies is that they can be sure

* But even the measurement of smell should not be thought of as beyond the
realms of possibility. As a result of much experimentation in Sweden it now
appears that 'Through an instrumental technique ... it has proved possible to
measure objectively the concentration of evil-smelling sulphur compounds with
a precision and sensitivity comparable with those of the nose', according to the
Bulletin of the Swedish Water and Air Pollution Research Laboratory, Vol. 1, No. 1,
1972. Similar progress, but with a different technical approach however, has been
reported in Britain, in *Pollution Monitor*, August/September 1972.

that the target for clothing output will be produced, whereas if they had left it to the market mechanism actual clothing output might have fallen below or above the target. Now this is quite true, but the accuracy with which one hits any target is not, in itself, a desirable objective of policy, irrespective of the extent to which it is the appropriate target. The advantage of the price mechanism is precisely that if the output of clothing is too high its price will fall, thereby discouraging its production (and encouraging its consumption) until the correct amount is produced. But with a production quota, and, in addition, no market (as would be the case with pollution), producers would continue to produce the target level of pollution and nobody would know whether or not it was the correct target. By comparison, with the charge method, if the charge failed to produce the level of pollution at which the marginal social damage were equal to the charge, this would itself constitute evidence for the fact that the initial estimate of optimum pollution could not have been correct, so that some adjustment in the charge would be appropriate in due course.

(vii) A seventh argument often advanced against charges is that, while polluters will accept rough-and-ready measurements for purposes of direct control, only very precise measurements will be publicly acceptable if they are to be the basis of a tax. But this is manifest nonsense, for innumerable taxes, fees and charges of one sort or another are levied in a rough-and-ready manner without giving rise to any general refusal by the public to pay them. To take obvious examples, local rates are not only calculated on the basis of very rough-and-ready formulae for rating valuations, but they are not even revised very frequently to allow for changing circumstances. And charges such as those made for bus fares, telephone calls, parking meters, and innumerable other services where it would be relatively easier to adjust the charge according to some very finely graduated scale are, in fact, arranged according to a scale with relatively large steps. With most pollutants it would be even more desirable to vary the charge according to relatively large steps in the pollution load.

Quite apart from the difficulties of precise monitoring (which apply to any system of control) the damage done by any amount of pollution varies considerably according to many other physical parameters, such as the composition of the effluent, the air conditions, the river flow, the time of day or night, and so on. It would be foolish to try to be any more perfectionist about a charging scheme than about direct control schemes. *

Related to this is the argument that a pollution charge requires continual monitoring. But a charge scheme no more requires continual monitoring than does a direct control scheme. If, for example, the direct control takes the form of a weekly check on the flow of a firm's effluent in order to ensure that it is within the consent limit, the same readings can be used as a basis for the charge. It is absurd to argue that, with the charge system, the firm can always seek to cheat by disposing of its pollution at some other time of day or week, when the flow is not being measured for the charge purpose. For it could do exactly the same to avoid being caught when the flow is being measured for the purposes of checking whether it is respecting the direct regulations. Thus, it is not true that the use of the charges scheme depends on technical improvements in monitoring arrangements. Such improvements will make it easier to control pollution by any means, and are irrelevant to the choice between the direct control and other methods.

There are, of course, many practical problems involved in introducing a charge scheme, such as the role of the various authorities in determining the target levels of pollution in each case, and in settling the charges, and so on, but these matters lie outside the scope of this book.† In many cases it may be too

* It is not widely realized that the current practice of concentrating on the content of SO_2 and smoke, as far as air pollution is concerned, is largely a matter of convenience in that these two particular pollutants are regarded as being very good indications of air pollution in general, as well as being pollutants in their own right.

† For a discussion of some of these ideas see the Third Report of the Royal Commission on Environment Pollution (H.M.S.O. London, 1972), pp. 82–5. I do not cover, in this chapter, some of the more absurd anti-charge arguments, such as those put forward in an editorial in *Pollution Monitor*, October–November 1972, to the effect that the charge scheme is undesirable because it would require

costly, in relation to the benefits thereby gained, to try to implement any scheme. But it is more important here, where we are concerned with basic principles rather than their detailed implementation in individual cases, to move on to other major items concerning the role of the public authorities in pollution control. These include the relative contribution of collective purification facilities, such as sewage works, as against pollution charges, as a means of reducing pollution, and the relationship between the revenues from pollution charges and the number of public purification facilities that should be provided.

Collective purification facilities and 'public goods'

One important alternative to pollution charges or direct controls as a means of reducing one of the most common forms of pollution, namely water pollution, is to allow firms (and households) to pour their effluent into some collective drainage system and then purify the water to the desired degree in some collective sewage works. It might be much cheaper to do this when there are economies of scale in treating effluent on a large scale, instead of obliging each firm or household to install some small-scale purification process. (This applies chiefly to water pollution; there are few such possibilities as regards most other forms of pollution.) But it is wrong to regard collective facilities or pollution charges as mutually exclusive alternatives. In an optimal system for controlling pollution both have their part to play, together with many other ways of reducing pollution, according to their respective cost conditions.

The supply of clean water from collective sewage, or other purification facilities, together with the supply of clean water determined by the amount of pollution produced in individual sources, constitutes the total supply to the community, and its

---

such a wide variety of charges. This is like arguing that the allocation of motor-cars by a price mechanism is undesirable because there is such a wide variety of prices. Anyway, the direct regulation system also involves extensive variation from firm to firm in the composition and quantity of the pollution they are allowed to produce.

price should be the same for all users and to all suppliers. Individual firms will have to pay for using the collective facilities to purify their effluent, and this charge should correspond to the tax they would bear on their pollution. In this way they will tend to find the optimal allocation as between reducing their pollution themselves, paying for the collective facilities to do so, and paying a tax on their remaining pollution.

The case for collective facilities to deal with pollution does not rest solely on possible economies of scale. Whether collective facilities are under public ownership or not is nothing to do with the existence of economies of scale,* and it may well be that the collective facilities will be entirely privately operated, as are, for example, many water works. Thus the provision of collective facilities on the grounds of economies of scale is quite a separate issue from the provision of publicly operated collective facilities on the grounds that such facilities provide what are known as 'public goods'.

There are various criteria by which certain activities are classified as 'public goods'. One of the most important is that provision of the good or service to one person, or many people, automatically makes it available at no extra cost to other people. The classic textbook example of a public good is the lighthouse, where, as long as the light is made available to one ship it can be seen, at no extra social cost, by other passing ships, at least up to the point where the area concerned becomes congested. National defence is another example, in that once the army or navy is established to defend some of the people in society, the others are automatically equally defended. The two cases are not identical, since some of the defended people might not want to be defended at all, but they will be so just the same, whereas only sailors that *want* to look at the light need do so. But the common feature of both cases is that, once the service is provided for some users, society need incur no extra opportunity cost in order that others may enjoy it. Hence, it would be sub-optimal to charge any consumer for the use of

* Apart from the usual problems of optimal pricing policy in industries where average costs of production decline as output rises.

6*

the service in question, since such a charge would merely reduce his consumption and welfare without adding to the possible consumption level of anybody else.

At the same time it is usually impossible to prevent anybody from using a public good – for example, to prevent any part-cular ship from taking navigational bearings from the light-house. This means that it is usually impossible to charge anybody for using it. These two features of public goods mean that the free market mechanism is hardly likely to produce the socially required amounts of them. The public sector con-sequently has to step in and fill the gap.

Now pollution is a form of public 'bad'. That is to say, the fact that, for example, one individual may breathe some polluted air, or smell some polluted river, does not usually reduce the amount of polluted air or smell available for other people. Conversely, clearing up pollution is a form of public good in the sense that, say, reducing health hazards from poor sewage for some people in any given locality will, at the same time, reduce the health hazards for other people in the same area or for visitors. Hence in the same way that the public-good character of, say, lighthouses, or defence, implies that the price mechanism cannot ensure the socially optimum output of the service in question, it might appear that the public-good character of, say, a sewage works or other pollution-prevention device necessarily implies that it must be supplied by the public sector. But this is not the case; the analogy between the public-good character of pollution prevention and purification, on the one hand, and the classic public goods, on the other, is not complete.

The difference between the two is that with, say, the light-house, the only way that the dark can be mitigated is by build-ing the lighthouse, whereas with currently produced pollution there is always the alternative of taxing the polluter. Currently produced pollution is something that can be reduced at source, whereas this is not the case with, say, darkness or the hostility of some enemy country (real or imagined). Only if darkness could be reduced by taxing God might this be preferable to building a lighthouse.

However, this does not apply to previously produced pollution, so that the case for a 'public-good' approach to, say, the restoration of derelict land, or beaches that have been polluted by some previous oil-spillage at sea, is much stronger. But as far as currently produced pollution is concerned, the case for public facilities is by no means conclusive and the optimum amount of pollution abatement can often be achieved by a pollution charge, supplemented by collective facilities (possibly privately operated) when there are economies of scale. Of course, even with pollution charges, the market mechanism may still fail to ensure that the socially most economical system of reducing pollution is introduced. There are too many imperfections in the market, as well as the expenses involved in obtaining the requisite information or in conducting the appropriate transactions. Hence, the appropriate collective facilities that would be required in an optimal solution may simply not be constructed by anybody, so that the public authorities will often be obliged to intervene. But where they do so, they should still charge for their service as if they had been some large-scale commercial firm supplying 'clean water' (or other medium as the case may be) to those who found it cheaper to obtain it this way than to produce their own.

Who pays and what happens to the money?

There are various other issues of principle which arise in connection with optimum pollution policy, and which deserve a mention here, but are not worth treating even as sketchily as the previous issues have been treated above. One of these is the question of whether, instead of making the polluters pay, it would not be preferable to make the beneficiaries pay. After all, it may be argued, in so far as some people benefit from a cut in the pollution of, say, water, should they not be charged for the clean water in order to discourage them from wasting it? Why give them a free gift?

And it is perfectly true that, in so far as public authorities can charge for any clean product they supply as a result of their pollution-abatement or purification facilities, and in so far as these do not have a pure 'public-good' character (notably that the more any person uses of it the less is available for others), then a charge should be made. This would be the case, for example, with the supply of piped drinking water, or with access to special recreation facilities that would otherwise become congested (thereby involving an opportunity cost). In the same way that a firm will waste the pollution 'input' if it is free, consumers will waste clean water if it is free.

But this does not mean that the polluter should not be charged also; one does not exclude the other. The price of clean water should be the same for all users of it, whether the user is the consumer who washes in it, the factory that uses it for industrial purposes, or the factory that pollutes it. Thus, charging those who benefit from the purification of the water by no means implies that polluters should not also pay for their pollution. Both should pay, for both are, in effect, users of the clean water, and only if they face the same charge will the optimum total supply of the clean water be obtained and allocated between them in the optimum manner. Apart from the case of the pure public good, all users of a scarce clean medium should pay for it, whether they use it as final consumers or destroy it through their pollution.

Another minor point concerning charges for public facilities is the question of how far the revenue from the charges should determine the amount to be spent on environmental improvement (as with the French Agence des Bassins system). The answer is that there should be no connection between the amount received from pollution charges (or from the provision of clean water) and the amount spent on purification or other environmental protection. How far the public sector reduces pollution, or cleans it up, should be determined by the principles set out above – i.e., the relative cost and feasibility of collective facilities, or the 'public-good' character of pollution treatment (notably where it is a matter of cleaning up some past pollution). It has nothing to do with the revenue that would be derived from either pollution charges or charges to users. These revenues are relevant only in connection with their impact on the overall level of demand, as discussed above (see pp. 160–61). That is to say, the revenues from pollution charges must be offset by reductions in other government tax revenues (or increases in government expenditures) in so far as the government wishes to maintain the same pressure of demand in the economy. But which particular taxes should be reduced or which alternative government expenditures should be increased should bear no relation to the origin of the extra pollution charges.

Conflicts between environment policy and other policy objectives

So far we have been concerned with the principles of pollution abatement only from the point of view of the optimum national allocation of resources. We have examined the way in which these principles would be served by means of policy instruments that, in one form or another, make the polluter bear the full social costs of the pollution for which he is responsible. However, economic policy is designed to serve more than one economic objective – though perhaps not quite as many as is often believed. One of the most important objectives of economic policy during the last few decades or so has been to maintain full employment, both nationally and regionally – i.e., to ensure that resources are fully used, rather than to worry about *how* they are used. Governments are also very concerned with income distribution, that is, with the way that the output produced by all our resources is allocated between people. And this is often closely bound up with the impact of policies on local employment situations, or on specific industries or sectors of the economy.

Political concern with regional differences in prosperity may well be as much a reflection of the political constraints on all governmental policies than a concern with overall economic welfare. For it is not obvious why, other things being equal (including duration of unemployment, and so on), total economic welfare is reduced if a given total number of unemployed tend to be concentrated in one region or one industry rather than spread over the country. But in the former case the political pressures on governments to act are likely to be far greater. Hence, there may often be instances where a reduction in pollution in the interests of better resource-allocation appears to conflict with other objectives, in that it would have a particularly damaging effect on employment in a locality or a particular industry, or that it would hit old and/or small firms in particular.

One very obvious example of a frequent conflict between the optimum allocation of resources nationally and a possible loss of welfare (through loss of jobs) for those engaged in a particular industry or region arises in cases where decisions have to be taken concerning the protection of industries against foreign competition. The pure theory of international trade might demonstrate that a reduction in barriers to trade is desirable in the interests of world welfare, or even of the welfare of individual countries, but the theory nowhere suggests that it is always necessarily desirable in the interests of the welfare of all individual groups. A reduction in tariffs, on some particular imports for example, might raise national economic welfare if the gains to the consumers outweigh the losses to the producers (which will usually be the case). But what is to be done about the losers? It is little consolation to them to be told that the economy as a whole is better off and that it would have been possible, *in theory*, for them to be compensated for their losses by the consumers, leaving the latter better off than they were to begin with. The same principle applies if individual industries face higher costs as a result of some need to reduce pollution. Governments will obviously be under pressure not to introduce anti-pollution measures that could create difficulties of this sort. In the next chapter the argument that pollution abatement would impose a heavy burden on the country on account of a loss of competitiveness in international trade is discussed, and it is argued that there is no such burden at the national level. But this does not dispose of the problems that could arise at the level of the individual industry, firm or region, and governments will, in these cases, face a conflict of objectives.

Broadly speaking, there seem to be three types of solution to adopt in the face of such a conflict of policy objectives. First, the measures that would be appropriate on resource-allocation grounds can be modified or relaxed; secondly, they can be maintained, but with a time-lag to allow for a transitional period of adjustment; thirdly, they can be implemented without any qualification, but accompanied by additional policy measures designed to minimize the conflict with other policy objectives.

For example, consider the case where the appropriate policy for pollution abatement meant that considerable extra costs were imposed on some firms or industry in a certain area, with the result that their competitive position was badly threatened (nationally or internationally) and considerable local unemployment ensued. In such a situation many authorities would be under pressure to abstain from the appropriate anti-pollution measures and replace them by others that would be less efficient, from the resource-allocation point of view, such as a subsidy to the industry concerned to install techniques of production that involved less pollution. This would be the first type of response to the conflict of objectives. It is open to the usual objection that, in so far as resources are misallocated, total national output is less than potential output. If, instead, output were maximized (by optimum resource-allocation) it would, at least in principle, be possible for the losers from the anti-pollution policy to be compensated, or more than compensated, while the rest of the community would still be better off. Whether the losers would, in practice, be compensated, however, is another matter, and would depend on social and political circumstances. While economists may have no expert knowledge of these circumstances, it is important that they draw attention to this aspect of the problem, rather than give the impression that there is absolutely no reason known to economic science why the resource-allocation objective should ever be sacrificed in the interests of income distribution.

The second type of response to the conflict of objectives is to permit some transitional period during which firms have time to take appropriate measures to adjust to the introduction of pollution-control policies. This is the very common practice whenever tariffs on internationally traded goods are reduced. For example, the various internationally agreed rounds of tariff reductions and also the arrangements for the establishment of customs unions of one kind or another (such as the E.E.C.) invariably allowed transitional periods. The rationale of this is usually that it is inequitable to suddenly remove some protection from domestic firms in the interests of resource-allocation, since the growth of the industries concerned, the investment of capital and the acquisition of skills and other ties by the labour force therein, have been developed in a situation in which tariffs did exist. Hence, workers must be given time to find other outlets, other job opportunities, or other ways of adapting to the changed market conditions, which have been brought about through deliberate governmental policy rather than through the normal uncertainties of economic life. *

A third reaction is to implement the policy to restrict pollution to the (assumed) optimum and to deal with the other problems that may then arise by entirely different policy measures. For example, it might be thought that the best procedure would be to implement the pollution-abatement policy and to accompany this by measures to improve labour mobility, or re-training, or to inject alternative sources of employment into the region. Of course, in some of these cases the accompanying measures might involve even more resource misallocation of a new form than did the initial excessive pollution. For example, measures to artificially stimulate the entry into a region of new industries that do not, otherwise, find it economical to go there will often involve resource misallocation, unless they can be justified in terms of dynamic effects in the long run, or extra economies of scale, and so forth. On the other hand, some measures to minimize the local-employment effects of anti-pollution policies might only involve improvements in information, at little cost, which would thereby increase the efficiency of national resource-allocation.

* While profit-receivers might be expected to bear the risks of uncertainty on the grounds that this is what profits are the reward for, it is difficult to justify bearing the notion that labour should bear any of these risks.

In principle, this third means of reconciling conflicts in policy objectives is likely to be the most efficient economically.* If the objective of reducing pollution conflicts with the employment objective it is generally preferable to persist with the pollution abatement with the aid of the most appropriate instrument for this purpose (namely, a pollution charge), but to accompany this by an additional instrument, such as a fiscal or monetary or institutional instrument, designed to bear on the level of employment.

But apart from recognizing that, in principle, the third response to the conflict of objectives is preferable, it must be recognized that, in practice, the appropriate policy instrument may not be at hand, particularly when it is local employment that is affected. Where pollution abatement means a loss of jobs and where the only immediate alternative is unemployment, the true cost, to society, of the labour employed in the industries concerned is less than the wage – that is, it is less than the nominal market price of the labour. This is because the use of labour in the industries concerned does not imply that it has been taken away from some alternative activity and that society, hence, is deprived of the output of this alternative activity. As explained earlier in this chapter, what matters for resource-allocation are 'opportunity costs' – i.e., what output is sacrificed in one part of the economy as a result of using resources elsewhere. In the case in question here, if the labour would not have been employed in some other way the social 'opportunity cost' – which is the true social cost – of using it in the polluting industry is nil.

In such cases, the resource misallocation from excessive pollution, in the short run, is reduced and might be zero, or negative. For although the nominal market costs of the goods concerned fail to allow for the external costs of the pollution generated in their production they exaggerate the true social cost of the labour employed. In such a situation, the second response to the conflict of objectives might be appropriate,

* This corresponds to the well-known principle of economic theory to the effect that it is impossible to achieve several targets successfully without an equal number of policy instruments (that independently affect the different objectives).

namely the use of a transitional period, accompanied, as far as possible, by some measures to minimize the transitional difficulties, provided that these did not tend to perpetuate the resource misallocation.

On the whole, this procedure would appear to be preferable to the first type of response, such as subsidies to firms on pollution-abatement equipment. In general, such subsidies are not likely to be very effective, except where accompanied by other measures to enforce or stimulate pollution abatement, and will anyway not lead to the most economical means of pollution abatement, as would be the case with the pollution charge. They are also likely to be diverted partly to subsidize investment in general (though this side-effect may not always be entirely undesirable). While economists are reluctant to stick their necks out over questions such as whether any particular policy is necessarily desirable from a welfare point of view, they do have a duty to draw attention to some of the fallacies that are behind many of the anti-pollution-abatement arguments.

For example, the fact that it might mean a loss of jobs does not necessarily mean that the policy should not be adopted; for, as pointed out above, it is at least necessary to be sure first that no other means can be adopted to remedy the employment problem. If no such policy can be devised, so that a chronic, quasi-permanent, increase in local unemployment would result, that is another matter. But the relevant facts must be established in the first place. The unemployment argument has been used throughout the ages to oppose all sorts of measures to reduce international tariff barriers, to introduce safety regulations or other improvements in working conditions in factories, to abolish child labour, and so on. But in the end these measures have been adopted; some short-term local effects on employment may have been felt in some cases (and in some cases the effects were acute and long-lasting), but this has not led to increasing unemployment over all; and, in the long run, standards of living have risen.

Thus, apart from short-term adjustment problems, or problems arising out of longer-term structural rigidities in the economy, which should be tackled by appropriate measures to increase the flexibility of the economy, there is no fundamental choice to be made between jobs and pollution abatement. In so far as policies lead to a reduction in pollution they imply a shift in the way the economy uses its resources, not a change in the overall level of resource use. If, for a given use of resources, total final output changes in response to a reduction in pollution, the authorities may have a minor problem of controlling the pressure of demand in the economy. But governments are constantly concerned with this problem anyway, since, in addition to continuous changes in the pattern of demand and output, the variables determining the overall pressure of demand are constantly changing. In any case, as is shown in the next chapter, the total macro-economic burden of environmental protection is probably negligible.

7 The Economic Burden of Environmental Protection

Introduction

In the previous chapter we considered the economic policies that are required to protect the environment from excessive pollution. The next question is, 'How much will this cost?' If the costs of pollution abatement were to rise rapidly as economies grow, the price to be paid for a cleaner environment in terms of economic growth might be substantial. This is precisely what *The Limits to Growth* study (see p. 113), for example, maintains, i.e. that even if economic growth is not constrained by shortages of raw materials or food, it would eventually run up against a pollution constraint. And many other people who do not necessarily subscribe to the analysis or conclusions of the doomsday school of thought fear that the burden of pollution-abatement expenditures will become very heavy, so that there will be insuperable social and political obstacles to the policies required to protect the environment. Some people fear that a choice has to be made between the environment and jobs, on the grounds that if industry is forced to reduce pollution this will raise its costs and lead to unemployment in the industries affected, or will lead to a loss of competitive power in relation to other countries that might not be prepared to go as far in protecting their own environments. Others fear that heavy expenditure on protecting the environment must slow down economic growth, since less will be available for investments of the more conventional kind. Policy-makers will often feel that they are caught in a squeeze between the environmental lobby on the one hand and the difficulties, on the other hand, of imposing heavy burdens on industry or on the national use of resources for other competing purposes.

The object of this chapter is to try to put the burden of

environmental-protection policies into some sort of perspective, and to show that the optimum amount of environmental protection will cost very little, if anything. To do this we concentrate on pollution rather than other aspects of the environment, since (i) this is, and will continue to be, for some time, by far the most important component of environmental-protection expenditure; (ii) it is the pollution constraint rather than, say, the increase of litter or derelict land, which is believed to constitute a constraint on economic growth; and (iii) it is the area in which the concepts are clearest and where most work has been done to make numerical estimates of the costs involved and of the likely benefits.

First, we shall consider how pollution-control expenditures affect national product as conventionally measured, both in the short run and in the long run; and how much substance there is in fears of unfavourable effects on unemployment, or foreign-trade competitiveness. Finally, we shall consider what the magnitude of the expenditures and benefits is likely to be in the light of various recent attempts that have been made to put a figure on these items.

It is important to recall at the outset the distinctions made in earlier chapters between three concepts:

(i) welfare
(ii) gross national product (GNP)
(iii) the growth of GNP over time

There is little need to dwell on the first of these three concepts here, since it follows from the principles of pollution policy as outlined in Chapter 6 that welfare would rise if pollution were reduced to the optimum level. This conclusion holds even if the expenditures on pollution abatement lead to a cut in national product. This is another facet of the obvious proposition that, ideally, the value of the costs of pollution abatement should be less than the value of the benefits to be derived from it. These benefits should be defined very widely, and include (i) all the additions to consumers' welfare, including the so-called 'intangible' benefits, such as improved amenity, (ii) the direct economic benefits accruing to some firms, such as reductions in costs caused by pollution (for example, corrosion from air pollution, or water-treatment costs), and (iii) benefits, such as improved health, which may fall into an intermediate category. The effect of pollution-abatement expenditures on GNP depends only on the balance of abatement costs and those *economic* benefits that are included in the measure of GNP.

The short-term direct effect on national product (GNP)

IGNORING THE BENEFITS OF POLLUTION ABATEMENT

Some common sense tells us that if resources are used to reduce pollution, they cannot be available for other purposes, notably consumption. Hence although, for the reasons set out in the preceding chapters, expenditures incurred to reduce pollution to the optimum level must, by definition, lead to higher *welfare*, they must also lead to lower consumption *as conventionally defined in the national accounts*. For consumption is defined in the estimates of national product to include only items that can be valued. It includes, therefore, items such as consumers' expenditures on food, clothing, motor-cars, books, records, tobacco, and so on, but it does not include the welfare that people may derive from admiring beautiful scenery, swimming in a clean river (unless a charge is made for doing so), walking by the side of a clear stream, enjoying the peace and quiet of a day in the country, good health, and so on. But one of the objects of reducing pollution is to increase human satisfactions of this kind. Hence, if resources are transferred from the production of the goods and services that are included in the measurement of consumption in order to make a net addition to welfare of the non-measured kind, measured consumption will appear to fall even though welfare has risen. And the cut in measured consumption, other things being equal, will mean a corresponding cut in GNP as measured.

But it is not quite as simple as that. Pollution-abatement

expenditures may be of different kinds, with different effects on national product as conventionally measured. If the pollution abatement requires only capital costs (for example, a water-purification plant), then, other things being equal, GNP will not fall.* What happens is simply that the pattern of output in the economy has changed, with investment occupying a larger share of a given total level of output. In the longer run, however, this will make GNP, or consumption, lower than it would otherwise be. But if, on the other hand, the resources used to abate pollution took the form of current costs, measured GNP would fall in the short run.† To take an extreme example, suppose the pollution were reduced entirely by using more labour in some factory in order to clean the effluent. Clearly, other things being equal, less labour is available to produce the final output of the economy, which is what GNP measures, so that GNP will fall.‡ In practice, pollution abatement is likely to be a mixture of various kinds of costs, so that it is impossible to say how far GNP will be cut. But in the end, whichever particular combination of abatement costs is involved, private consumption as conventionally defined and measured must be cut sooner or later, although this does not conflict with a rise in consumers' welfare.

ALLOWING FOR THE BENEFITS OF POLLUTION ABATEMENT

In reaching the conclusion that GNP would be cut if private firms had to incur current costs in order to reduce pollution we have not yet taken account of the way that measured national product might gain from a cut in pollution. In particular, there would be a saving in costs for some firms, who had hitherto been the victims of excessive pollution. In other words, some firms would require *less*, not more,

* Assuming no change in the pressure of demand. In other words, the discussion here is about the change in GNP *for a given pressure of demand*. The possibility that the pressure of demand may change is discussed later in this chapter.

† The economist will recognize that the principle involved is that resources are being shifted, in this case, from final demand to intermediate output.

‡ If the extra labour is used in a public sewage works, however, GNP is unaffected, since all public expenditure is part of the final output of the economy and hence adds to GNP.

resources, to produce a given output if other firms are obliged to reduce pollution. For example, if following the introduction of anti-pollution policies, an upstream firm is obliged to use more resources in order to purify its effluent, the cut in its pollution might lower the cost of water use to some down-stream firm, which could then cut its water-treatment costs. In other words, firms that had hitherto been 'victims' of pollution will be able either to release resources for use else-where in the economy or to expand their output for a given use of resources. In either case, total GNP will tend to rise and hence tend to offset the extra resources used by the polluter in order to cut his pollution. Another way of looking at this is to say that, leaving aside all considerations of the unmeasured ingredients of consumers' welfare, etc., if pollu-tion were to be reduced only to the point where, at the margin, the tangible economic benefits of the abatement to firms that had been victims of pollution matched the costs of the abate-ment, then, subject to various qualifications arising out of changes in relative prices, GNP would necessarily rise. For the total cost-savings of the victims (i.e. the benefits) would add to national product more than the extra costs of the polluters subtracted from national product. If, however, pollu-tion were abated to the point where, at the margin, abatement costs equalled *all* social benefits, including the non-measured components of welfare, it might well be that the cost-savings obtained by victims in the productive sector of the economy would be less than the costs of the pollution abatement, so that national product would fall even though welfare, of course, would still rise.

The indirect and longer-term effect on national product

The possibility that measured national product may rise as a result of the economies reaped by firms that had hitherto suf-fered excessive pollution is not a remote theoretical notion.

Over the past few years several estimates have been made of the benefits of pollution abatement, and though the methodology used is necessarily still in a primitive stage (as the authors of the various studies would be the first to point out) there is little doubt that the direct economic benefits of pollution abatement are at least comparable to the costs. These estimates of costs and benefits are surveyed later in this chapter. But meanwhile, the story about the effects on measured national product has to be taken a little further.

So far, we have considered only the *direct* impact of pollution costs and benefits in the short term (apart from noting that a short-term cut in conventional investment means a longer-term cut in consumption). But there will also be indirect effects on national product as conventionally measured, and on its longer-term growth rate. For example, a reduction of pollution might, and no doubt would, increase the productivity of labour as a result of better health.[1] Although the scientific data relating air pollution to health are still far from conclusive, there is considerable evidence that pollution of the air in some cities has reached a point where it does harm health. In so far as air pollution is reduced, therefore, not only will some resources be released from health expenditures for use in other ways, but the productivity of labour would also probably rise. This might simply take the form of less working days lost through sickness, but there might also be an increase in the productivity of the working day. For example it has been estimated that a 50 per cent reduction in air pollution in the U.S.A. 'would be worth about $2 billion per year in terms of the increased benefits of (a) increased work days, and (b) decreased direct health expenditures'.[2] And there are other obvious ways in which a reduction in air pollution can raise measured GNP. For example, the reduction of smogs will not merely add to welfare, it will reduce traffic congestion and hence cut transport costs, some of which will be borne by firms, so that the cut in these costs will raise GNP.

The longer-term effect of more pollution abatement on measured GNP is uncertain, as with the short-term effect. This is partly because they are related via the short-term effect of extra pollution-abatement expenditures on the rate of profit. And it is partly because the implementation of tighter pollution policies could well accelerate technical progress generally and hence cause GNP to grow faster.

However, given the uncertainty as to the short-term effect on national product, further discussion of the various possible longer-term effects is of limited interest. Furthermore, in view of the estimates discussed in the next section, which suggest that pollution-abatement costs will be comparatively modest anyway, refined analysis of the possible effects on the growth rate would seem to be out of place.

The costs of pollution abatement: data problems

It has been argued above that the need to incur costs to reduce pollution does not necessarily mean that GNP must fall, even before allowing for the economic benefits from reduced pollution. In the next section we shall show that the costs of pollution abatement are, in any case, likely to be small and of the order of magnitude of only about 1 per cent of GNP for most countries. But some preliminary qualifications to the available estimates must first be discussed.

First, one of the implications of the analysis of optimum pollution policy set out in the previous chapter is that, ideally, what we would like to know is how much it will cost to reduce pollution to the *optimum* amount. But in order to make such estimates we would require information both on the costs of achieving different degrees of pollution abatement and on the benefits (i.e., the damage done by existing levels of pollution). And, as indicated in the last chapter, we do not know enough about either the costs or the benefits of pollution abatement to be able to identify the precise point at which pollution is optimal.

Hence, the available estimates of anti-pollution expenditures are most unlikely to represent the costs of achieving the optimum level of pollution. But this does not mean that these estimates are on the low side; they might be on the high side, for we simply do not know whether they are above or below the optimum. Taking the available figures as a whole it appears that, whether or not they represent the optimum levels of pollution abatement, substantial improvements in the environment will be achieved in the countries in question at relatively low costs in terms of the shares of national product that have to be devoted to pollution abatement.

Secondly, the optimum degree of pollution abatement will vary from country to country according to the particular costs and benefits of pollution in the individual countries. These will depend, in turn, on the precise structure of industry in each country, since some industries pollute the environment far more than others. Economies that are heavily dependent on relatively pollution-intensive industries, such as iron and steel, oil-refining, pulp and paper, chemicals, brewing, certain metal-working processes, and so on, would probably need to spend more on pollution abatement than economies heavily dependent on say, tourism, banking, and insurance services.

Even for a given industry, the damage done by a given emission of pollution will vary from country to country for a variety of reasons. The damage depends, in the first place, on how far pollutants are absorbed, dispersed and diluted. It does not matter greatly how much carbon monoxide is produced in British cities by the motor-cars if it is all rapidly dispersed thanks to the favourable climatic conditions in Britain and the absence of temperature inversions such as those experienced in Los Angeles and other American (and European) cities. Similarly, a given amount of polluted effluent does less damage if it is poured into an ocean where the tidal and wind conditions are favourable than if it is poured into a river, or a relatively sheltered and enclosed stretch of water such as the Great Lakes or some parts of the Baltic.

Furthermore, in the case of, say, water, even if local conditions (ambient standards) are equally affected in two areas, if one area is better provided with alternative supplies, the loss of welfare caused by a given fall in local 'ambient standards' in one of its many sources of water supplies will be less.*

A third source of incomparability in pollution data as between different areas, let alone different countries, is that what we want to know in the end is how much damage is done in terms of loss of human welfare, not in straight physical units of amounts of smoke or pollutants in the water. One obviously important variable determining the size of the damage to human welfare caused by pollution is simply the number of humans affected. If high concentrations of SO_2 are produced near power-stations in a country where power-stations are remote from centres of dense population the damage done will be less than if the same effect is produced in a country where power-stations have been sited closer to large cities. This difficulty cannot be overcome by converting emissions of pollutants to some sort of *per capita* basis. The 'public bad' character of pollution rules out this adjustment, for the amount of pollution suffered by one person is not reduced by virtue of the fact that many other people also suffer from it.

On the side of the cost of pollution abatement there are also many incomparabilities between countries. For example, in some countries (such as Japan) the relatively high level of abatement expenditures now envisaged may have little relevance for other countries partly because of differences in environmental factors such as those discussed above, but partly because the environment has been allowed to deteriorate more than in certain other countries. Countries such as Britain

* This is in accordance with the law of diminishing marginal utility. For the point is that the damage done by a given degree of pollution can be looked at as its marginal disutility, and the marginal disutility of a given amount of pollution is the counterpart of the marginal utility of the clean air or water that has been 'used up' or destroyed by that pollution. And the marginal utility of the clean water used up by pollution will be smaller the more of that water is available. If there is plenty of clean water available its *marginal* utility will be low so that it does not matter so much whether some extra units of it are 'used up' through pollution. This amounts to saying that the marginal disutility of pollution will be low; which corresponds to the above proposition to the effect that the damage done by, say, water pollution will be less in a region where there is plenty of water. This applies not merely because of the greater dispersion and dilution capacity of a larger body of water but also because of the larger number of alternatives available to the population in question.

that have been active in this field over many years, not to say decades, will not need to embark on such major new programmes in order to achieve the sort of standards that are deemed to be socially desirable. Consequently, since the available data on pollution-abatement programmes are largely in terms of the new programmes now being considered or introduced in various countries, they may differ between countries on account of differences in the starting level – i.e., in the amount of anti-pollution expenditures that are already being incurred, or that were incurred in the more distant past (for example, when sewage works were installed).

Furthermore, the conceptual basis of the cost data will vary from country to country, according to factors such as the degree to which they relate only to capital costs, or include maintenance and operating costs, and the precise coverage of the programmes – such as how far they are confined to water and air pollution and how far they allow for the treatment of garbage, noise reductions, land reclamation, pesticides, radioactive waste disposal, and so on.

However, the problems of the international comparability of environmental-protection expenditures are problems for international organizations, and this is not the place to embark on a full-scale study of the difficulties involved. All that is needed here is to emphasize that no claim is made that the expenditure data available represent the optimum expenditure in each country, nor that the data are sufficiently comparable conceptually to provide the basis for firm generalizations. But in spite of these reservations it does appear from the evidence surveyed below that there is a surprising degree of uniformity in the various national estimates and that the costs of major improvements in the environment in the main industrialized countries will be of the order of only 1 per cent to 2 per cent of GNP.

Finally, it should be emphasized that these estimates are probably over-estimates of what expenditures are likely to be in the long term, when the full effect of technological progress in pollution-abatement equipment has been achieved. For pollution abatement is a relatively new preoccupation of governments, and hence of industry, in most countries, and now that a far greater incentive to find cheap ways of reducing pollution has been provided it is possible, indeed probable, that rapid technological progress will be made to find cheap abatement techniques.[3]

The costs of pollution abatement: the 'facts'

The only country for which estimates of anti-pollution expenditures are relatively abundant is the U.S.A. Here the various estimates that have appeared over the last two years or so have been revised upwards, but the latest upward revision to the figures is chiefly due to a big increase in the estimated expenditure on the reduction of air pollution from motor-cars, corresponding to the adoption of what many people would regard as extremely ambitious targets for reducing motor-car pollution. In 1972 the Environmental Protection Agency reported that the costs to private industry of implementing the Clean Air Act (and amendments) would amount to about $35 billion over the period 1973–77, compared with an estimate published the previous year of only $10·5 billion.* But of this $25 billion increase, about $20 billion reflected an upward revision of the estimated cost of achieving the more stringent motor-car emission standards laid down in the 1970 Clean Air Act Amendments.[4]

In the light of this latest estimate for air-pollution abatement costs the present position on environmental-protection expenditures in the U.S.A. (at the time of writing) is that total cash expenditures over the period 1972–76 would amount to $127 billion. This represents about 2·1 per cent of national product.[5] But this figure lumps together the actual capital expenditures incurred during this period with the current costs, which implies an overestimate of the *annual* costs, since the capital costs will, to some extent, enable an improved environment to be obtained over a long period. When one is

* By comparison with the costs expected to be borne by private industry the costs expected to be incurred by the public authorities in the U.S.A. are negligible.

considering the 'burden' of buying a motor-car, for example, one does not divide the whole capital cost by one year's income; rather one annualizes it by spreading the cost over the time-period during which one expects to own the car (less resale value at the end, if any). On this basis the annualized costs (comprising operation, maintenance, interest and depreciation) of the latest U.S. programme amount to only about 1·5 per cent of GNP.

Furthermore, these costs include the costs that are already being incurred as part of the current pollution-abatement effort, as well as the additional costs of achieving improved standards as laid down in recent American legislation concerning air and water pollution. It is arguable that the economic burden that matters in the context of the problem of how far economic growth can be sustained is the additional burden over and above that which is already being borne by the community and to which the growth rate has already been adjusted. And it appears that about half of the annual pollution-abatement expenditures anticipated in the U.S.A. over the period 1972–76 (inclusive) are already being incurred. So that the addition to current pollution-abatement costs will only be about $60 billion, or about 1·0 per cent of GNP. If these were also to be put on an annualized basis, the figure would be further reduced to possibly about 0·8 per cent of GNP over the next few years.[6]

Another way of looking at this figure is as a percentage of the total cumulative addition to GNP during this period – i.e., the cumulative sum of the additional output produced in each of the years over the base year. Thus if, for example, the national product of the U.S.A. were to rise by $50 billion each year (which would be about 5 per cent per annum), the cumulative total of extra output produced after five years would be $750 billion.* On this basis, according to an O.E.C.D. calculation, the annualized cost of the new pollution-abatement expenditures that are to be introduced over the next few years amount to only 5·1 per cent of the cumulative additional output produced over this period.[7] Furthermore, the O.E.C.D.

* For it is the sum of $50 billion, $100 billion, and so on.

analysis of the expected time-path of the planned expenditures shows that, in terms of the burden as just defined, it will decline to only 4·4 per cent of the cumulative addition to GNP over the period up to 1980.

Another aspect of the estimates that is brought out in the O.E.C.D. study is that the capital-cost component of the total pollution-abatement expenditures will represent an almost negligible fraction of total investment in the various countries covered in the study. In the U.S.A. it is estimated that over the period 1970 to 1980 pollution control investment will amount to only 3·7 per cent of total investment. Clearly this cannot have a significant effect on the growth rate of the American economy. Even if no allowance is made for efficiency gains, and assuming that growth rates are proportional to investment rates, this would only reduce the annual growth rate of the American economy from about 5 per cent to about 4·83 per cent. Obviously, such changes are well within the margin of error of any predictions of growth rates, as well as the margin of error of any simple relationship between investment and growth rates.

This confirms the estimates shown in another study carried out for the O.E.C.D. by a group of technical experts on the costs of reducing air pollution. This study, which is confined to air pollution, but which also covers a number of countries, showed that the total costs of reducing SO_2 and nitrogen-oxide emission levels to their 1968 levels by 1980 would be negligible by comparison with the national products of the countries concerned.[8] (This, incidentally, is in striking contrast to the impression one might gain from a report in one British newspaper, as is discussed in Chapter 2.)

As the O.E.C.D. study stated, 'the capital investment [for the SO_2 programme] represents some 0·5 per cent of the gross domestic fixed asset formation' in the O.E.C.D. countries in question. Since investment is only about 20 per cent of total national product in the O.E.C.D. countries, this means that the capital investments required to carry out this programme for SO_2 would amount to only about 0·1 per cent of GNP. Even if the nitrogen-oxide abatement expenditures are included, and all operating costs are added the total burden is still only about 0·2 per cent to 0·3 per cent of the GNP of O.E.C.D. countries, as shown below.

TABLE 7.1

Costs of Reducing Air Pollution to 1968 levels by 1980 in O.E.C.D. countries ($ billion)[9]

	Operating Costs	Capital Costs
Sulphur-dioxide (SO₂)	2·2 to 4·2	5·8 to 15·6
Nitrogen-oxides (NO$_x$)	0·8	3·9
Particulates	0·25	1·5
TOTAL	3·25 to 5·25	11·2 to 21·0

As the O.E.C.D. study points out, in so far as programmes along these lines have either not yet started or are only just starting, it would be safer to assume that the costs will, in fact, be incurred over the six-year period, 1975 to 1980 inclusive, so that the *annual* capital costs would amount to between $1·9 billion per annum and $3·5 billion per annum. The sum of the *annual* operating costs and *annual* capital costs during this period would thus amount to between $5·15 billion and $8·75 billion per annum, i.e. between $(3·25 + 1·9) billion and $(5·25 + 3·5) billion.

The relevant national-product figures would be as shown below. These projections are based on the conservative assumptions that the Japanese economy grows at only 8 per cent per annum, and that Europe and North America grow at only 4 per cent per annum over the period to 1980 (which in both cases is below the trend rates of growth over the last decade). Given these projections the final figure is that total costs of bringing air pollution down to 1968 levels by 1980 would be between 0·2 per cent and 0·34 per cent of national product of the countries concerned.*

* For the ratio of costs to GNP is the ratios of between $5·15 billion and $8·75 billion (the figures referred to in the text above) to the GNP figure of about $2,600 billion arrived at in the final column of the table.

7

TABLE 7.2

Projected GNP of O.E.C.D. countries, 1970–80; ($ billion at 1970 exchange rates and prices)

	GNP 1970	Projected GNP 1980	Average GNP (1975)
Europe	775 ⎫	2,720	2,280
North America	1,067 ⎬		
Japan	198 ⎭	512	356
TOTAL	2,040	3,232	2,636

It may be asked why the above figure of about 0·2 per cent to 0·3 per cent of GNP for air pollution in all O.E.C.D. countries is well below the figures of about 1·0 per cent for the U.S.A. taken direct from the American national sources. The difference might suggest that the cost figures for the other countries covered by the O.E.C.D. report are too low. But the reason for the apparent discrepancy is partly (i) that the lower figures just shown related only to targets in the field of air pollution from stationary sources, and so excluded air pollution from motor-cars, and (ii) the current legislation and air pollution programmes in the U.S.A. are far more ambitious than the targets implied in the O.E.C.D. figures just shown. For example, by 1977 the United States SO_2 emissions are to be reduced by 89 per cent below the level that they would otherwise have achieved by then, and particulate emission by 86 per cent.[10] Similar dramatic reductions are expected in the other major air pollutants, such as carbon monoxide and hydro-carbons.

These official U.S.A. estimates do not differ significantly from earlier private estimates that had been in circulation.*

* They are also consistent with the implications of a completely different approach to the problem, namely that used by Wassily Leontief in a recent study which estimated, among other things, the effects on prices, in ninety individual industries, of conformity to the 1967 Clean Air Act standards. Out of these ninety industries, the effect was less than 1 per cent in seventy-five cases, between 1 per cent and 5 per cent in thirteen cases, between 5 per cent and 10 per cent in three cases and above 10 per cent in only one case. The weighted average for all the ninety industries is below 1 per cent, and in so far as this measures the extra

For example, Allen Kneese, who is one of the world's fore-most authorities on pollution, estimated that the costs of 'making a substantial improvement on all fronts (air, water, solids – including a lot of cleaning up of problems inherited from the past) would be between $11 billion and $19 billion per annum in 1972–73, which would have represented between 1 per cent and 1·8 per cent of U.S.A. national product.'[11]

In the U.S.A. protection of the environment has only become an important objective of policy relatively recently, so that many kinds of pollution had been allowed to reach serious proportions. Furthermore, stringent control pro-grammes have now been adopted. Hence the figures for other countries are likely to be rather lower than these U.S.A. figures. One exception to this proposition is Japan. Here, according to the O.E.C.D. data, total current and capital expenditures on new pollution-control programmes during the next few years are estimated to be about 2·6 per cent of GNP. But given that the Japanese national product is likely to grow much faster than the U.S.A. national product, these new programmes are estimated to account for only about 1·7 per cent of the cumulative increase in GNP (compared to the base year) by 1975 (compared with a U.S.A. figure for the same period and concept of 5·1 per cent).

At the other extreme, if one takes a country such as the U.K., where considerable efforts to preserve and improve the environment have been made for very many years and where new tough legislation has been progressively introduced since the 1950s, new expenditures required to achieve further improvement in rivers and in the air do not seem to impose any great strain on national resources, and would amount to only about 0·7 per cent of GNP. The major component of these expenditures includes the amounts that would be required to bring the effluents discharged to the rivers in England and Wales up to the standards that the various river authorities

---

resources used by industry to meet air-pollution standards laid down in the 1967 Act it is a measure of the loss of real resources available for other uses. ('Environ-mental Repercussions and the Economic Structure', *Review of Economics and Statistics*, August 1970).

believe to be desirable and attainable by 1980. These expenditures would lead to the following changes in the quality of the rivers.

TABLE 7.3

Effect on Quality of Non-tidal Rivers in England and Wales of Estimated Expenditures on Improved Effluent Discharges, 1970–1980[a]

| | 1970 | | 1980 | |
	miles	%	miles	%
Class 1 (free of pollution)	17,000	(76)	(18,200)	(81)
Class 2 (mildly polluted)	3,290	(15)	(3,250)	(15)
Class 3 (badly polluted)	1,070	(5)	(670)	(3)
Class 4 (grossly polluted)	952	(4)	199	(1)
	22,312	(100)	22,319	(100)

[a] Joint Department of the Environment Circular 64/72 and Welsh Office, Circular 127/72, *Vol. 2 of the River Pollution Survey of England and Wales*, July 10th, 1972.

Compared to the costs of improving the rivers, the costs of further improving the air in Britain would be negligible. The O.E.C.D. technical report on air pollution suggested that it would cost only about £45 million by 1980 (capital cost) to achieve a very substantial reduction, in Britain, in SO_2 (the most costly form of air-pollution abatement), to which has to be added about £15 million per annum for operating costs.[12] Even if generous allowance is made for other forms of air pollution from stationary sources, the total would still amount to only about £30 to £40 million per annum, compared to GNP of over £50,000 million at market prices in 1970.

It is true that these estimates do not include any allowance for reduction in air pollution from motor-cars, but this should not greatly change the order of magnitude of the figures. For although steps are being taken to tighten up on motor-car exhausts in Britain the situation in Britain, in this connection, is much less serious than in the U.S.A. or certain other countries, on account of more favourable climatic conditions. The low estimates for the costs of reducing air pollution from stationary sources in Britain may appear to be surprising, but it should not be forgotten that the dramatic improvement in the London air during the 1950s was obtained at a cost of only about £0·15 per annum per head of the London population.[13] Power-stations, oil refineries and certain chemical processes are important sources of SO_2 emissions. But their impact on ground-level SO_2 concentrations has been greatly reduced, in Britain, by the policies described in the previous chapter. And given the shrinking dependence on coal-fired power-stations in the U.K., which tended to be sited near coal-fields for obvious reasons, the scope for siting power-stations, and other plants that make considerable use of relatively sulphurous fuels, well away from congested regions, has been increasing. In this way, ground-level concentrations of air pollution in densely populated areas can be reduced relatively cheaply.*

Furthermore, the main source of ground-level concentrations of SO_2 (not to mention particulates) in Britain is still domestic, commercial and public-service sources, on account largely of the low level of their emissions. Hence, in so far as the fuels with high sulphur content can be channelled to the power-stations and so on, and low-sulphur-content oil and natural gas can be channelled to domestic users, and other users that have to be close to urban areas, a further considerable reduction in the pollution to which people are exposed will be achieved at comparatively small cost compared with the expensive techniques of de-sulphurization and the like.

The benefits of pollution abatement

There is no doubt that the benefits of pollution abatement have not been very well described so far in the literature of the subject. This is partly because it is so difficult to measure the damage done by pollution (which is the same thing as the benefits from *reducing* pollution). It is possible to say how

---

* Of course, if deliberate environmental policy leads to such plants being sited in remote areas on account of environmental considerations a social cost would be incurred (i.e. the excess of the total cost of the products concerned over what they would have cost if such considerations had not affected the plant location). These costs are not included in the above calculations.

much will be spent on reducing pollution over a specified period without this being related in a precise way to the actual reduction in ambient pollution levels that will be achieved. But it is not possible to value the benefits from any pollution-abatement programme without making assumptions, first, about the way the programme will actually change the pollution in the environment, and then about the effect of these changes on the damage done by pollution.

Nevertheless, as pollution-abatement policies are increasingly implemented there will be increased pressures to quantify the benefits, and progress will no doubt be made in the methodology of such estimates and in the collection of the requisite data. Some items of pollution damage will no doubt be easier to measure than others. For example, the tangible effect of air pollution on the corrosion of metals is likely to be more amenable to measurement than the effect on the pleasure that ordinary people may get from walking by a river that does not smell and does not have its bank littered with plastic bottles.* But the history of science is full of concepts that could not easily be measured at first, and that may even have seemed impossible to measure at first, but which gradually become amenable to quantification with the gradual develop-

* This does not mean that the estimation of the tangible damages will be easy. Many of the difficulties are summarized in the recent report by the Atomic Energy Authority's Programmes Analysis Unit as follows: 'There is virtually no data which enables one to say that exposure of commonly used materials in specified polluted atmospheres will lead to given rates of "damage". Where data do exist they frequently relate to materials in forms which are not commonly used, and/or excessively high pollution levels so different from the ambient air as to make extrapolation foolhardy, and/or relates to properties that have no relevance to the practical use of the material, and/or contains complicating variables whose effects are not or cannot be disentangled. For example textile damage is measured by strength loss when exposed to a mixture of pollutant, sunlight and humidity. The relationship between strength and usefulness and the synergy effects of the causes of degradation need to be known before the damage functions can be expressed explicitly. Plant studies are generally done with very high pollutant doses under conditions which have little relevance to long-term low level exposures. It is not known how the extent of damage varies with pollution level and the ranges normally experienced. How does prolonged exposure to low levels compare in significance with short exposure to high levels? Does the stage at which exposure occurs during a plant or animal's lifetime matter and how much?' *An Economic and Technical Appraisal of Air pollution in the United Kingdom* (H.M.S.O., London, 1972), p. 204.

ment of the appropriate techniques. For example, the measurement of heat was a problem that baffled scientists for centuries before it was solved.

It is true that many of the concepts involved in pollution damage are intrinsically much more difficult. For some of them are of an aesthetic nature, and the difficulties of breaking them down into measurable components would appear to be insurmountable for the foreseeable future. But it may well be that some of these difficulties will never have to be faced for practical purposes, as long as some methods can be found which will provide indicators of any monetary value that the public would attach to the amenity in the particular circumstances. And it is only this that is required for the purposes of any specific decision regarding pollution damage. For example, it may not be necessary to know exactly *why* some people prefer to spend a day at some particular lake rather than another as long as methods can be found, such as those pioneered by Marion Clawson and others, to evaluate how much they are prepared to pay in order to go to one lake rather than the other.[14] And the fact is that although concern with the measurement of pollution damage is a relatively recent phenomenon, much progress has already been made in the techniques of measuring it.

One of the first serious attempts to evaluate the damage done by pollution was the 1954 'Beaver' report on air pollution in Britain.[15] In this pioneering work the damage done by pollution was divided into two classes:

The direct costs include laundry and domestic cleaning; the cleaning, painting and repair of buildings; the corrosion of metals, which entails the cost not only of replacements but also of providing protective coverings etc.; damage to goods; additional lighting and extra hospital and medical services, etc.; and, secondly,

The loss of efficiency includes, for example, the effects on agriculture of damage to soil, crops and animals, interference with transport, and reduced human efficiency due to illness.[16]

The report concluded: 'After examining all the evidence we have been able to obtain we feel justified in stating that air pollution is at present costing the nation about £250 million a year in terms only of losses that can be given a monetary value.'[17] Since the Beaver report estimates excluded items such as loss of amenity and many other items to which they could not put a monetary figure, they are confined largely to the economic damage done by pollution (i.e., damage that would tend to reduce national product). They found that this damage would far outweigh the costs of abatement, and that 'air pollution as it occurs in this country today is a social and economic evil ... it not only does untold harm to human health and happiness; it is also a prodigal waste of material resources. Expenditures on curing it would be a fraction of the savings which would result from the cure.'[18] In other words, if this pollution were reduced, national product would rise.

In recent years further basic data have become available which have enabled fresh estimates to be made of the benefits of air-pollution abatement in Britain. These estimates, which have a somewhat wider coverage than the Beaver report, show that the economic damage done by air pollution in recent years is of the order of magnitude of £400 million per annum, of which £130 million represents damage to health.[19]

While the authors of these two sources of estimates emphasized very clearly the margins of error involved, the consistency between them (allowing for various factors that have changed over the years) and the fact that they have both been obliged to exclude many items of pollution damage on account of lack of data, suggest that they are not likely to be serious overestimates of the 'true' economic costs of air pollution. If anything, they are likely to be on the low side on account of the omissions through lack of data. Hence, given the modest costs of reducing air pollution in Britain mentioned above, there is little doubt that the further reduction currently envisaged would not merely raise welfare, it would also raise national product.

Estimates of the damage done by pollution in the U.S.A. are more readily available than for the U.K., and a convenient summary of findings has recently been published by the U.S. Council on Environmental Quality,[20] and in the 'RECAT report'.[21] According to the latter, the *annual* damage done in the U.S.A. from air pollution alone amounted to about $16 billion in 1968 and would rise to about $24 billion by 1977.[22] This compares with the estimated cost of about only $7 billion per annum for achieving the targets laid down in the Clean Air Act mentioned above. However, not all of the $24 billion damage from air pollution in 1977 would be directly reflected in national product, since about $9 billion of the total consists of the damage done to health. It is not possible to say how much of this reduction in damage to health would raise GNP, so the gain to GNP from the total elimination of all air pollution in the U.S.A. might be of the order of only about $15 billion.

Of course, the Clean Air Acts programme, which is expected to cost about $7 billion per annum (on a crude cash basis, which will overestimate the annualized costs) is not intended to eliminate air pollution entirely, although, as indicated above, the targets are ambitious. Hence, it is not possible to draw firm conclusions to the effect that the achievement of the current targets would cost less than the benefits to be derived, and thus lead to a direct rise in GNP (at equal pressures of demand).

In fact, the RECAT report suggests that the costs of the programme envisaged for reducing motor-car pollution will exceed the total benefits, even if the benefits are defined to include some that are not part of national product. This would imply that the current programme for reducing motor-car pollution must have gone well beyond the optimum point.* For the total costs attributed to mobile sources of air pollution in the U.S.A., of which the motor-car is overwhelmingly the chief culprit, are estimated to amount to $2·15 billion by 1977 (or 8·6 per cent of the total damage from air pollution), and this figure is far below the latest estimate of the expected annual *additional* expenditures on the abatement

---

* This is defined, as in the previous chapters, as the point where *marginal* costs of abatement equal *marginal* benefits.

7*

of air pollution, namely about $4 billion per annum.[23] But while it may well be true that automobile-pollution abatement will lead to a net fall in national product, the amount involved is negligible by comparison with American national product of over $1,000 billion. Furthermore, as regards the *total* air-pollution programmes, it appears from the above figures that the direct economic benefits will exceed the costs of the current programmes and hence lead to a slight rise in national product.

It is more difficult to make an assessment for water pollution. Expenditures on this item are expected to increase by about $25 billion between 1972 and 1976 – i.e., about $5 billion per annum – but official estimates for the total national damage from water pollution are virtually non-existent.[24] The Council on Environmental Quality reported that 'water pollution may cause recreational losses extending into many billions of dollars nationally',[25] which suggests that the welfare gain would certainly outweigh the costs, but much of this gain will not be included in measured national product.

No attempt has been made here to prove that pollution abatement will be costless, and more than offset anyway by the direct economic benefits that would follow from reduced pollution. The object of the above survey has been merely to demonstrate that the orders of magnitude of the costs are small, and that they could quite plausibly be expected to be exceeded by the resulting economic benefits. Furthermore, as will be shown below, even if there is, after all, some small cut in GNP as a result of the diversion of resources to reduce pollution, this need not have any of the adverse effects on employment or on the country's gains from foreign trade that are often feared.

Effects on employment

Even if national product is reduced as a result of greater pollution-control costs, this does not mean that unemployment must rise (contrary to the results given in a recent American study of the economic impact of pollution-control expenditure).[26] The reason for this is that if anti-pollution policies reduce national product this will effect a diversion of resources (to current pollution-abatement costs), not a fall in demand, hence there is no fall in the *pressure of demand* in the economy, and it is the latter that determines the level of unemployment. It is true that measured real income falls, but this is the counterpart of a fall in potential real output. There is no fall in the *degree* to which the production potential of the economy is utilized; merely a change in the *way* it is utilized. More is devoted to raising welfare and less to producing the goods that add to GNP. But the resources are still used.*

Consider, for example, the case of some natural disaster, such as a flood, hurricane or earthquake. This might reduce the level of real output in the economy and hence the level of real incomes that the population could enjoy, but would not necessarily mean a rise in unemployment. It could simply lead to the use of more time and resources for repairing the flood damage or clearing up the rubble. People could still be busy, but not busy producing the same consumption and investment goods and services that they had been able to produce before.

This conclusion may seem paradoxical at first sight, since one of the more obvious first effects of a rise in pollution-abatement expenditures by firms will be a rise in their costs, which will be passed on to varying degrees (depending on market conditions) in the form of higher prices, which, in turn, can be expected to reduce their sales. But the rise in their costs represents a rise in sales by other firms or individuals supplying pollution-abatement equipment or services. Even where national product must fall (other things being equal), therefore, this is not because fewer resources are employed in the economy but simply because they are redeployed in such a way that fewer of them are available for final output.

* A change in the efficiency of the economy, in terms of the relationship between inputs and outputs, does not imply any change in the level of unemployment. Otherwise, given the continued rise in productivity and efficiency over the ages, the level of unemployment would have been rising continuously, which is clearly not the case. And a diversion of resources to pollution abatement is like a fall in productive efficiency in a narrow sense; more resources (inputs) are now needed to produce a given final output.

Effects of pollution abatement on foreign trade

One aspect of pollution policy which seems to trouble many people, particularly those in industries in which pollution-abatement expenditures might have to be relatively large, is the effect on a country's trading position. It is often argued, for example, that if a country introduces tougher anti-pollution measures, the industries of that country will be placed at a competitive disadvantage compared with those of other countries where the anti-pollution measures might be less severe, or cost less money anyway on account of different natural environmental or other factors, and that this will lead to a threat to employment in their industries, particularly if these are export industries.[27] This fear has led many people and institutions, such as the E.E.C., to suggest that common standards should be adopted by countries with respect to their pollution-abatement targets. For example, it would be argued that the U.S.A. or Britain should not impose more stringent regulations on its own producers of chemical products or iron and steel than those imposed by other countries, since otherwise the latter will have a cost advantage.

Such arguments are, of course, very much like the protectionist arguments that have been heard through the ages against imports from 'cheap labour' countries, and so on, and which are now generally agreed to have been examples of illogical special pleading. For a country does not necessarily gain by selling its goods to foreigners at relative prices that do not correspond to relative social costs. These relative social costs include the disutility of work and the social valuation of leisure, amenity, and the safety and health of the population. Of course, we might be able to export more coal if we cut the wages of the miners, sent children back down the mines, or simply sell the coal at a loss. But it will be the overseas buyers who gain, since they will be acquiring our resources cheaply. We incur the real social costs – they get the benefits in the form of the cheap coal.

In general, the pattern of exports should correspond to the pattern of social costs of producing the various goods and services. Purely to illustrate the argument, suppose we are able to export steel very cheaply because we do not make our steel-producers pay for their pollution. What we would then be doing, in effect, is selling steel cheaply because we do not require the proceeds from steel exports to cover the full social costs of their production, *including the damage done by the pollution*. In effect, the victims of this pollution are subsidizing our steel exports (and hence are subsidizing overseas steel-consumers). From the point of view of the welfare of society as a whole, steel production has been pushed too far; at the margin the benefits (which equal the extra imports that can be bought from the proceeds of the steel exports) will not cover the full social costs of producing steel.

Of course, if stricter anti-pollution measures are introduced, it is possible that, in addition to a change in the relative costs of different industries, bringing them more into line with genuine comparative social costs, there will be an overall rise in export costs (though this is not necessarily the case, in so far as some exporting firms may benefit from reduced pollution). This may make the foreign balance deteriorate. But this cannot be a valid reason for not introducing the policies – it merely indicates that the old exchange rate was not appropriate, given a correct pattern of export prices (i.e. one that reflected their true social costs). The exchange rate will have to be allowed to depreciate, but this is merely handing back to overseas countries the initial improvement in our terms of trade that resulted from the rise in our export prices to take account of pollution-abatement costs.* Our terms of trade need not deteriorate over all, and the economic welfare of the country as a whole rises. For resource allocation has been improved, corresponding to the fact that the pattern of exports will now reflect more accurately the pattern of comparative *social* costs, including damage done by pollution.

If other countries do not follow suit and choose to export

* Before allowing the exchange rate to depreciate the country concerned was, in effect, trying to make the rest of the world pay for its higher pollution-control costs by improving its terms of trade *vis-à-vis* the rest of the world.

their chemicals, steel, pulp and paper, and so on, relatively cheaply because they do not wish to reduce their pollution, and prefer their own national victims of their pollution to subsidize their exports, then we should not try to stop them from, in effect, handing us this free gift, any more than if they wanted to sell us their butter or television sets at prices that do not correspond to their relative costs. We should gratefully accept the gift, provided we can shift our resources out of the industries concerned into other activities where overseas suppliers are less generous.

But here's the rub, of course, for here we run up against a major qualification to the pure free-trade doctrine implied in the above argument. For the above argument implies that, in order to maximize economic welfare in the *economy as a whole*, pollution should be reduced according to the principles set out in the preceding chapter, irrespective of what other countries are up to. But this does not detract from the problem of unemployment in the *particular industries or regions* that might be adversely affected by the introduction of tougher anti-pollution measures. And there are numerous obstacles, rigidities and imperfections in the labour market, so that labour put out of a job as a result of tougher pollution policies may not be immediately employed elsewhere.

In other words, the above application of the free-trade doctrine to the pollution problem is designed only to demonstrate that welfare would be increased in so far as relative export prices reflected more accurately the full relative social costs of production, including pollution damage costs, (a) if resources displaced from one use were re-employed, and (b) if resources were employed for society as a whole, not necessarily every member of it. But in the first place, failure to re-absorb any displaced labour rapidly could lead to an under-utilization of resources, and hence failure to achieve potential welfare for society as a whole. Secondly, even if full employment is maintained, the overall social gain is still likely to mean that the gain in welfare by some sections of the community (notably those who had been victims of excessive pollution) more than offsets the losses of welfare of others (notably those who are obliged to take less attractive jobs, or whose profits are cut).

The former problem can only be tackled by measures to remove rigidities in the economy and to improve the working of the labour market. These measures are, of course, desirable anyway. The latter problem concerns the effect of pollution policy on income distribution, which we have already touched upon, and illustrates the sort of conflict of policy-objectives which is at the heart of the economic policy, and which has been discussed in a more general context in Chapters 1 and 6.

Here we are concerned with the specific foreign-trade effects of environmental policies. In particular, one of the arguments commonly used as an objection to the introduction of pollution-abatement policies is that if other countries do not follow suit international trade will be 'distorted'. An extreme, and possibly important, form of this doctrine has been put forward by the Commission of the European Economic Community at Brussels as follows: 'Marked disparities between the measures taken by the authorities in Member States ... reflecting a very different evaluation either of the nature and harmfulness of pollution, or of the desirable quality objectives for the environment ... are bound to cause distortion of competition and diversion of investment incompatible with the proper working of the common market';[28] or: 'Measures taken by a single country are liable to penalize certain sectors of the economy and industry of that country vis-à-vis competitors less attentive to the adverse effects of pollution. It is advisable to preclude such distortions by international agreement.'[29]

As regards the effect on the competitive position of a country embarking on more stringent anti-pollution policies, we have already discussed this particular fallacy in detail. As regards the other point, namely that trade would be distorted if each country pursued a policy that seemed to be appropriate given its own evaluation of the damage done by its pollution and of the importance of the environment in its ranking of objectives, nothing could be further from the truth. If industries are made to pay for their pollution then one of the many sources of divergence between their costs of production and the full social costs of their output will be removed, as will one of the many divergencies between export prices and the true pattern of their relative costs of production. In this way international trade will, in turn, tend to reflect somewhat more accurately the varying cost and demand conditions in the different countries, as it tends to do with other goods.

If the damage done by, say, air pollution in some country, say the U.K., is less than in another country on account of, perhaps, different climatic conditions, the U.K. will have a comparative advantage in the production of goods that are intensive in that particular form of pollution. But to attempt to cancel out this comparative advantage would be like attempting to cancel out the comparative advantage that, say, the French or Italian wine producers have on account of a favourable soil and climate for grape cultivation, or the favourable conditions for winter sports in Switzerland by comparison with Scotland. Each country should use the environment (i.e. pollute it) according to its costs and benefits, and it is only if countries fail to do so that trade is distorted. At present countries fail to do so to varying degrees simply because they have only recently begun to introduce pollution-abatement policies, so that an additional distortion is included in export price-patterns (i.e. additional to other distortions, such as those arising out of monopoly conditions). But another form of distortion could arise if countries were obliged to accept common pollution standards, since these too would prevent their export prices from accurately reflecting the varying relative costs of pollution control in each country.

The costs that matter are not merely those determined by technical considerations, such as the influence of geographical and climatic factors on the damage done in any country by air pollution or water pollution. The costs that matter, as the preceding chapter has shown, are those *at the optimum level of pollution*, where, at the margin, the costs of abatement equal the benefits. And this depends also on the relative importance that countries attach to pollution abatement. In a country where other things are much more important, it would be wrong to push abatement far even if it were relatively cheap to do so.

Costs of pollution abatement will also vary on account of different techniques of production in the various countries. For pollution depends, in any given industry, on the particular product-mix, the type of raw material used (for example natural gas as against high-sulphur-content oil), the type of capital equipment installed, the location of the production in relation to the centres of urban concentrations, and so on. Suppose, to take an extreme example, steel can be produced in one country, in isolation from any possible victims of pollution, whereas in another country the only possible location – taking into account access to raw materials and so on – is in the centre of urban areas. Clearly, taking the two countries together, it is preferable for steel output to be concentrated in the former, where it will do far less damage. This corresponds to the usual international division of labour according to which it is preferable for output to be concentrated in areas where the comparative costs are least.

In this particular case, the former country has a relatively abundant supply of the factor of production 'environment', and the best international allocation of output requires that the environment be most used where it is most abundant and hence, other things being equal, cheapest. But if uniform technical standards were laid down, the steel plant in the former country would be obliged to reduce its air pollution as much as in the latter country, so that its costs of production would be raised to the level of the latter. This would constitute an artificial increase in steel-production costs in the former country, since the costs it would have to incur to reduce pollution would exceed the damage done by it. And in the latter country, if it were to be excused from covering its full social costs of production so as to avoid some of the price rise that would otherwise take place, its costs would still not fully reflect the social costs of its air pollution. Instead of demand and output being diverted to the former country to take advantage of its lower social costs of production they would tend to be more equally divided, thereby reflecting the artificial distortion of costs in both countries.

In short, the whole notion of imposing common standards to avoid a distortion of trade on account of the international differences in environmental conditions and priorities is quite nonsensical, and has no basis at all in economic theory or in accepted international practice as regards other forms of trade. If every country had to iron out differences in cost conditions arising out of differences in climatic factors, topological factors, techniques of production, relative abundance of all factors of production, taxation policies, relative unemployment rates, and so on, in order that no country had a comparative advantage in any product or service at all, either it would be impossible ever to reach agreement on any trade conditions, or there would be no trade.[30]

There is, however, one major exception to the doctrine that countries should implement the pollution policies that are justified in terms of their own national conditions. This concerns 'trans-national' pollution, by which is meant pollution that crosses national boundaries. For this is a form of international externality. There are many examples of trans-national pollution. One example is the use of common water-resources by both Canada and the U.S.A., which has been the subject of discussions and negotiation over very many years and which is regulated to some extent in various treaties between these two countries (notably the Boundary Waters Treaty). Another old-standing form of water pollution affecting principally two or three neighbouring countries is the pollution of the river Rhine, which is largely blamed by the Germans and Dutch on French potash mines in Alsace. In this case, there has been much acrimonious dispute among the countries concerned and not much progress towards an agreed solution can be reported so far. Of course, water pollution may not be limited to its effects on nearby neighbours. Certain forms of pollution of the rivers and the seas (and, after all, almost all rivers flow into the seas) can be transmitted throughout the world's oceans, as in the case of certain persistent chemical compounds – notably PCBs, DDT – or heavy metals; and oil spillages at sea can harm fish life or amenity at points far removed from the original discharge.

Air pollution, too, can cross national boundaries. This problem is probably not serious for countries such as Britain or the U.S.A., which are both relatively far removed from other countries' pollution and which are not likely to be responsible in a big way for polluting other countries' air either (although the U.K. has been held responsible for some of the air pollution in Scandinavia),* but it is likely to be very important for the countries clustered around the industrialized region of north-west Europe. An analytically related problem is the problem of over-fishing of the world's fishery resources. This may not look as if it has any connection at all with pollution, but the connection is a very close one from the point of view of economic theory, since it is just another special case of an 'externality', namely one where the benefits to any one country of abstaining from further fishing would be shared out (diluted) among all other countries. Hence no individual country would have the correct incentive to reduce his fishing in order to conserve fish stocks; for other countries could then simply take advantage of the given country's generosity.

In such cases, as with trans-national pollution, the best result from the point of view of everybody concerned will only be achieved if they co-operate. In the past this has, in fact, been done for some of the main forms of ocean pollution, and international treaties have been negotiated which have helped to reduce various forms of dumping at sea, such as the International Convention for the Prevention of Pollution of the Sea by Oil, or the international convention to prevent the dumping of numerous toxic wastes at sea negotiated in London in November 1972. Furthermore, a Law of the Sea Conference, under the auspices of the United Nations, is to be held in 1973. On a smaller scale, concerted action has been taken by

* The particular allegation is that the SO_2 from Britain contributed to the acidity of the atmosphere in Sweden, but British scientists are doubtful about this on account of the fact that SO_2 has a comparatively short life in the atmosphere – two to four days – so that not more than one-third of British SO_2 is believed to be exported, and then most of it will be absorbed by chemical interaction in the humid air over the North Sea.

the countries having an interest in the pollution of the North Sea. All such co-operation should certainly be encouraged. The difficulties of reaching agreement are enormous (the 1972 London conference mentioned above ran over its time-limit by three days) and the implementation of agreements is by no means an easy matter, as is known to be the case, for example, with the implementation of international agreements to restrict the discharge of oil at sea. * But there is a clear need to pursue this line of action as far as trans-national pollution is concerned, unlike the negotiation of common standards for dealing with purely national pollution.[31]

The arguments that will no doubt continue to be heard in favour of the international adoption of common pollution standards are largely just a new form of old-fashioned protectionism. Protectionist interests have invariably disguised their true motives behind the façade of concern for the sweated labour of other countries, or the health hazards of importing foreign livestock, or distortion of foreign trade in one way or another. Policies to reduce pollution in individual countries will only be delayed if they are to be made dependent on agreement over common international standards which are entirely without any foundation in economic theory anyway. The danger now is that some countries will seek to protect their industries by keeping out imports of certain goods which, they will allege, fail to live up to their own high anti-pollution standards.

In certain cases this may be justified. For example, there is no reason why European motor-cars *sold in the U.S.A.* should not meet the same exhaust requirements as are imposed on

---

* What is needed, of course, is not merely that countries should sign conventions, but that they should be ratified and implemented by enough of them and without undue delay. There is little doubt, for example, that progress now depends on enough of the contracting parties to the 1954 International Convention for the prevention of Pollution of the Sea by Oil adopting the 1969 amendments, which tightened up the regulations. In the light of these amendments British tankers will now be forbidden to discharge oil within fifty miles of the nearest land, and are subject to various other new restrictions under new rules that come into force on January 5th, 1973, under 'The Oil in Navigable Waters (Exceptions) Regulations, 1972', but unless other countries follow suit the impact will be quite inadequate.

American cars in the same country, for the damage done by the motor-car pollution is done to American citizens. But there is absolutely no reason why European cars sold in Europe (or American cars sold in Europe) should follow suit. The same applies to European steel sold in the U.S.A., since here the pollution caused arises in the course of the steel production, which takes place in Europe, not in the U.S.A. Thus, broadly speaking, if the pollution arises in the course of production only (and does not transcend the frontiers), the importing and consuming country has no valid basis for insisting on any particular level of pollution abatement; but if the pollution arises in the course of the consumption of the goods concerned, then each importing country has a right to impose standards on the products appropriate to its own conditions and priorities. Failure to distinguish between these different cases will tend to lead to the emergence of new forms of non-tariff protection, and hence needs to be vigilantly resisted.[31]

Conclusion

No attempt has been made here to prove that pollution abatement will be costless. All that has been attempted is to show that the costs are likely to be, at worst, a very small proportion of national product and, at best, to be more than offset by economic benefits from pollution abatement, so that national product will probably be raised. Although the data are still in a relatively primitive and crude state, since interest in this subject is of a fairly recent character, the orders of magnitudes of such estimates as are available tend to show that the costs of likely pollution-abatement programmes are somewhere in the region of about 1 per cent of the national products of the U.K. and the U.S.A. And the direct economic benefits that can be expected to flow from the abatement programmes in question – which are relatively ambitious programmes – are at least as great as the costs, with the possible exception of the U.S.A. programme to reduce motor-car pollution drastically.

Furthermore, it has been shown that even should national product decline somewhat, as a result of the diversion of resources to pollution abatement, this does not necessarily entail any rise in unemployment. Nor does it provide any valid grounds for protectionism against countries with less stringent pollutant policies, or for the introduction of common internationally agreed pollution standards.

8 Resources for Growth

The problem

One of the anti-growth arguments that can easily impress people is the 'finite Earth' argument. This is that since the resources of the globe are not infinite, they must all be used up one day, and that the rate at which the consumption of many resources is increasing – compared with the size of existing known reserves – suggests that that day may not be very far off. Dr Mishan, for example, wrote: 'And though in the constructs of economists there are always substitute resources waiting to be used whenever the price of an existing resource begins to rise, there is no knowing yet what, if anything, will substitute for a range of such apparently essential metals – lead, mercury, zinc, silver, gold, platinum, copper, tungsten – that will become increasingly scarce before the end of the century.'[1] People who concede that the pollution scare is unfounded since they recognize that the technology to deal with pollution is now available or is being developed and that the pollution problem now is simply a matter of implementing by no means revolutionary policies, still fail to see any way out of this finite-resources constraint on growth. Many people worry about the longer-term supplies of raw-materials resources in general and some people worry about the particular problem of the availability of adequate food supplies to feed the world's rising population. Other people just feel, in a vague sort of way, that growth cannot continue much longer at the sort of rates that have been experienced during the post-war period. As John Stuart Mill said, in 1848, 'It must always have been seen, more or less distinctly, by political economists, that the increase of wealth is not boundless; that at the end of what they term the progressive state lies the stationary state, that all progress in wealth is but a postponement of this, and that each step in advance is an approach to it.' But, as Mill went on to point out, 'We have now been led to recognize that this ultimate goal is at all times near enough to be fully in view; that we are always on the verge of it, and that if we have not reached it long ago, it is because the goal itself flies before us.'[2]

There are several reasons why the fear that growth will be brought to a fairly sudden halt on account of raw-material shortages is unfounded. One is that it is usually based on a misinterpretation of the published estimates of available reserves; another is that it fails to recognize the many favourable feed-back mechanisms in society for adjusting to changes in the demand and supply for materials; another is that it simply takes no account of the way these adjustment mechanisms have operated in the past; another is that it takes no account of current techniques already known to scientists that will overcome some of the more immediate needs for certain materials; and so on. In the next section we shall survey some of the facts about the way supplies of resources have matched demand in the past, the known prospects for further increases in supplies, and for technological progress affecting the demand and supply of raw materials. This purely factual survey should suffice to dispel fears on this subject. Nevertheless, it is followed by some discussion of the general *prima facie* reasons why there is no need for anxiety about reserves in general and why, in particular, there is no case for slowing down growth on account of raw-material exhaustion, even if it were true that, some day, raw materials will be exhausted.

Past responses of reserves to rising demand

Prophecies of impending difficulty, or doom, on account of the exhaustion of raw materials are not entirely new. Just over a hundred years ago, a distinguished occupant of my chair in Political Economy at University College London, the great economist Stanley Jevons, predicted an inevitable shortage of coal within a short space of time.[3] But, although coal demand has since increased far more than Jevons anticipated, known coal reserves are now estimated at about 600 years' supply. In 1908 President Theodore Roosevelt was alarmed at the impending exhaustion of mineral reserves in the U.S.A., and called for a survey of resources which soon turned up many more reserves. Similar surveys in response to similar alarms have often been conducted since.[4] One of these, which was carried out in 1944, gave estimates of available reserves which, had they been correct, would have meant that by 1973 half of the products on the list would have already been exhausted. In particular, the U.S.A. would have already run out of tin, nickel, zinc, lead and manganese. In the event, more deposits have been found in the U.S.A. during the 1950s than during the previous twenty-five years.[5]

A recent World Bank report quotes a 1929 study that concluded 'assuming a continuity of present techniques and a London price of 3 cents per pound it is clear that the world's resources [of lead] cannot meet present demands', and adds that now, forty-three years later, nobody is worried about lead shortage. In fact, people are more worried that too much of it is around. The same 1929 report concluded that 'the known resources of tin ... do not seem to satisfy the ever increasing demand of the industrial nations for more than 10 years.'[6] But, over forty years later, the authors of *The Limits to Growth* are worried because existing 'known' reserves of tin are only enough to last for another fifteen years. Still, that is better than in 1929 when they were only supposed to be enough to last us for ten years. At this rate we shall have to wait millions of years before we have identified enough tin reserves to last us for ever. Meanwhile we shall just have to go on using up that ten years' supply which was all we had back in 1929.

Soon after the war the famous 'Paley report' was prepared in response to a fear in the U.S.A. concerning increasing scarcity of domestic mineral supplies. This report confirmed that domestic supplies would be inadequate, so that rising demand for increasingly scarce imported supplies would raise their prices in relation to the prices of manufactured goods and move the 'terms of trade' against the industrial nations of the world. In the end, of course, nothing of the sort has happened; indeed, one of the main, and justified, complaints of the underdeveloped countries has been that much of the aid they have received has been offset by a deterioration in their terms of trade.

One of the main reasons why these earlier predictions of shortages have proved to be unfounded is that estimates of reserves at any moment of time never represent true reserves in the sense of being all that can ever be found, irrespective of the demand and the price. As the report by the World Bank team has pointed out, the usual estimates of known reserves of raw materials (namely those published by the U.S. Bureau of Mines) are 'conservative contingency forecasts by the exploration companies and they are related to a certain price: if the price is higher, more resources can be exploited commercially'.[7] In other words, the known reserves represent the reserves that have been worth finding, given the price and the prospects of demand and the costs of exploration. Again, as I have pointed out already elsewhere,

> ... the existence of only fifty years' supply of material X at current rates of utilization or seventy years' supply of some other material is no cause for concern for the simple reason that there is rarely any point in companies' employing geologists to prospect for supplies to last Mankind to the end of eternity. For example, is it seriously imagined that, if there were already 20,000 years of known reserves of copper, any geologists would be employed in looking for new copper supplies?[8]

At any time in the past the level of known proved reserves has been in terms of some time-period which could be measured in decades (with some exceptions, such as iron ore or coal), yet as the decades passed by and existing reserves were gradually drawn on it became profitable to seek for new ones and to develop techniques to exploit them.

At no point of time is it worth prospecting for enough to last to the end of eternity, or even some compromise period, such as a 100 million years, or even 1,000 years. New reserves are found, on the whole, as they are needed, and for reasons set out below, needs do not always rise exponentially at past rates. In fact, given the natural concentrations of the key metals in the earth's crust, as indicated by a large number of random samples, the total natural occurrence of most metals in the top mile of the earth's crust has been estimated to be about a million times as great as present known reserves.[9] Since the latter amount to about a hundred years' supplies this means we have enough to last about one hundred million years. Even though it may be impossible at present to mine to a depth of one mile at every point in the earth's crust, by the time we reach the year A.D. 100,000,000 I am sure we will think up something.

This same point has been confirmed in the World Bank report, which stated: 'The reason why we do not know the absolute limits of the resources we have is simple and does not even require recourse to elaborate arguments about the wonders of technology. We do not know because no one has as yet found it *necessary* to know and therefore went about taking an accurate inventory.'[10]

And, as a matter of straight fact, it has usually been the case in the past that, however fast demand expanded and for however long, new mineral reserves were found (or some other painless corrective mechanism came into operation). For example, iron-ore reserves have risen fivefold in the last twelve years. Bauxite reserves have risen sevenfold in the last twenty-two years. And it is no answer to say that those of us who refuse to be alarmed have 'overlooked' the fact that growth is 'faster' than in the past, or that world demand is on a 'much higher level' altogether, or to bandy about some other such vague adjective. Even when true, which is not always the case, such propositions are irrelevant since they tell us only about the relation between the growth rate of some entity now and its growth rate in the past. They still tell us nothing about what we want to know, namely the relationship between the growth of demand for the product in question in the future and the growth of supply of it, also in the future. The same sort of irrelevant proposition has been true in the past anyway, without being followed by exhaustion of supplies.

For example, copper consumption rose about fortyfold during the nineteenth century, and demand for copper was accelerating, around the turn of the century, from an annual average growth rate of about 3·3 per cent per annum, taking the average of the nineteenth century as a whole, to about 6·4 per cent per annum during the period 1890 to 1910. Annual consumption had been about 16,000 tons in the first decade of the nineteenth century, and was over 700,000 tons in the first decade of the twentieth century. Given the rapid growth of consumption the 'known' reserves of copper at almost any time in the nineteenth century would have been exhausted many times over by subsequent consumption if there had been no new discoveries. But at the end of the nineteenth century known reserves were bigger than at the beginning.[11]

And even in the post-war world, with what are believed to be unprecedented rates of economic growth, the story is the same. From the supply point of view, faster rates of economic growth have taken place precisely because of faster rates of growth of technical progress of all kinds, and faster development of the basic resources required. Resources have still increased to match demand. For example, in 1945, estimated known copper reserves were 100 million metric tons. During the following twenty-five years 93 million metric tons were mined;[12] so if one were to accept the eco-doomsters' sort of analysis, there should be almost no copper left by now. But no, present known reserves are over 300 million tons, i.e. three times what they were twenty-five years ago. In fact, copper consumption has trebled during the last twenty years, and we still have more copper left in the 'known' reserves than we had at the outset. The same applies to zinc, known reserves of which were 63 million tons in 1949 and production of which in the following years up to 1970 amounted to 75 million tons.

The way in which figures of known reserves have fluctuated, but have been maintained in the long run, in spite of rapid increases in demand, is illustrated below for iron ore and coal, two of the most basic ingredients of economic growth in the past:

TABLE 8.1

Reserves of Iron Ore and Coal[a]
('000 million metric tons)

Iron Ore			Coal [b]		
Year	Actual	Potential	Year	Actual	Potential
1910	33·1	212·5	1913	1,088	7,141
1925	55·0	n.a			
1937	60·0	n.a	1936	1,102	8,298
1944	35·2	164·8			
1947	58·8				
1971	n.a	'Probably more than 200 billion tons'	1967	8,610	15,180

[a] Sources: E. W. Zimmerman, op. cit.; W. H. Voskuil, op. cit. (see note 11, p. 220); J. H. Ronaldson, *Coal*, Imperial Institute Monograph (London, 1923); J. Darmstadter, et al., *Energy in the World Economy* (Washington, 1971); Chambers' *Encyclopedia*; and UNO *Statistical Yearbooks*.

[b] Including brown coal and lignite.

During the period 1913 to 1967, in which actual known coal reserves have risen eightfold, annual coal production has doubled. And over the period since 1937, when known iron-ore reserves have stayed about the same, iron-ore production has trebled.* In neither case has the rise in demand made even a significant dent in the incomparably greater reserves, and that is without trying particularly hard to find new reserves, since there is already much more than enough for immediate and foreseeable needs.

* The rate at which the growth of demand for iron ore has slowed down during the course of the century is a striking example, in fact, of the dangers of simple extrapolation of past trends, as even Barbara Ward, who generally expresses concern at the prospects of continued growth, has pointed out. She notes that between 1900 and 1910 the annual increase in the production of iron ore in the U.S.A. was 7·8 per cent, which would have meant doubling output every 8·9 years. This, in turn, would have implied that output now would be 256 times as great as in 1900. In fact it is only three times as great. ('The end of an epoch', by Barbara Ward [Lady Jackson], *The Economist*, May 27th, 1972).

Future prospects for raw materials

A prediction that took account of the preceding data on the way that resources have always matched demand in the past, however fast the rise in demand, would have to indicate a similar capacity to meet demand in the future. Hence there is little need to dwell on particular raw-material prospects. Indeed, the essence of the above argument is that the world is rarely likely to know, at any moment of time, how much 'total' reserves it has, since it never needs to know this. It needs only to find enough reserves to supply foreseeable demands at reasonable costs. In the past this has always sufficed, even though there have been spectacular discoveries or increases in known usable reserves sometimes, often through advances in techniques of extraction or utilization. Nevertheless, the prospects for certain materials are worth mentioning, if only as illustrations of the fantastic size of supplies of certain key materials.

One of the most exciting new sources of minerals appears to be the recently discovered manganese nodules that apparently litter the sea-bed. According to the World Bank, 'literally vast quantities of minerals can be obtained from the as yet unexploited sea-bed, through the mining of so-called manganese nodules'. It appears that within the next decade or two it will be possible to collect these nodules very cheaply, and that they could produce, if required, nearly six times current 'free-world' consumption of manganese, over three times the nickel consumption, twelve times the cobalt consumption, and so on. According to the World Bank report, reserves of 'in the order of "hundreds of billions of tons" and a mining rate of 400 million tons per year is possible for a literally unlimited period of time' at 'production costs estimated at a fraction of current costs'.[13] Apparently, at one of the international conferences held to discuss nodule mining the focus of the conference was on 'how to prevent potential drastic declines in mineral prices resulting from nodule mining'.[14]

Furthermore, as pointed out in the Sussex University's Science Policy Research Unit study, 'A large portion of the earth's land mass has hardly been looked at in any detail ... and the technology of underground mining has been changing fairly rapidly over the last decade, especially in contrast to the relative stagnation of the last few centuries ... new concepts are being explored such as softening rock through chemical or vibrational techniques, or the use of induction heating or hydraulic jets',[15] and so on. In addition, these changes in mining techniques have been accompanied by changes in treatment and extraction techniques, such as those already mentioned above. For example, as a result of certain technological improvements the low-grade porphyry copper ores that have been explored only in the past twenty years will now provide enough copper to last for six or seven hundred years at present rates of use.[16]

But there are two resources which, perhaps, give rise to slightly more serious concern. The first of these is food; it is the most important of all. This is discussed in a later section in conjunction with population, as these two problems go together. The second is energy. Here, it is probably true – notwithstanding the way such predictions have proved to be wildly wrong in the past, and the way oil seems to be found wherever one looks nowadays, provided one looks deeply enough – that supplies of oil will fail to keep pace with rising demand for oil *at the present price*.

It is true that known reserves of oil are always expanding rapidly. As demand rose, oil has been sought in more remote areas, first offshore, then in the North Sea, the Arctic, and so on. In fact, the oil under the sea-beds has hardly been touched yet. Also, there seem to be enormous possibilities in the extraction of oil from tar sands (and shale), and one single deposit alone (in Alberta) has been estimated to contain more oil than the whole of the oil-reserves figure in *The Limits to Growth*.[17] Nevertheless, although there is considerable doubt as to how much oil reserves might still be found (since oil companies naturally tend to be secretive about their own reserves, and because vast areas of Soviet Russia and China are possible major sources of new oil discoveries) there appears to be a fair measure of agreement among the experts that, at present prices and hence at present rates of increase in demand, supplies would not increase correspondingly. This seems to be the view recently expressed, for example, by Dr Warman, the Chief Geologist of the British Petroleum Company, and is shared by other authorities.[18]

But what are the implications of this? They are the same as for any product, material or otherwise, the supply of which *at the initial price* cannot keep pace with the rise in demand: the price rises.[19] This tends to slow down the rate of increase in demand, as well as provide a further stimulus to increases in supply or the development of substitutes. For example, this has been the path followed for decades now by the demand, supply and price of numerous personal services. The supply of domestic services failed to match the rising demand (in fact, it fell), and this divergence, at the initial price, spread to numerous other services. As pointed out quite correctly in a scientific journal, although oil may be the most vulnerable of the resources used at present, it does not 'follow from this simple-minded calculation that there will come a time when, to everybody's surprise, petroleum deposits are worked out and industry is forced to grind to a halt. Is it not much more likely, about a century from now, that prices for petroleum will be found to be so high that even the least successful nuclear-power companies will find themselves able to sell reactors more easily?'[20] The same journal had earlier written:

> In the long run, the United States will most probably have to pay more, possibly much more, for petroleum than it does at present and the consequences will be considerable although not catastrophic. After all, there are few who would seriously consider that the United States would grind to a halt if the price of crude petroleum were doubled from its present cost of just over $2·50 a barrel ... Even the prospect that imported oil might cost two or three per cent of the GNP in foreign exchange – a gloomy estimate – is not insupportable.[21]

As the relative price of oil rises, the growth in world demand for oil will, of course, be slowed down. Dr Warman suggests that it might slow down to an annual increase of about 4 per cent as compared with almost twice that rate during recent years.

This will obviously not create terrible difficulties for economic growth. Of course, even leaving aside the possibility of some technical breakthroughs in mining deep beneath the sea, or gigantic new oil discoveries in the yet unexplored parts of the earth (particularly in the Communist countries), perhaps less oil would be used for many purposes, such as heating and the production of electric power, for which there are easy substitutes that can be produced by numerous other means. For there is also general agreement among the scientists that, taking energy as a whole, the longer-term prospects are, if anything, more favourable than they have ever been in the whole previous history of mankind.

To begin with relatively conventional alternative sources of energy, figures have already been given above of the world's enormous coal stocks. Even assuming that demand for energy doubles in the U.S.A. by 1985 and that electricity demand quadruples by 1990 it has been estimated that there is still at least 600 years' supply of 'fairly easily accessible coal in the U.S. ... Three times that amount – not at present economically recoverable – also lies underground.' In fact, coal constitutes almost 90 per cent of the U.S.A.'s proved energy resources, although, at present, it supplies only about 20 per cent of its energy requirements.[22] Other estimates of conventional substitutes for oil as a major source of energy are slightly less optimistic. They suggest that allowing for annual production rates to rise to nearly eight times current rates, we have only about three hundred years left in which to find some other source of energy.[23]

Fortunately, the scientists also agree that we won't need the whole of the 300 years, and that in fact thirty should suffice since, by that time, less conventional sources of energy will have become economically viable. The Nobel prize-winner Dennis Gabor has stated: 'Since about 1966, we know that fission power is virtually inexhaustible.' The World Bank report states:

8

Much has been heard recently of an energy crisis in the developed countries, particularly the United States. This is not of course, an ultimate crisis for the availability of sufficient energy sources to meet demand, but is more a crisis of *policy* on what sources of energy those countries should be reliant on, at which prices, and from where these sources should be obtained. There is still a vast potential of energy which could be tapped with changed economic circumstances or technological advance. They include discovery of new reserves, improved recovery of proven energy reserves, exploitation of the Athabasca tar sands and Arctic oil and gas in Canada, the Orinoco tar belt in Venezuela, nuclear energy, solar energy and perhaps the use of hydrogen as fuel extracted from water by nuclear energy.[24]

The tremendous prospects for energy production, particularly given the probability of major breakthrough in the next fifty years in nuclear fusion (which will not even create problems of storing radioactive waste, as with fission) and other techniques means, of course, that the unlimited resources of energy will enable the other problems, such as those of pollution and the supply of other raw materials, to be overcome relatively easily. As Fred Singer (Professor of Environmental Science at the University of Virginia) has rightly pointed out, energy can be substituted for materials or for pollution in the sense that the energy can be used to convert materials more easily and to clean up pollution.[25] Some scientists are reported as being sufficiently optimistic about energy supplies that they postulate a future in which the planet can comfortably carry 20 billion people at current American living standards simply by using the virtually limitless resources that exist of atomic energy, water, air, and the minerals locked up in common rock.[26]

Others have put the population sustainable for the same reason at a very much higher figure than this.[27]

General flaws in the resources argument

FAVOURABLE FEED-BACKS

There are two types of general flaw in the argument that economic growth should be slowed down or brought to a halt on account of the danger that, otherwise, the limits to raw materials will be reached suddenly and with drastic consequences. The first is that the argument fails to allow for the various feed-back mechanisms at work in society, which, as shown above, have always tended to ensure that supplies and demands are matched one way or another (not necessarily always by finding new supplies – the mechanism may involve reducing the rate of growth of demand).

As I have written elsewhere, in connection with the first point, 'it is true that if tomorrow the world were suddenly to wake up and find that there was no more oil or iron ore, like in some science fiction story in which some bug from Outer Space feeds on minerals or destroys all the vegetation and so on, we would be in a mess. But this sort of thing happens only in science fiction.'[28] The main reason why this will not happen in reality is the favourable economic feed-back mechanisms – i.e., the incentives to new exploration, recycling, and the use of substitutes, that would all be occurring gradually as the increasing scarcity of any product led to an upward trend in its price.

Mention has already been made of the limitations on the most commonly used estimates of 'known' reserves, notably that they represent estimates of what is known to be available, given present prices. The original source of these figures (the U.S. Bureau of Mines) has estimated how far some of these figures would have to be revised upwards if it were assumed that prices rose on account of a rise in demand. For example, known iron-ore reserves would apparently be doubled at a price 30 per cent to 40 per cent higher than the current price. And the reserve estimates for copper which are now about 3·5 times higher than in 1935 would be expected to rise eightfold if the price were to rise threefold.[29]

One of the favourable feed-backs in the economic system

has been technical progress. Sometimes this takes the form of just technical progress in mining or exploration, so that new reserves have been found when needed, or lower-grade ores prove to be economically useful. But it also often takes the form of the development of completely new materials, or new uses for old materials.[30] As Professor Beckmann has pointed out, it is important not to confuse 'non-renewable' resources with 'non-replaceable' ones.[31] In particular, the development of synthetic products and major technological breakthroughs of one kind or another have rendered obsolete some of the classic uses of many basic materials. Synthetic rubber is one of the best examples: it was produced in response to urgent needs, during the Second World War, for a substitute for natural rubber; for almost all purposes it is as good as natural rubber and for some purposes it is better. Synthetic materials such as plastics are even replacing many metals.

Of course, as Professor Beckmann rightly adds, if the attention of the average eco-doomster is drawn to the way that synthetic materials have vastly added to society's range of resources, he will usually complain that such synthetics only add to pollution since they are indestructible. 'If it is non-renewable, don't use it, use something indestructible instead, [but] if it is indestructible, don't use it either. Nothing is feasible except the two possibilities he has set his heart on; a return to the caves or doomsday.'[32]

In other cases, technical progress means that many materials may hardly be wanted at all within the next few decades. For example, the tungsten that appears on Dr Mishan's list, which is used in present-day electric light bulbs, can probably never be synthesized economically in the foreseeable future; but the light bulbs currently in use will probably hardly be made at all by the end of the century, since they are extremely inefficient in electrical-engineering terms compared with fluorescent strip-lighting, which does not need any tungsten.[33] The same applies to certain uses of other metals, such as copper and aluminium in telephone lines. It is highly probable that telephone lines in future will not need the electrical conductivity

of these materials at all, since they will all be made of glass
fibres acting as wave-guides for laser beams.[34]

Another form of technical progress has been in the means of
producing materials from raw materials that are abundant. An
example given by Beckmann is aluminium, which was a
precious metal until well into the nineteenth century, so that
only the rich could afford aluminium cooking utensils. But
the discovery of methods of extracting aluminium from
bauxite, reserves of which are astronomical,[35] has made
aluminium so cheap that it is now used for hundreds of mis-
cellaneous products that are thrown away after little use. The
World Bank report gives the example of similar kinds of
technical progress, namely the way that the 'fixing' of nitrogen
by separating it from liquefied air, and the French process of
recovering sulphur from 'salt domes' (plus advances in
recovering the latter from chimney stacks) have literally
eliminated the problem of resources in these two cases.[36] And
there are innumerable other examples of radical changes in
techniques of extracting or refining materials from ores that
have enabled lower and lower grades of ores to be handled
economically, such as the reduction in the lowest grade of
copper which could be handled economically from about 3 per
cent in 1880 to almost 0·4 per cent now.[37]

The above are just a few examples out of thousands that
could be quoted of the ways that continual progress in various
forms, often in response to increasing demand for certain
materials, has prevented the emergence of shortages, even of
materials the demand for which has risen very substantially
over the past. But this is not a book on technology, and the
above examples combined with the illustrations given already
of the way that reserves have kept pace with rising consumption, must suffice here. What is important here is that they
illustrate the basic methodological fallacy in the eco-doomsters
analysis, namely a failure to realize that ' ... the concept of
resources itself is a dynamic one: many things *become* resources
over time. Each century has seen new resources emerge. The
expansion of the last hundred years could not have been sustained but by the new resources of petroleum, aluminium and

energy. What about the possibilities of tomorrow – solar energy, sea-bed resources, and what else?'[38]

Technological progress of the many kinds that have helped to increase resources *pari passu* with demand has, in other words, proceeded exponentially throughout the past. Since knowledge of the past must provide the basis for predictions of the future, the best prediction of the future would be that this technological progress would continue exponentially in the future as well. As the World Bank report points out, exponentiality is a double-edged sword 'for if technical progress were, for example, to reduce the rate of use of some mineral from 4 per cent per annum to only 1·5 per cent per annum this would have an effect equivalent to that of lengthening the life of the mineral fivefold.'[39]

Resources cannot be usefully measured just in terms of physical amounts of certain minerals that may exist at any moment of time. This is a fundamentally misleading way of looking at them. There are many physical elements in the world which are of absolutely no use at all given present costs of exploration and utilization, present techniques for using them, and the present demand for the products in which they might conceivably be used. But tomorrow all these things may change. What is a 'resource' depends on the economic conditions determining the usefulness of the materials in question. If economically worth while, unused land can be turned into a usable resource by irrigation, drainage of swamps, clearing of forests, and so on.[40] A hitherto useless mineral, such as the bauxite mentioned above, is transformed into a useful resource by the development of techniques for converting it into aluminium. Sea water contains unlimited supplies of uranium for use in nuclear-power production, and already it is thought to be possible to extract the uranium from sea water at a not astronomic cost. It has been estimated that sea water contains about a billion years' supply of sodium chloride and magnesium, 100 million years' supply of sulphur, borax and potassium chloride; more than one million years' supply of molybdenum, uranium, tin, cobalt; and so on.[41] Yet who would have thought of including sea water in the list of resources available to us thirty or more years ago? This sort of process of adding to the resources available to society has been going on throughout history. There could hardly be more conflict between the lip-service paid by many eco-doomsters to the need for imaginative, forward-looking vision and the static, unimaginative nature of their concept of resources, with its failure to take account of the vast increases in resources over the past. To understand the future it is desirable first to take a look at the past.

THE CONSEQUENCES OF SHORTAGES OF MATERIALS

A purely logical error in the anti-growth school of thought is the assumption that if the world did run out of some useful resource this would be a catastrophe. Suppose that none of the economic feed-back mechanism described above came to our rescue in time – i.e., no new discoveries of accessible deposits (even at higher prices); no new techniques for producing the end-products in question with the aid of substitute materials; no technical advances in re-cycling; and so on and so forth – so that we did run out of supplies of some material. Well, what would happen? The answer is that far less of the end-products in which the material was used would be consumed. The price would have become too high. Production of the end-product in question would be limited to what could be produced by means of reclaiming and re-cycling the old products. This would, of course, become a highly profitable business, since the price of the product in question for re-cycling purposes would have risen to relatively high levels and the re-cycling industry would have received a great boost.

True, the absence of new supplies would mean that economic growth could not proceed quite as rapidly as if supplies had been available. But this situation has existed in the past. For example, over the ages, economic growth has often been limited by the exhaustion of timber resources in what, in the distant past, were the more developed parts of the world. Hence, it may well be that, if many important materials were exhausted in future, economic growth would be slowed down. But, in the first place, it should not be thought that the slowing down need be significant. For, as I have written elsewhere already ' ... economic growth has managed to keep going up to now without any supplies at all of Beckermonium, a product named after my grandfather who failed to discover it in the nineteenth century. In fact we manage very well without an infinite number of products that have never been discovered ... In other words, is it really likely that if, say, nickel had never been discovered, modern civilization as we know it would never have emerged?'[42]

And secondly, if economic growth does slow down significantly in the distant future, what of it? Society still has to face a choice problem, namely, to what extent is it desirable to slow down growth deliberately now in order to postpone an eventual slow-down that *might* otherwise be needed on account of the remote possibility that, against all the evidence, we might run out of some materials. In other words, if we let economic growth continue, and if the more pessimistic forecasts turned out to be correct, this merely means that one day economic growth will be more difficult, and hence slower, than would otherwise be the case. Materials will become less easily accessible; more and more resources of labour and capital will have to be devoted to extracting them, and so less can be devoted to further increases in output per head through investment in ordinary equipment or in research and technological progress. As long as one accepts that it will not happen suddenly, and will not happen to *all* materials simultaneously, economic growth will simply gradually slow down. This has happened before in human history, sometimes for centuries. And if exhaustion of all raw materials is inevitable – that is, if we really have to face the implications of so-called 'finite' resources in a time-horizon that is relevant from the point of view of taking present-day decisions, then why should zero growth now be of any help in the long run?

WHY NOT STOP PRODUCTION NOW?

In other words, one cannot have it both ways. Either resources are finite in some meaningful sense, in which case even zero growth will fail to save us in the long run, and as long as we go on using up these finite resources we must run out of them some day. Or, resources are not really finite in any meaningful sense, in which case this argument for slowing down growth collapses. *

This whole issue takes us back to the economic problem of the choice of optimum-growth path, introduced in the first chapter of this book. For if we accept (i) what are now seen to be wholly unrealistic assumptions concerning the relationship between currently 'known' reserves and their rates of utilization, so that we are driven to the conclusion that some, and possibly many, or even most, resources will be used up some day, and (ii) the equally unrealistic assumption that this is not matched by extensive re-cycling techniques, changes in demand patterns and so on, so that it really does bring growth to a halt, and (iii) that this will actually lead to an abrupt cut in output, and hence in living standards, on account of the suddenness of the whole sequence, we still have to decide whether it is better to give up some output now, which is what zero growth means, in order to have more later.

And it is not obvious that this is desirable. First, this is a matter of weighing up the relative values attached to the welfare of future generations against that of the present generations who would be deprived of greater output if we renounce the growth that is currently feasible. What is superior: that ten million families should be better off over the next hundred years or that a hundred families should be better off over the next ten million years? How much of the former is one prepared to sacrifice for a very uncertain chance of the latter? And the choice is not merely between maintaining recent rates of growth now (with the prospect of drastic cuts later) and stopping growth altogether. For why stop at zero growth now? Why not *cut* output? After all, what is so special about the figure 'zero'? Why not slow down growth to 1 per cent per annum, or to minus 2·2 per cent? Those who are worried about

---

* In *The Limits to Growth* this dilemma is avoided by cutting off the computer print-out at the year when it becomes clear that even their proposed stationary state would still be untenable on account of exhaustion of what they assume to be a finite supply of resources.

8*

the exhaustion of resources must face up to this choice, which, as pointed out above, depends partly on the relative weight attached to the welfare of society at different points of time.

Secondly, the choice also depends on the *probability* that failure to slow down growth will lead to an exhaustion of resources in the future. If we could be certain that maintenance of current growth rates would lead to a sudden and general exhaustion of resources, then it might be perfectly reasonable for society to decide that it was prepared to make some sacrifice of increased living standards for generations alive today in order to avoid the certainty that, otherwise, future generations would suffer a sudden and drastic cut in output and hence a socially catastrophic fall in their living standards.

But if the probability of such an eventuality is very low, it would be irrational for society to embark on a *certain* cut in living standards for people alive today in order to minimize an already very small chance that future generations would be deprived of the wherewithal for survival. We have already seen some of the reasons for believing that the risks are negligible. These include, notably, the absence from the doomsday analysis of adequate allowance for the various *prima facie* favourable feed-backs that prevent resource shortages, notably in discovery and exploration for new resources, technological progress in finding substitutes, in developing new products, and in re-cycling, and so on.

Thirdly, both these elements in the choice – i.e. the relative weight attached to the welfare of the world's population at various times, and the probability element – depend on exactly *when* the catastrophe is expected to occur. As Professor Fred Singer has pointed out, there is little point in a proposition to the effect that increasing use of resources must, *some day*, come up against finite supplies 'unless it contains a specification, backed up by data, when to stop growing. How useful is a forecast that it is going to rain *some time*?'[43] In other words, if we believed that there was a serious risk of running up against resource limitations in the lifetime of our children or grandchildren then we might be worried and prepared to do something about it. But if the limit is to be reached in 100 million years, we might not feel personally involved in the problems of the people alive at that time, and we might well assume that some way out of the difficulty would have been found by then. After all, when one ponders on the fantastic technological progress that has been made in the last twenty or fifty years, the mind boggles at the progress that will be made over the next 100 million years. Tautologies about finite resources, therefore, although they are apt to be triumphantly repeated over and over again by eco-doomsters, are really not much help in the decision-making process.*

There is one area, however, where we know already that supplies are not enough to meet 'demand', namely food supplies. For it is a fact that a large proportion of the world's population is inadequately fed, and that, in spite of this, population is rising. Hence, a rise in price doesn't help; it only makes the poor even poorer, and there is no close substitute for food in total. Some eco-doomsters, therefore, frighten people with visions of starving hordes rampaging over the world, or of people standing ten per square yard as a result of exponential growth of population. How serious are these fears? And what are the implications for economic growth as an objective of policy?

Food and population

There is no doubt that rising population in many parts of the world is one of the most urgent and serious problems to be faced by the world as a whole. A large proportion of the world's population cannot be fed properly even now, and in many countries fast rising populations are the greatest obstacle to rapid increases in their standards of living. At the same time the gap between living standards in these and other

* The same point is made by Carl Kaysen in writing that 'The earth is finite, to be sure, and without broaching the larger question of whether the universe is or is not, it can be shown that the finiteness of the earth does not in itself set limits to what technology might accomplish that are relevant to the time horizons of the kind of argument with which we are concerned.' (P. 226, note 27.)

countries, and the population pressures in the former, are a constant source of tension and friction. Hence, from a humanitarian point of view or from the point of view of self-interest and expediency, it would be foolish to pooh-pooh the population and food problem. It is a far more real problem than the pollution problem or the non-renewable minerals problem. But again, hysteria never helps to find reasonable solutions to problems, and it is necessary to put the food/population balance into perspective.

In the first place, the mere fact that these predictions have been made in computerized studies, such as *The Limits to Growth* (see p. 113), does not necessarily guarantee their accuracy. If one makes the assumption that population will continue to rise exponentially but that food supplies will only rise at a constant arithmetical rate (i.e., that there will be a constant addition to supplies every year instead of a constant *percentage* rise in supplies) then clearly it does not need a computer to reach the conclusion that, one day, population will outrun food supplies. After all, Malthus made exactly the same prediction, on the basis of the same assumptions, about 150 years ago, long before computers were invented. Secondly, it is quite unreasonable to extrapolate far into the future the birth-rates of the poorer countries in the past. The phase of rapidly rising population that the underdeveloped countries are now experiencing corresponds to a similar phase that the developed world passed through at various stages over the last fifty years or more. The key feature of this is that, first, advances in incomes lead to a fall in death-rates and an extension in the average length of life. Hence, with birth-rates unchanged, there will obviously be rapid increases in population. But this is then followed by a phase in which the higher incomes are accompanied by higher standards of literacy, education, and different economic and social motivations, which all lead to a fall in birth-rates, so that eventually the rates of increase in population slow down. It should not be forgotten that, for very poor people in many parts of the world, a large number of children is the only available form of old-age insurance, particularly when the infant mortality rate is high.

When the latter is reduced, there is less economic incentive to have such large families. This is only one of the many ways that rising incomes – i.e. *continued economic growth* – will help to reduce the rates of increase of population in these countries.

And this is, of course, what is happening. As the World Bank report points out ' ... the recent demographic trends indicate that fertility has already started declining in a number of countries. Of the 66 countries for which accurate data are available, as many as 56 show a decline. Most demographers are agreed by now that the 1970s will see the population growth rate reach a plateau so that by 1980 population growth rates will tend to decline, slowly at first and rapidly thereafter.'[44] In fact, there are very good *prima facie* reasons for believing that the poorer countries of the world will reach the phase of declining birth-rates much faster than was the case in the Western world.

In the first place, birth-control techniques have been greatly developed over the past few decades, and the need for them generally accepted (except by the Pope, which probably partly explains why Latin America has lagged behind in reducing the birth-rate). Secondly, when the Western world was passing through this phase there was no help from outside; there were no other richer countries to give aid and advice on birth-control devices. And, indeed, this *prima facie* expectation does look like being borne out by the events. For there are already reports that in some developing countries birth-rates are being cut more rapidly than had been the case in the Western world at a comparable stage.[45] Of course, population projections are notoriously prone to error. There have been many cases in the past of grotesque errors in population and birth-rate projections, including many that, thirty or more years ago, predicted alarming prospects of depopulation in many Western countries. Nevertheless, there seems to be little doubt that nothing can be done now to prevent world population from more or less doubling by about the end of the century. In spite of the slow-down in birth-rates in most of the world, in many countries they will still not have fallen to the point where population growth is stabilized. What does this imply for (i) the adequacy of food supplies, and (ii) policy with respect to economic growth?

Perhaps it is better to take these two questions in the reverse order. For since it is generally agreed that the progress now being made to reduce birth-rates cannot prevent the world population from doubling by about the end of the century, there seems to be no alternative but to continue economic growth. For economic growth provides the only hope of being able to provide all these extra people with the basic means of survival. In the long run, of course, it is imperative that current efforts to help the poorer countries to reduce their birth-rates continue to be given high priority. But we did not need a computer to tell us that, and in any case, such predictions do nothing whatsoever to solve the population problem *in the countries where it is acute*. Although the evidence of widespread poverty and starvation is used by some eco-doomsters to persuade us that we should face up to realities and take them seriously, this evidence does not confirm their predictions, it refutes it! It is precisely because there is already, and has been for some time, a problem of over-population in many countries that these countries have already been making intensive efforts for many years (and with considerable success in many of them) to reduce their birth-rates as well as to step up their food outputs. What contribution does a prediction, such as that in *The Limits to Growth*, make to help them solving their problems?[46] It is hardly likely that the Indian authorities will now start trying to get their own population under control solely because the Club of Rome has drawn their attention to the prospect of over-population in the rest of the world by the year 2050.

Finally, it may be asked, 'All right, there is little doubt that population-growth rates are declining in the poorer countries in the same way as they did in the Western world at a corresponding stage in our economic development, and there is little doubt that we have to maintain economic growth for the time being – at least of food – in order to feed the extra three billion or so people who we all agree are certain to be alive by about the turn of the century. But can it be done?'

Now this is a perfectly good question, and if it were true that there was little prospect of increasing food supplies, there would really be a drastic problem on our hands, assuming we accept the objective that the extra three billion people should be fed and not left to 'solve' their problem by starvation or some other Malthusian 'solution'. Clearly the expansion of food supplies to meet the rising population will not be easy. The evidence is simple enough; it suffices to note that food supplies are not adequate *now* to provide a sufficient and properly balanced diet for a large part of the world's population (and have probably never been adequate). If the adjustment mechanism hasn't worked so far, there is no reason to assume that it will work perfectly in the future. But there are reasons to assume that it will work *better* in the future.

First, the present imbalance between food supplies and population growth is partly because of the unprecedented rates of growth of population in the poorer countries, for the reason set out above. Hence, given the same rate of increase in food supplies, the projected slowing down of the population increase will make it easier for food supplies to catch up with population. Secondly, as with birth-control, the problem is not a new one, and experience is continually being gained in techniques to raise agricultural productivity. Thus, as Marstrand and Pavitt correctly point out, the food-supply problem is not essentially a technical problem; it is an economic and social problem.[47]

As regards the physical limitations in food supplies, there seems to be general scientific agreement that this does not constitute the real constraint. For example, the Professor of Organic Chemistry in the University of Cambridge has stated that if all the land *now* cultivated (i.e. without making allowance for the vast tracts of land not yet brought under cultivation in Latin America, Australia and other parts of Asia) were to be cultivated as efficiently as it is in the Netherlands, the world could support 60 billion people – i.e. ten times as many as are expected by the end of the century.[48]

The vague counter-argument that more intensive cultivation will ruin the soil is hardly convincing in view of the fact that

the soil has been farmed with increasing intensity in Western
Europe for about 2,000 years, and there is still no sign that it
is exhausted. Most of the world's cultivatable areas are, by
comparison, either hardly touched or not yet touched at all.
Nor does the need for more fertilizers for purposes of modern
agricultural methods pose any problem, as there are ample
supplies of phosphate and potash. The more intensive farm-
ing methods do, it is true, tend to aggravate certain crop and
animal diseases, but again this has still not posed any insuperable difficulties in Europe.[49]

In some parts of the world, remarkably rapid increases in
agricultural yields have already been obtained as a result of the
'Green Revolution'. The expert plant pathologist and Nobel
prize-winner Norman Borlaug draws attention to the way that
the wheat yield has doubled in India and in Pakistan in the
six years from 1965. Similar remarkable progress has been
achieved in rice yields.[50] Of course, if extrapolated into the
future, exponential growth rates like this would still spell
disaster; within a century the world would be covered in rice
to a depth of three feet!

In fact, increases like this will not be maintained for long
enough, or even in enough countries, to solve the food
problem by the end of the century in the absence of investment, and adequate economic and social planning. But these
constraints on economic development are not new. They are
constraints on the attack against poverty in all its forms in
most developing countries. They will never be overcome as
quickly as one would like – human problems never are. But
they can be reduced with the aid of higher output and higher
standards of living that, in turn, enable more resources to be
devoted to education and the acquisition of technical skills and
organizational abilities. It is difficult to see how zero economic
growth can help in solving such problems.

9 Conclusions

Review of the doomsday argument

My main argument has tried to show that there is no substance
at all in the main fears of the eco-doomsters. These include,
in particular, the fear that rising pollution and declining
supplies of raw materials will bring economic growth to an
end in a sudden, and hence catastrophic manner, within a
relevant time-period, unless unspecified measures are taken to
bring economic growth to a halt now. It has been shown that
the assumptions underlying these fearful predictions bear no
relation to actual trends in pollution control or policies, to
the continual development of new materials and technologies,
to the increases in food supplies and to the reductions in birth-
rates, and so on, that have taken place in the past, that are still
taking place, and that can be clearly anticipated for the foreseeable future. It has also been shown that the link between
economic growth on the one hand and 'welfare' or 'happiness'
on the other hand is far stronger than simple arguments in
terms of increasing 'needs', or artificially stimulated needs,
would suggest.

At the outset, it was also argued that this rejection of the
anti-growth school of thought by no means represented any
particular 'economist's' tastes or preferences. The economist's
contribution was merely to show how society should make
choices that were in the best interests of society. These choices
depended on, first, society's preferences as between the alternative uses it could make of resources both at any point of
time and over time, and secondly, the technical possibilities
open to society to switch resources from one use to another
or from one point of time to another. The former is a matter
of taste and the latter is a matter of fact. And most of the
factual evidence presented has, of course, been obtained from
the work of scientists and other authorities in the individual
topics covered. There is no clash here between economists

and scientists; but there is a conflict between good science and bad science. As Professor Mellanby has written: ' ... many of those who spoke in the name of "ecology" were telling so many half truths, that they were destroying the credibility of the scientist, and that by denigrating technology and the technologist they were accelerating rather than preventing the onset of the disasters about which they wrote.'[1]

It has been further argued that one of the most recent and widely known of the doomsday predictions, namely those associated with Professors Meadows and Forrester, and the 'Club of Rome',[2] have been guilty of various kinds of flagrant errors of fact, logic and scientific method. The detailed facts have been surveyed in earlier chapters, as well as some of the detailed defects in the methods used. Here, it will suffice to summarize some of the general features of these defects. First, as pointed out already, the reason why these doomsday models arrive at the conclusion that there is no escape from catastrophe sooner or later is that they allow any assumed 'bad' trends, such as pollution or the use of raw materials, to continue to rise exponentially, while the 'good' variables, such as techniques for reducing pollution, or for adding to raw-materials supplies, or reducing demand, and so on, are only allowed to increase by finite amounts. This, as anybody could see without a computer, must mean that, some day, the 'bads' will outrun the 'goods'. Many eco-doomsters talk of 'exponential' growth as if it were some great new discovery that had, once and for all, demonstrated the impossibility of continued economic growth.

But, of course, if every past trend were projected to continue exponentially into the future, one could arrive at any sort of absurd conclusion one liked. Rudolf Klein has pointed out: 'It would not be too difficult to show that at the present rate of growth, by the year 2000 every new graduate student will be either an ecologist or a futurologist', or that:

In fact, it is tempting to go much further still in drawing up an alternative exponential vision. In place of an apocalyptic view of a globe ravished by famine and environmental decay, it would not be too difficult to sketch out a vision of a world where the main problem was to persuadé people to work in factories – where the revolt against materialism had gone so far as to produce a pot-smoking population too dozy to engage in either pro-creation or production. Looking at the phenomenal increase in conviction rates for pot-smoking in recent years, any school-child – let alone a computer – could produce the appropriate statistics to support the alter-native vision. It would, of course, be an utterly absurd one.[3]

There are, of course, unlimited examples in the natural physical world, as well as in the social and economic world, of exponential growth rates being brought down to tolerable limits by some corrective process or other. The interesting questions are: what are the corrective processes? how have they worked in the past? and is there evidence to believe that they will fail to work in the future?

If the population of the world appears to be increasing exponentially, or if its consumption of iron ore or its pro-duction of disposable bottles seems to be increasing exponentially, it requires no flair for prophecy but merely a simple understanding of the differential calculus to know that exponential growth will sooner or later be replaced by some other and more moderate law of growth. The interest of prophecy in matters like these lies in the extent to which it may be possible to guess how exponen-tial growth will at some stage be attenuated.[4]

In the above chapters we have surveyed the main ways in which exponential growth of 'bads' has, in fact, been brought to a halt in the past, and the ways in which the process is likely to continue in the future. Essentially, these safety mechanisms represent society's responses, in one way or another, to the growth of some 'bad', whether it be pollution or increasing use of some material.[5] These responses take diverse forms; in some cases they are mainly the introduction of governmental policies, as with the rapid spread of measures to control pollution during the last few years, which are already reducing pollution at far faster rates than allowed for in the most 'optimistic' assumptions of the eco-doomsters. In other cases, these favourable feed-backs take the form of automatic market responses to changes in the demand and supply of raw materials. The failure to take account of the more than adequate information concerning these favourable feed-backs is characteristic of the static and unimaginative approach of the doomsday predictions. One minor, but very typical example of this, as pointed out by Kneese and Ridker, is the argument in *The Limits to Growth* to the effect that it will never be possible to reduce pollution adequately since certain forms of pollution, like asbestos from brake linings, are hard to control. There is no need to add to Kneese and Ridker's comment on this, namely, 'Asbestos brake linings in a hundred years?'[6]

The details of many of the favourable social and economic feed-backs that have been omitted from most doomsday predictions have been given already, and there is no need to repeat them here. They are not new discoveries, and one would be entitled to suspect that they were actually already known to Professor Meadows and his colleagues in view of the trouble they have taken to erect secondary and tertiary lines of defence in case their front line – namely their assumptions concerning pollution, food supplies, raw materials, and so on – is easily breached. These include supplementary defences such as that society must protect itself against the *risk* that their predictions turn out to be more or less correct. The fallacy in this has already been pointed out, namely that it overlooks the matter of the price that has to be paid in order to avoid some risk in the future. No prudent rational person would be prepared to pay *any* price now to insure himself against some future risk, however small. And the evidence assembled above suggests that the risk of future catastrophe on account of the sort of factors that the eco-doomsters are talking about are insignificant by comparison with the enormous economic and social costs – not to mention political costs (since democratic government would have to be sacrificed) – of trying to stop economic growth.

The final line of defence of *The Limits to Growth* has been: 'Perhaps its figures are awry – but they must be proved to be so.'[7] The best comment on this is by John Kay, as follows:

> One day Professors Meadows and Forrester wheel a vehicle into his [i.e. the social scientist's] workshop. How do you like our car, they say: we made it up last night, before we went to bed. He looks at it in horror. Several of the subsystems seem quite incapable of effective operation. No thought at all has been given to the way in which they should fit together. Difficulties which keep him awake at nights have not even occurred to them. Nothing is more certain than that it will leave the road at the first bend, killing all the occupants. Gently he points this out, only to meet with sharp rebuff. It's not completely satisfactory, Forrester and Meadows concede, but it's the best car we have. We shall be grateful for suggestions for improvement, but tomorrow we intend to take the Club of Rome for a ride in it. We attach little weight to your criticism, since you have so far failed to produce a car of your own.[8]

The real issues

The anti-growth movement and its accompanying excessive concern with the environment not merely leads to a regressive change in the distribution of resources in the community, it also distracts attention from the real issues of choice that society has to face.

First, large sections of the community are still not adequately provided with the conventional necessities of modern conditions of living, and economic growth needs to be maintained as a necessary, though by no means sufficient, condition for improving the standards of living of the vast mass of the world's population. As one trade unionist stated clearly, 'It was all very well for learned academic colleagues to suggest the slowing down of the rate of technological advance and the use of raw materials to reduce pollution and conserve resources, but they could not put back the clock to before the industrial revolution.'[9] We have not yet reached a situation in which scarcity has been banished from the face of the earth so that there would no longer be any point in trying to increase output. For the same reason there is still some point in trying to find ways of increasing output at relatively low cost.

If increasing total incomes is a necessary condition also for increasing the equality of income distribution then growth must continue to be pursued by those who rate equality highly in their ranking of objectives. It is true that it seems that there has been little correlation between growth rates and equality of income-distribution in the past. But such evidence is ambiguous. For it is difficult to find anything that has been highly correlated with greater equality of income-distribution, or to find any policies, whether they be in the field of economic measures or educational or social policies, that have had much effect on income-distribution. Hence, small marginal contributions to equality that may be traced to economic growth must not be despised. When so few easy remedies for inequality can be discovered it is important to hang on to what is likely to be, after all, at least a necessary condition for greater equality, and possibly more than that. For both these reasons, therefore, growth is still an important objective of policy, though it should not be overrated (for the reasons given in the first two chapters). Hence, the precise means by which growth can be maintained at reasonable cost is a valid and important area of enquiry, where there are many questions but few answers. It is more important, therefore, to return to the study of these questions than to futile debates about whether – as a matter of principle – we want growth or not.

In the study of the costs of growth it is important not to limit these to the conventional economic costs. The social costs and the economic costs that escape the national accounting measures must be brought into the picture as far as possible – though, as pointed out in Chapter 4, such work as has been done in this area suggests that, on balance, these social costs are not as great as had been thought. Clearly much more work needs to be done on this issue.

At the same time it should not be thought that only growth imposes social and political costs. The social and political costs of trying to stop growth would be incalculable. For there is no prospect, in a democratic society, of any party winning an election on a no-growth ticket, so that 'to talk of aiming at an economic equilibrium without discussing its political and social implications, is to indulge in meaningless rhetoric'.[10] Nor is there any prospect of winning over the public to support an anti-growth policy in due course. The notion that mankind can now be made to abandon his age-old continual rise in aspirations and needs and to accept the self-denying rejection of goods and services that has been preached for thousands of years by the inspired leaders of great religions, without any effect on the vast mass of the population, is unrealistic. Those of us who are confident that society will continue to find the means and the technology to overcome the problems of pollution, to increase food supplies, to reduce birth-rates, and to find raw materials or synthetic materials, and so on, are invariably accused of being 'Micawbers', and myopic or complacent optimists, but, as the preceding chapters have shown, our predictions are firmly based on a study of the way these problems have been overcome in the past. And it is only the past that gives us any insight into the laws of motion of human society and hence enables us to predict the future. By the same token, any extrapolation into the future of the degree of success achieved by efforts to make mankind renounce worldly goods can only take the form of assuming that the degree of success will be as small in the future as has been the case in the past. It is particularly absurd to assume that societies will be too timid to enforce pollution-abatement technologies on industry but will be bold enough to carry out the vast political and social transformations that zero growth would require. For, as Rudolf Klein rightly asks, 'Do the anti-growth advocates assume that the existing social and economic structure of society will somehow be frozen – and that the present inequalities ... will become happily accepted? Or do they assume a political system which insures that non-growth does not become a synonym for perpetuating existing inequalities – that economic stagnation can be reconciled with social change?'[11]

Thirdly, as we have not yet eliminated scarcity, we are still faced with real problems of raising output at reasonable cost, and we must also face up to many problems concerning the allocation of resources. As long as there is scarcity there are problems concerning who gets what and how resources are allocated. The anti-growth issue must not be allowed to divert attention from the more serious allocation problems. Of course, for the reasons set out in detail in earlier chapters, governments need to adopt policies to increase the amount of resources currently devoted to environmental protection. Of course, as also argued earlier, the free-market system will not achieve an optimum allocation of resources to the environment. Society must intervene in the environmental choice. But the decisions must be taken by bodies that are representative of society as a whole, not solely or even mainly of the middle classes, with their special interests in the matter.

The middle-class obsession with certain aspects of the environment must not be allowed to divert attention from more serious allocation problems. These include, first, the distribution of income, both internationally and within countries. They also include major problems such as those of education, housing, health services, and working conditions, and in the poorer countries they include even more basic ingredients of life. So, as Anthony Crosland has put it, 'we can move away from the recent sterile argument of growth versus anti-growth, and resume the real argument. How do we use and direct our growth?'[12]

Postscript:
The Oil Crisis and
Economic Growth

Soon after the final draft of this book was completed the world was hit by the so-called oil crisis. Those who had maintained for some time that economic growth would sooner or later lead to the exhaustion of key raw materials lost no time in proclaiming that the oil crisis had proved them to be right. In Britain, for example, *The Times* carried numerous letters from people such as the Bishop of Stepney or Lord Gladwyn stating that the oil crisis demonstrated that they and like-minded people had been correct in the forecasts they had made years ago – in the face of opposition from most economists, or apathy from the public or governments – to the effect that we should soon run out of key resources, and the only correction required to their predictions was that the crisis had come sooner rather than later. The conclusion that many of them have drawn from the oil crisis, therefore, is that it is more urgent than ever to change our way of life and to go back to the pursuit of the simple life.

In fact, the oil crisis demonstrates nothing of the sort. If anything, some of the reactions of producers of oil or other energy resources (outside the Arab world) to the rise in the oil price tend to support the arguments set out in Chapter 8 of this book to the effect that the capacity of supplies of resources to be augmented if the price rise is much greater than is generally supposed. But before coming on to this aspect of the question, it is necessary to explain what the oil crisis is really all about and what it is *not* about.

First of all, to listen to those who are now proclaiming the accuracy of their foresight one would imagine that the sharp rise in the price of oil and the alleged cut in supplies to the Western World had resulted from an exhaustion of oil reserves in the Middle East. In other words we are expected to believe that the Arabs have simply begun to run out of oil – for it is an exhaustion of supplies that had been forecast by the anti-growth lobby. But in fact the sharp rise in the oil price and the cutback in certain supplies were both caused by the outbreak of the 'Yom Kippur' war in the Middle East and the formation by the Arabs of a cartel to push up oil prices. And I am not aware that this was ever part of the gloomy predictions of the anti-growth lobby.

What they had predicted was an exhaustion of supplies at economical prices. The predicted cut in oil supplies was to have taken the form of an increasing scarcity of oil reserves (most of which were believed to be in the Middle East) so that it would be impossible to produce the same flow of oil at the same cost as before, since more and more inaccessible sources of oil would have to be exploited. (In the jargon of economics, the 'supply curve' of oil shifts backwards.) But oil is not being sold now by the Arabs (and various other countries who naturally follow suit) at about $10 per barrel because the costs of extracting it have risen to something like that level. In fact, the total direct real costs of producing oil in the Middle East are still only about 10 cents per barrel – i.e. one hundredth of the price being asked! Nor has output of oil actually fallen taking the world as a whole. In 1973 total world output actually rose by over 8 per cent (and in the fourth quarter of 1973 British crude oil imports were 17 per cent higher than in the first quarter of the year). Total oil tanker loadings from six major Middle East oil terminals during the last quarter of 1973 were 31 per cent higher than in the same quarter of 1972. Some exhaustion of supplies!

So what has actually happened? The answer is presumably fairly obvious to anybody but those who are so determined to prove that the world is on a collision course that even the most well-known facts have to be ignored. It is that, under the conditions provided by the Middle East war, the Arab oil producers found a unity – which may not last – that enabled them to change the marketing conditions in which their oil was sold. The point to note about the oil market is that there are really two markets. The first is the market in which a few giant oil companies, who also control most of the transport, refining and distribution networks, buy oil from various sources. The second is the market in which they sell oil to numerous final consumers. Neither market is a very competitive one, to put it mildly, and in both the oil companies can exert a certain amount of monopolistic power.

This means that in the first market – where they buy the oil – they can exploit their bargaining position to buy it cheaply from very low-cost suppliers, notably in the Middle East, although they pay a higher price to higher-cost suppliers. In the second market, where they sell the oil, they can average out the price to some extent, allowing for differences in transport costs, refining and distribution costs, and their particularly intricate tax arrangements. In the first market they can get away with this system as long as the low-cost producers cannot make alternative arrangements – e.g. to sell the oil at a higher price to other customers. The low-cost producers cannot do this since the companies have more or less tied up the transport, refining and distribution networks so that it is very difficult for large amounts of oil to be marketed without going through the major oil companies in one way or the other. In the economics jargon the oil companies can buy cheaply from the low-cost suppliers on account of their near-'monopsonist' buyers' position (i.e. the buyers' equivalent of a 'monopolist' seller). They are in a similar position to that of a monopolist seller, who can charge different prices in different markets, according to people's capacity to pay, provided that it is impossible for any customers to buy from them in the cheap market and to re-sell the product in the higher-price market.

Faced with this sort of situation one possible way in which the low-cost oil producers can extract a higher price is to form some sort of cartel to restrict supplies to the companies except on more generous terms than they had previously enjoyed. In other words, they try to match the near-monopsony power of the companies with some monopoly power of their own. In such a situation the final price depends very much on sheer bargaining strength of the two sides. By forming such a cartel after the 'Yom Kippur' war the Arabs have thus been able to expropriate some of the profits that had previously been made by the oil companies (some of which were, of course, passed on to consumers in the form of lower oil prices than would otherwise have been the case).

In other words, the sharp rise in oil prices and the limitation on supplies has absolutely nothing to do with any exhaustion of oil reserves in the countries concerned, but reflects a change in the relative bargaining strength of the various participants in the oil market. This is no more related to a genuine shortage than would a sharp rise in the price of colour film on account of the establishment of a monopoly in its supply indicate an imminent exhaustion of supplies of the chemicals used in their production. Changes in market conditions must be sharply distinguished from changes in the *real* costs of production.

As to the question of how long the Arab oil producers can maintain their monopoly position, it is possible to have serious doubts. Within two or three months of their actions signs have appeared of divergence of interests and of some difficulty in preventing some of them from breaking ranks as far as their output and supplies are concerned. The relaxation of the embargo announced in January 1974 is widely believed in oil and governmental circles as being merely a recognition of the facts – i.e. that some suppliers had failed to restrict supplies as much as had been agreed. This is confirmed by the way that most of the major oil consuming countries, particularly those such as the Netherlands and Japan or Italy, which had been expecting catastrophic effects on their economy and dire shortages of oil, have found themselves, in the end, relatively little affected. Already in January 1974 spot prices for oil and oil products were beginning to fall back.

Furthermore, differences of interest with respect to oil prices policy between the various Arab oil producers have also begun to come to light, as could have been expected given their different situations as to the size of their reserves and their capacity to use large revenues in the near future. For example, Saudi Arabia has relatively very large reserves compared, say, with Iran, and relatively small capacity to make much productive use of far greater oil revenues in the short to medium run. Hence, it is less in Saudi Arabia's interest to force up the price of oil, since she cannot use the money now and it would only stimulate greater output of oil and oil substitutes in other countries (such as North America), so that, in the longer run, when she will still have plenty of oil, its price may be relatively low. But whilst these and other (particularly political) considerations suggest that an oil cartel will face at least as many – and possibly far more – difficulties as are faced by a cartel in the long run, they are not directly relevant to the problem under consideration here. What is more relevant is the light that the recent developments have shed on the scope for alternative sources of energy supply.

One of the useful by-products of the recent events has been a renewed interest in the possibilities of finding alternative sources of energy in the medium run – i.e. before nuclear energy becomes important. In the first place it is necessary to put into perspective the role of oil in total world energy resources from fossil fuels. In a study completed before the end-1973 rise in the oil price, Professor William Nordhaus of Yale University converted the various sources of fossil fuels into comparable units in terms of energy equivalents (given usual conversion processes).* These showed that, taking units of one thousand billion billion British Thermal Units, fossil fuel reserves known at that time (they have since been revised upwards sharply in many cases) were approximately as shown in the table on page 254.

It is true, of course, that oil is used for many purposes other than energy and that some of the other energy resources may be relatively expensive to extract. But this is precisely why oil has been increasingly used for energy purposes where it could be replaced by other fossil fuels if the oil price were to rise relatively. We have become accustomed to cheap oil which is

* *The Allocation of Energy Resources*, preliminary draft of study supported by the U.S.A. National Science Foundation, November 1973.

Petroleum	8,000
Coal	60,000
Shale Oil	25,000
Natural Gas	6,000
Total above	99,000
Annual world consumption (1965)	154

also a convenient fuel for many purposes, but there is nothing sacred about the past very low price of oil, and should it rise significantly it will become increasingly economic to use other fuels for energy purposes, thereby reserving oil for uses for which there may be no close substitutes, as well as to economize on fuel use in general. No special measures would be required to bring this about – the change in the relative price of oil would automatically lead to fuel economies and to increased use of alternative fuels in those areas where such alternatives are viable. Various industrial surveys in some European countries at the end of 1973 showed that savings in oil consumption of up to 15 per cent could be – and were being – made without any effect at all on output. If the price of oil were to stay high, the longer-run scope for economies in its use would presumably be far greater.

Nor is it true that the cost of some of the alternative fossil fuels would be prohibitive, and, as the above table shows, conventional oil reserves are dwarfed by the amount of coal and even of oil from shale (not to mention tar sands). As a result of the oil crisis much more attention has been paid to shale and tar sands, and there is a general convergence of views amongst the experts to the effect that the extraction costs of shale oil would be about $7 per barrel, compared with the 'posted price' of oil at the beginning of 1974 of over $11 per barrel. And it is estimated that in the western U.S.A. shale oil reserves amount to about 90 billion tons (or about as much as known world oil reserves and about twice as much as the oil reserves of the Middle East) – and possibly several times as large as this. Similar reserves of oil from tar sands exist in Alberta in Canada, and the cost at which oil could be extracted from this source is estimated as being about $5 to $6 per barrel. Of course, there are various constraints on the desirability of exploiting shale and tar sands, but, on the other hand, the technology for doing so is relatively new, and the whole history of technological developments shows that when larger-scale production is introduced in such activities and there is a market incentive to expand to an economical scale the advances made in technology produce considerable reductions in costs. Up to now it has not been worthwhile engaging in large-scale production of oil from such sources – with Middle East oil costing about 10 cents per barrel plus about another two dollars per barrel for the host government taxes and share of royalties. But with the host governments now asking nearly $10 per barrel the whole situation has drastically changed – at least it would be drastically changed were the oil price to stay at anything like this level.

Of course, it is unlikely that the oil price will stay at anything like its latest (January 1974) level for very long, partly for the reasons given above concerning the difficulties of maintaining a cartel in the Arab oil producing countries, and partly because of the scope for substitution by other sources of oil and other energy resources such as coal and natural gas. But a third reason is simply the prospect of major increases in the world's known reserves of conventional oil deposits, particularly in the U.S.S.R. and China (reserve estimates of which are, naturally, not widely publicized), not to mention countries such as Brazil – the potential of which has been barely scratched. But already estimates of reserves in the Communist countries are emerging that suggest enormous increases over previous estimates. For example, a recent study by the Atlantic Institute, which is shortly to be published, suggests that Soviet oil reserves may be as great as 45 billion tons (i.e. about as much as the Middle East) by comparison with earlier estimates of only about 10 billion tons. Various statements by Russian ministers, referring to 53 new oil deposits discovered during the last three years, as well as to gigantic new reserves of natural gas and, in general, to the availability of fossil fuels over the very long run, support the view that the potential for finding new reserves in the U.S.S.R. is very far from being exhausted. Other sources suggest that, if offshore reserves are included, the oil reserves of China may be about as big as those of the U.S.S.R. In Africa, too, known oil reserves almost doubled during the one year 1972.

Nor is it enough to answer that oil demand is rising faster in contemporary economies than in the past. Such vague statements have held true for oil for decades, yet the fact remains that, without even allowing for all the recent increases in prospective reserves such as those indicated above, whereas proven world oil reserves were only about 15 times annual oil production before the war, they had risen to 25 times annual production by the 1950s (when demand was already twice the pre-war level) and now stand at about 35 times world production in spite of the demand having trebled again.

Thus, not only does the recent rise in the oil price have nothing to do with any exhaustion of already known supplies, but it has, on the contrary, provided further support for the general argument in Chapter 8 of this book to the effect that figures of reserves at any date always turn out to be very conservative underestimates, and that insofar as the supplies of any material did fail to increase more or less in line with demand at the prevailing price, the search for new resources and the development of techniques for finding alternative supplies would be greatly stimulated.

But there is a final moral to the oil crisis story. This concerns the light it throws on the mentality of the anti-growth lobby. It is argued in this book that the anti-growth movement, for all its self-righteous and ostentatious display of moral fervour, represents very much the reaction of the wealthier section of the world community that finds its privileges threatened by further economic growth, and fears – often mistakenly – that those aspects of the quality of life which it can afford to value relatively highly are likely to be sacrificed to increased output of the goods that are still vital for the provision of decent standards of living for the poorer members of advanced societies and for the desperately poor that make up the majority of the world's population. In this connection it is striking that they have seized on the rise in the price of oil as a decisive argument for abandoning the goal of economic growth and for a re-thinking of our basic values. But over the last two or three years the economies of many of the poorer countries of the world – such as India – have been hit quite as badly by the sharp rise in the price of wheat. We did not hear the same outcry about this as we have been hearing lately as a result of the oil crisis. The reason – if only subconscious as far as most people are concerned – is not hard to imagine. The rise in the price of wheat (partly caused by the American policy of subsidizing farmers to reduce wheat output!) only meant starvation for a few more million people in backward countries a long way away. Apparently, that does not provoke the men of spiritual sensibility to righteous indignation about the values of society as much as does a rise in the price of petrol for automobiles.

Notes and Sources

Chapter 1: An Economist's View of the Growth Issue

1. *Pollution: Nuisance or Nemesis*: a report presented to The Secretary of State for the Environment, February 1972. This report was drawn up by a working party under the chairmanship of Sir Eric Ashby, of which the present writer was also a member. It did not represent, therefore, the unanimous views of all the members, and the quotations here are from the section of the report in which the case *against* growth was given. It should be added that this was followed by a section consisting of the case *for* economic growth.

2. The O.E.C.D.'s Secretary-General's Ad Hoc Group on New Concepts of Science Policy, under the chairmanship of Harvey Brooks, writes: 'Many aspects of developed societies are approaching a condition that may be described as the precursor of saturation, in the sense that things cannot go on growing much longer in some lines without reaching fairly fundamental limits. Indications of saturation are present in conglomerations, in traffic, in information overload impinging on the individual, even in higher education and perhaps, in the view of some people, the production of new knowledge.' – *Science, Growth and Society* (O.E.C.D., Paris, 1971), p. 21.

3. Lord Robbins, 'Growth and anti-Growth', *The Financial Times*, December 2nd, 1971.

4. E. J. Mishan, *The Costs of Economic Growth* (Staples Press, London, 1967), p. xvi.

5. E. J. Mishan, 'Making the Future Safe for Mankind', *The Public Interest*, No. 24, Summer 1971, p. 49.

6. Frank Fraser Darling, *Wilderness and Plenty*, The Reith Lectures 1969, (B.B.C., London, 1970), p. 17. It should be noted that Sir Frank's book does not share, however, many of the misconceptions of the more extreme environmentalists, such as the notion that pollution is a new problem and that it is getting worse everywhere. Furthermore, Sir Frank does insist that, in the final analysis, 'The resources of the planet were for man, without a doubt', (p. 35), a view which conflicts with that of some conservationists, who attach independent value to the animal world or the natural environment.

7. Aubrey Buxton, 'Concern for nature', *The Times*, November 2nd, 1972. Mr Buxton is careful to point out that the new philosophy which he advocated should also not go to the other extreme and put protection of the countryside and resources above all else.

8. Arthur Cordell, 'The Costs of Economic Growth', *The Canadian Field-Naturalist*, April–June 1970. Dr Cordell is Economic Adviser to the Science Council of Canada.

9. See for example an excellent commentary on this belief by Joe Rogaly, 'Alternatives to God of Growth', *Financial Times*, December 16th, 1969. In *The Diseconomies of Growth* (Earth Island Ltd, London, 1972), H. V. Hodson

says: 'The economists lectured the politicians about growth ... they were more eagerly listened to because of the apparent success of Keynes's admonitions ... the cult of growth had spread, like some feverish infection of which economists were the carriers ... ' (p. 33).

10. *Sinews for Survival*, Report of a Working Party under the chairmanship of Mr R. B. Verney (H.M.S.O., London, 1972).

11. Dr Sicco Mansholt, 'Pollution Politics', *The Guardian*, April 7th, 1972. This does not mean that the E.E.C. Commission as a whole shared Dr Mansholt's views; far from it. In fact, one of the most penetrating and categorical critiques of the anti-growth school of thought is that by Monsieur Raymond Barrel, who was Vice-President of the E.E.C. Commission at the time, in his 'Reflexions sur la lettre de Mr Mansholt à M. Malfatti' (Brussels, June 9th, 1972).

12. Dick Taverne, 'Not-so-sacred cow', *The Observer*, May 28th, 1972. Mr Taverne reaches the conclusion that 'maximization of GNP should not be our prime aim ... ', that industrial nations cannot continue doubling their GNP every thirty years, and that 'It seems impossible to envisage any conceivable substitution of resources or technological breakthroughs that could enable the world to support a future population of over six billion (the very lowest at which we might remotely hope to see population stabilized) if all countries attain the standards of living of the developed world.'

13. See also my chapter on 'The Logic of Environmental Choice' in Nigel Calder (editor), *Nature in the Round: A Guide to Environmental Science* (Weidenfeld and Nicolson, London, 1973), and my article 'Environmental Policy: The Contribution of Economics', *O.E.C.D. Observer*, September 1972.

14. Also, the primary uncertainties here relate to the scientific aspects of pollution, which are not fully understood by any means. (See paper by Dr Martin Holdgate, 'The Basis for Standards', in *Pollution Abatement*, edited by K. M. Clayton and R. C. Chilver (David & Charles, Newton Abbot, 1973).

15. See also Royal Commission on Environmental Pollution, *First Report* (H.M.S.O., London, 1971), Chapter II.

16. J. K. Galbraith, *The Affluent Society* (Hamish Hamilton, London, 1958). This was the first statement of Galbraith's characterization of modern economies as consisting of private affluence and public squalor.

Chapter 2: Passengers on the Anti-Growth Bandwagon

1. *Report of Joint Ad Hoc Group on Air Pollution from Fuel Combustion in Stationary Sources* (PAC/70.72), O.E.C.D., Paris, May 1972.

2. *The Observer*, July 9th, 1972.
1972.

3. See also comments by J. M. Barnes, 'The Dangers of Watching for Doom', *The Times Higher Education Supplement*, May 12th, 1972, on a particular example of misleading scientific commentary on environmental hazards.

4. Petr Beckmann, *Eco-Hysterics and the Technophobes* (The Golem Press, Boulder, Colorado, 1973), p. 27.

5. *The Ecologist,* January 1972.

6. Jeremy Swift wrote, of the *Blueprint for Survival,* that 'The Blueprint also leans heavily on the supposed stability of all natural ecosystems, and the cyclical nature of all biological processes. These notions, which are only partly true, tend to lead biologists astray when they talk about human societies. It is noteworthy that almost all the distinguished supporters of the document are natural scientists. The new environmental battle lines may be forming between them and the social scientists, who believe more strongly in man's uniqueness'; 'Flaws in the Blueprint', *New Scientist,* February 10th, 1972.

7. See Marshall Goldman, 'Ecological Facelifting in the U.S.S.R. or Improving on Nature', *Political economy of environment: problems of method,* with an introduction by Ignacy Sachs (Mouton, Paris and the Hague, 1972) for a detailed description of some of the damage done to the Soviet environment.

8. Professor E. Stuart Kirby, 'Environmental Spoilage in the U.S.S.R.', *New Scientist,* January 6th, 1972; Renée Short, 'Siberia's pollution problem', *The Times,* October 5th, 1972.

9. See Goldman, op. cit., for details of the depletion of water resources in the Caspian and Aral seas, as well as the pollution of the Siberian water resources. See also the references to Russian sources in Kirby, *op. cit.*: and references to complaints about pollution and the depletion of valuable environmental resources by various Soviet authorities and officials, quoted in 'Environment becomes an issue', *Financial Times,* December 10th, 1970.

10. See report 'New Soviet Drive to Fight Pollution', *Financial Times,* January 11th, 1973.

11. See report by A. H. Hermann, 'Production Before Cleanliness', *Financial Times,* May 20th, 1971.

12. 'The Clean-Up Gets Under Way', *Financial Times,* September 29th, 1972.

13. An interesting article on this aspect of China was 'La Chine Après La Revolution Culturelle', by Robert Guillain, *Le Monde,* September 21st, 1971.

14. See Petr Beckmann, *Eco-Hysterics and the Technophobes,* p. 71 for details of the way that controlled forests act as much more efficient air-purifiers (through consuming carbon dioxide and producing oxygen by means of photosynthesis and transpiration) than forests left to nature, filled with over-matured trees, which slow or stunt the growth of the younger trees.

15. This brilliant lecture by Keith Pavitt, *A European's view of the Environmental Crisis,* was given at the Woodrow Wilson School of Public and International Affairs, Princeton University, March 17th, 1971, in a series of lectures on 'Rescuing Man's Environment', sponsored by the Council of Environmental Studies of Princeton University. See also John Naughton, 'Doomsday Revisited', *New Statesman,* January 5th, 1973.

16. V. I. Lenin, *Left-Wing Communism: An Infantile Disorder,* p. 17.

17. E. J. Mishan's first full statement of his now relatively well-known opposition to economic growth was his book *The Costs of Economic Growth* (Staples Press, London, 1967). Re-statements of his views have appeared elsewhere in later years in various journals and in various issues of *Encounter.* References to some of these are given at the appropriate places.

18. This is essentially the argument put forward by Tibor Scitovsky in 'What Price Economic Progress', originally published in 1959 and reprinted in his *Papers on Welfare and Growth* (Allen and Unwin, London, 1964), Chapter 13.

19 As Rudolf Klein rightly puts it, 'Thus growth tends to threaten traditional middle-class values: it is felt to be disruptive and unpleasant precisely because it turns minority privileges into majority ones – because it means crowded roads, crowded beaches, and so on'. ('Growth and Its Enemies', *Commentary*, Vol. 53, No. 6, June 1972, p. 44.)

20. Peter Passell and Leonard Ross, 'Don't Knock the $2-Trillion Economy', *The New York Times Magazine*, March 5th, 1972.

21. Keith Pavitt, in a fascinating review of earlier anti-growth advocates, reminds us that Karl Marx clearly saw through Malthus's position on the growth issue and wrote: 'The hatred of the English working class against Malthus – the 'mountebank-parson' as Cobbett rudely calls him – is therefore entirely justified. The people were right here in sensing instinctively that they were confronted not with a man of science but with a bourgeois advocate, a pleader on behalf of their enemies, a shameless sycophant of the ruling classes.' (Quoted by Pavitt in 'The Ideological Background, Malthus and Other Economists; Some Doomsdays Revisited', in Part II of the University of Sussex Science Policy Research Unit's study of *The Limits to Growth*, *Futures*, April 1972.)

22. C. A. R. Crosland, *The Future of Socialism* (Jonathan Cape, London, 1956; paperback edition 1964, p. 222).

23. Professor J. R. N. Stone, 'The Evaluation of Pollution: Balancing Gains and Losses', *Minerva*, 1972.

24. Barrie Shermann, 'Free Air for All the Workers', *The Guardian*, December 7th, 1971. This article contains an excellent summary of various reasons why the working classes have been less concerned with the environmental debate than the middle classes, in spite of the fact that 'the bulk of pollutive problems fall on the working classes'.

25. *Pollution: Nuisance or Nemesis* (H.M.S.O., London, 1972), p. 41.

26. *Financial Times*, October 17th, 1972.

27. 'Ecology – Boom or Bust', *Daily Mail*, January 12th, 1973.

28. *Second Survey of Aircraft Noise around London (Heathrow) Airport* (H.M.S.O., London, August 1971).

29. Thomas D. Crocker, 'Some Economics of Air Pollution Control', *Natural Resources Journal*, Vol. 8 (1968), p. 242.

30. J. S. Mill, *Principles of Political Economy* (1848), Book IV, Chapter VI.

31. A recent example of exaggerated growthmanship is *L'envol de la France dans les années 80*, by Edmund Stillman and others, for the Hudson Institute (Paris, 1973).

32. John Maynard Keynes, 'Economic Possibilities for Our Grandchildren', in *Essays in Persuasion* (Macmillan, London, 1931), p. 367.

Chapter 3. National Product and the Quality of Life: Some Historical Perspectives

1. A. C. Pigou, *The Economics of Welfare* (Macmillan, London, 4th edition 1932), Chapter 1, para. 5.

2. Pigou, op. cit., Chapter 1, para. 6.

3. Ibid., para. 8.

4. J. de V. Graaff, *Theoretical Welfare Economics* (Cambridge University Press, London, 1957), p. 6.

5. A masterly early discussion of the desirability of growth is the Appendix to W. Arthur Lewis's *The Theory of Economic Growth* (Allen and Unwin, London, 1953). His main proposition is that economic growth is desirable chiefly in order to provide greater choice and that whether mankind uses this choice to make itself happier or not is another matter.

6. *The Memoirs of Chateaubriand* (Penguin, Harmondsworth, 1965), p. 141.

7. The Metropolitan Working Classes' Association for Improving the Public Health, *Drainage and Sewerage* (London, 1847), pp. 6-7.

8. Hector Gavin, *Sanitary Ramblings* (London, 1848), p. 20. Dr Gavin was a lecturer in forensic medicine and public health at the Charing Cross Hospital, and a member of the Committees of the Health of Towns and of London Association.

9. See Gavin's lecture, *Unhealthiness of London and the Necessity of Remedial Measures* (London, 1847), p. 33. See also E. C. Holland, *The Vital Statistics of Sheffield* (1843) and J. L. Hammond, *The Town Labourer* (1917), Chapter 3.

10. Health of Towns Association, *Report of the Sub-Committee on the Questions Addressed to the Principal Towns and England of Wales* (London, 1848), p. 7.

11. E. J. Mishan, 'Economic Growth: The Need for Scepticism', *Lloyds Bank Review* (October 1972), p. 18.

12. E. J. Mishan, 'On Making the Future Safe for Mankind', *The Public Interest*, No. 24, Summer 1971.

13. E. J. Mishan, 'Growth and Anti-growth', *New Scientist*, March 16th, 1972.

14. Hodson (op. cit.), p. 59 argues that GNP fails to allow for deterioration in the quality of goods and services. Not long ago it was fashionable to argue that GNP failed to reflect quality improvements. See discussion of objection to GNP estimates in W. Beckerman, *An Introduction to National Income Analysis* (Weidenfeld and Nicolson, London, 1972, paperback edition), pp. 190–201.

15. *Annual Reports of the Ministry of Health*.

16. *Statistical Abstracts of the United States*.

17. See E. P. Thompson, *The Making of the English Working Class* (Gollancz, London, 1963; Penguin, Harmondsworth, 1968), p. 360 of 1971 edition.

18. British data from *Annual Abstract of Statistics*, Vol. 108, 1971, and *Annual Reports of the Ministry of Health*. U.S.A. data from *Statistical Abstract of the United States, 1970*. The deaths relate to infants born alive.

19. E. J. Mishan, 'On Making the Future Safe for Mankind', p. 49.

20. *British Labour Statistics: Historical Abstract 1896–1968* and *Annual Abstract of Statistics*. This does not mean that conditions inside British factories and other places of work are entirely satisfactory. Quite apart from the noise, stench, and so on, the number of non-fatal accidents is still extremely high, and the evidence presented by the T.U.C. to the Robens Committee of Safety and Health at Work in 1971 contains estimates of the cost of work-accidents of the order of magnitude of £500 million per annum, which is probably far greater than the damage done in Britain by some of the forms of pollution such as noise or pesticides or DDT, which tend to cause such excitement in the anti-growth lobby. The point is that industrial accidents are taking place in a steady flow, day after day, so, as the T.U.C. evidence points out (p. 13n) it is only when there is some spectacular accident like the 1969 Glasgow fire

disaster that the public – and the authorities – become, temporarily at least interested in the subject of working conditions.

21. *Statistical Abstract of the United States* (the American data refer to all disabling work-injuries that prove to be fatal, and not just those occurring in 'industry').

22. E. J. Mishan, 'On Making the Future Safe for Mankind', pp. 53–4.

23. E. J. Mishan, 'Economic Growth: The Need for Scepticism', pp. 24–5.

24. Testimony by Robert Lampman before the U.S. Senate Subcommittee on Employment, Manpower and Poverty, 1971; quoted in Walter W. Heller, 'Coming to Grips with Growth and the Environment', op. cit. (see p. 62n).

25. The poll was commissioned by the National Wildlife Federation (reported in *U.S.A. Air/Water Pollution Newsletter*, April 1972).

Chapter 4. GNP 'Needs', and Welfare

1. Arthur Okun, 'Social Welfare has no Price Tag', *Survey of Current Business*, vol. 51, July 1971: anniversary issue on 'The Economic Accounts of the United States: Retrospect and Prospect'.

2. William Nordhaus and James Tobin, *Is Growth Obsolete?*, Cowles Foundation Discussion Paper Nò. 319, presented to National Bureau of Economic Research Colloquium, December 1970 (to be published).

3. Ibid., p. 12.

4. Nordhaus and Tobin, op. cit. (mimeographed version), p. 12.

5. Ibid., p. 14.

6. E. J. Mishan, *The Costs of Economic Growth* (Staples Press, London, 1967), p. 112.

7. Anthony Kenny, 'Happiness', *Proceedings of the Meeting of the Aristotelian Society* (February 28th, 1972), p. 102.

8. Kenny, op. cit., p. 95.

9. Henri Lefebvre, *Critique de la vie quotidienne* (L'Arche, Paris, 1958), p. 174. It should be added that Lefebvre thinks that modern capitalist society destroys man's natural needs, such as his need for space, pure air, solitude, and so on, and goes on to expound Marx's well-known view on this subject.

10. F. Nietzsche, *The Twilight of the Idols* (Penguin, Harmondsworth, 1968), p. 42.

11. Thomas Juster, *A Framework for the Measurement of Economic and Social Performance*, National Bureau of Economic Research, Conference on the Measurement of Economic and Social Performance, November 1971, p. 54 (mimeographed version). This document contains an extensive discussion of the whole question. On the whole, Juster takes the view that something can be done to arrive at a measure of economic welfare that is rather better than the existing conventional GNP estimates, a view which is obviously shared by Nordhaus and Tobin. For a contrary view, however, see Denison, op. cit., and Okun, op. cit. See also a superb summary of this and related debates in Heller, op. cit., pp. 16–18. For a technical discussion of the relationship between differences in environmental 'needs' and welfare comparisons in terms of indifference-curve analysis, see my 'Environment, "Needs" and Real Income Comparisons', *Review of Income and Wealth*, March 1973. An excellent

discussion of the welfare-oriented measure of GNP that concentrates on environmental needs and that goes beyond the general philosophical issue as raised above is contained in O. Herfindahl and A. Kneese, *Measuring Social and Economic Change: Benefits and Costs of Environmental Pollution*, N.B.E.R., Conference on the Measurement of Economic and Social Performance, November 1971.

12. E. J. Mishan, *The Costs of Economic Growth*, p. 120.

13. See, for example, C. A. R. Crosland's convincing denial of this and many other anti-growth arguments discussed as far back as 1956 in Chapter 2 of *The Future of Socialism* (Jonathan Cape, London, 1956).

14. I am indebted to Yoram Barzel for drawing my attention to this (and many other) points in a draft of my article on this subject in N. Kaldor (ed.) *Conflicts in Policy Objectives* (Blackwell, Oxford, 1971).

15. John Stuart Mill, *Principles of Political Economy*, Book IV, Chapter VI, 'The Stationary State'.

16. About half of the authors of this report were from the developing countries. See *Development and Environment*, report submitted by a panel of experts convened by the Secretary-General of the United Nations Conference on the Human Environment (Norstedt, Stockholm, 1971).

Chapter 5. Economic Growth and Pollution

1. Almost all economists recognize instantly the difference between problems pertaining to the allocation of resources at any moment of time and the problems concerned with growth over time. But one exception is Alan Coddington, who confuses the two issues completely in 'The Cheermonger, or, How to Stop Worrying and Love Growth', *Your Environment*, Vol. III, No. 3, Autumn 1972.

2. See also *Effects of Pollution Discharges in the Thames Estuary*, Chapter 5, 'Early History of Pollution', Water Pollution Research Laboratory Papers No. 11, and T. C. Sinclair's chapter 'Environmentalism' in the special issue on the Club of Rome's computerized predictions of global catastrophe, *Futures*, April 1973, Chapter 12.

3. See the brilliant article by Miguel Ozorio de Almeida, 'The Confrontation Between Problems of Development and Environment', *Environment and Development*, special issue of *International Conciliation*, published by the *Carnegie Endowment for International Peace* (New York, January 1972).

4. See Lord Zuckerman's paper 'Technology and Society: A Challenge to Private Enterprise', presented to the XXIIIrd Congress of the International Chamber of Commerce, Vienna, April 1971.

5. R. S. Scorer, 'New Attitudes to Air Pollution – The Technical Basis of Control', in *Atmospheric Environment* (Pergamon Press, Oxford, 1971), Vol. 5, pp. 903–34. Professor Scorer is not even correct in saying that an excess of speed *per se* is harmless; for an excess of speed increases the probability of an accident, which is something a rational society should be prepared to pay a certain amount to avoid.

6. H. Fish, Chief Purification Officer, Thames Conservancy, paper presented to the R.S.H. Congress, Eastbourne, April 1971. Mr Fish's definition of pollution is very close to that given by the Working Party set up to advise the

British government of pollution in preparation for the 1972 UN Conference on the Environment, which stated that 'Pollution means the deliberate or accidental contamination of the environment with Man's waste.' (*Pollution: Nuisance or Nemesis*, H.M.S.O., London, 1972). Of course, this definition is really circular in that much turns on the meaning of the word 'contamination'.

7. K. Mellanby, 'The Phoney Crisis', *Minerva*, Vol. X, No. 3, July 1972.
8. 'Prawnography', *The Guardian*, August 21st, 1971.
9. See A. E. J. Eggleton in *Atmospheric Environment*, Vol. 3, 1969, p. 355.
10. *Daily Telegraph*, August 11th, 1972.
11. This whole notion of the dependence of good or bad effects on the size of the dose is brilliantly described in Dr D. L. Gunn's Presidential Address to the Association of Applied Biologists, 'Dilemmas in Conservation for Applied Biologists', *Annals of Applied Biology*, Vol. 72, No. 2 (1972), pp. 105–27. See also 'Pollution: Plants Adapt to Toxic Metals', *The Times*, August 3rd, 1972.
12. U.S. Council on Environmental Quality, *Toxic Substances* (Washington D.C., 1971).
13. D. G. Hessayon, 'Homo Sapiens – the Species the Conservationists Forgot', *Chemical Industry*, May 20th, 1972.
14. Ozorio de Almeida, *International Conciliation* (New York), June 1972, No. 586, p. 43.
15. R. S. Scorer, 'New Attitudes to Air Pollution – The Technical Basis of Control', p. 932.
16. Eugene Rabinowitch, 'False Note in the Call of the Wild', *The Times*, April 29th, 1972. Also, as Harry Johnson rightly points out, 'Man's whole history has been one of transforming his environment rather than accepting its limitations. He has domesticated and raised animals for his own use, rather than relying on hunting them – and previously he invented weapons for hunting them made out of pieces of the environment, rather than relying on his original physical powers. He has cleared the ground for the planting of crops, rather than relying on what he could collect from nature's rather niggardly abundance ... The crucial question therefore, is not the fact of the transformation of the environment by man, and the presumptive undesirability of this transformation *per se*, but whether certain types of transformation have undesirable results, in the sense of worsening man's potential welfare.' – *Man and His Environment*, published by the British–North American Committee (London) and the National Planning Association (Washington).
17. Walter Heller, 'Coming to Terms with Growth and the Environment', pp. 3–4 of mimeographed version. Although Professor Heller left the White House long ago, the present U.S. administration at least shares his view on this optimization principle, judging by a report of a paper prepared by the Nixon Administration recently, which stated: 'Swimmable water quality, or elimination of pollutants, is neither necessary, economically feasible, nor possible in many cases. Such a goal would be undesirable and misleading to the general public.' – *Air/Water Pollution Report*, November 22nd, 1971, p. 473.
18. Dennis Meadows, Donella Meadows, J. Randers and W. W. Behrens, *The Limits to Growth* (A Potomac Associates Book, Universe Books, New York, 1972).
19. 'The Limits to Growth' by Peter Passell, Marc Roberts and Leonard Ross, *The New York Times Book Review*, April 2nd, 1972. See also the comment by Professor F. Singer on the original Forrester model lying behind *The Limits*

9*

to Growth, to the effect that it 'has the trappings of professionalism; there are flow diagrams, computer programs and more. Even the graphs are plotted by the computer. Unfortunately Forrester's model is constructed without benefit of valid data, without reference to economics, and even without demography or sociology' ('The Computer as Pallbearer', *The Nation*, March 13th, 1972); or Leonard Silk's comment in the *New York Times* (March 14th, 1972) to the effect that 'The M.I.T. group recognize that their data are weak ... Yet they do pour their scrappy data into the computer and find confirmation of their direct fears'; or *The Times Higher Education Supplement* (March 31st, 1972): ' ... the book ... has an unsatisfactory air of spurious scholarship throughout. It could be mistaken for an elaborate satire and is pseudo-science at its worst'; or Dr Martin Shubik in *Science*, Vol. 174, December 3rd, 1971.

20. Article by Professor Mellanby in *The Times Higher Education Supplement*, March 31st, 1973; see also similar comment made by Mellanby in 'The Phoney Crisis', *Minerva*, July 1972.

21. Lecture on 'Pollution in Perspective', given by Sir Eric Ashby to *The Times* 1000 Conference, 1972. See also the book *The Doomsday Syndrome* by John Maddox, who was editor of *Nature* for many years, and various articles in *Nature*, notably 'Another Whiff of Doomsday', Vol. 236, March 10th, 1972.

22. *Nature*, Vol. 235, January 28th, 1972. In a very similar vein, P. K. Marstrand and T. C. Sinclair write that *The Limits to Growth* ' ... advances neither our understanding of pollution, nor its interaction with other aspects of world behaviour. Furthermore, by concentrating attention upon contrived physical crisis situations, it diverts, or can be used to divert, attention from other social costs of economic growth such as work injuries, inadequate housing conditions and uncompensated adaptations to structural changes and the like which arise in contemporary industrial societies.' See chapter on 'Pollution Sub-System' in the major analysis of the Club of Rome's *The Limits to Growth* that was carried out under the direction of Professor Christopher Freeman at the University of Sussex, Science Policy Research Unit, and published in *Futures*, February and April 1973 (and also in book form by Sussex University Press/Chatto and Windus, under the title *Thinking About the Future*, by H. S. D. Cole, C. Freeman and others). Marstrand and Sinclair exposed many of the fallacies of *The Limits to Growth* treatment of the pollution problem, including, notably, the fallacy of aggregating all the world's pollution into one series, when most pollution is essentially a local problem. As they say, 'By aggregating all pollutants, and assuming that they behave in some composite way, attention is drawn away from what are urgent, and still soluble, problems, and diverted into speculation upon an imaginary race against time between "Life" and "Global Asphyxiation".'

23. See D. G. Hessayon, op. cit., p. 403.

24. See article by Lord Todd (Professor of Organic Chemistry, Cambridge University), *The Guardian*, January 26th, 1972.

25. D. L. Gunn, op. cit. (see p. 256, n. 11); D. G. Hessayon, op. cit.; 'DDT Condemned', *Nature*, Vol. 237, June 23rd, 1972; and Mellanby, 'The Phoney Crisis', p. 501.

26. 'Pollution and Worldwide Catastrophe', *Nature*, Vol. 236, April 28th, 1972; 'DDT Nailed Again', *Nature*, Vol. 233, October 1st, 1972. There is even disagreement among scientists on questions such as how far DDT does accumulate indefinitely in body tissues. The work done by Dr Coulson at Durham University suggests that the amounts in birds decrease almost as soon as the

quantities introduced into the environment are reduced (*The Times*, April 29th, 1972). Similar results concerning the elimination of DDT from humans have been obtained by Morgan and Roan at the University of Arizona (*Nature*, July 28th, 1972). Similar doubts have been cast on the accumulation hypothesis by work done by Dr Frank Moriarty of the Monks Wood Experimental Station (*New Scientist*, March 16th, 1972).

27. D. L. Gunn, op. cit., p. 122.

28. 'The scare tactics used by the Environmental Defense Fund,' says Dr Borlaug, 'based on unsubstantiated scientific data, questionable ethics, emotion and oratory, have been used very effectively for raising funds and gaining support for their battle against DDT.' (Cf. Petr Beckmann, *Eco-Hysterics and the Technophobes*, The Golem Press, Boulder, Colorado, p. 158.)

29. K. Mellanby, 'The Biological Effect of Pollution – An Ecological Problem'; Presidential Address to the Zoology Section of the British Association for the Advancement of Science, September 1972.

30. *The Times*, February 3rd, 1972.

31. Petr Beckmann, op. cit., pp. 163–4.

32. Lecture by the late Neil Iliff on 'Organic Chemicals', given to the Second International Symposium on 'Chemical and Toxicological Aspects of Environmental Quality', Munich, May 1971.

33. Sir Eric Ashby, 'Pollution and the Public Conscience', 51st Earl Grey Memorial Lecture (University of Newcastle, 1972), p. 7; *Financial Times*, November 25th, 1972; *Air and Water News*, May 10th, 1971, report on research carried out in the U.S.A. by Dr Stewart of the Medical College of Wisconsin, and by Dr A. W. Hoover of the Columbia University School of Public Health and Administrative Medicine.

34. *The Predicament of Man*, based on the Science Policy Foundation's third international symposium (published in Frimley, Surrey, 1972).

35. K. Mellanby, 'The Biological Effects of Pollution – An Ecological Problem'.

36. See reports in the *Daily Telegraph*, August 9th, 1972; *Nature*, Vol. 235, February 18th, 1972; and Mellanby, op. cit. See also the report on air pollution from lead that was communicated privately to the Greater London Council by the Medical Research Council's Air Pollution Unit; *The Guardian*, September 1st, 1972; and 'Is Lead Blowing Our Minds?', *New Scientist*, May 27th, 1972.

37. *Science*, Vol. 174, November 12th, 1971.

38. The phosphate story is well documented in Petr Beckmann, op. cit., pp. 182ff. See also *Water in the News*, December 1971. In the North Sea, into which there has been a vast increase in the discharge of pollutants of all kinds over the last twenty years, the fish catch has doubled over the same period. See 'Pollution of the Seas', by Dr H. A. Cole, Director of Fisheries Research at the Ministry of Agriculture, Forestry and Fishing Laboratory, Lowestoft, in *Chemistry in Britain*, 1971, 27 (6).

39. See, for example, 'The reliability of air pollution measurements in relation to the siting of instruments', by Marjorie Clifton and others (*Int. J. Air Poll.*, 1959, Vol. 2); 'Interpretation of data from air pollution in towns taking into account the siting of instruments', by Marie-Louise Weatherley; and 'Difficulties encountered in the measurement of air pollution in the interpretation of results', by J. Palletier (both in *International Journal of Air/Water Pollution*, 1963, Vol. 7). See also *Second Report of the Council of Environmental Quality*, Washington D.C., 1971, pp. 211–14.

40. Meadows and associates, op. cit., p. 69.
41. Barry Commoner, *The Closing Circle: Confronting the Environmental Crisis* (Jonathan Cape, London, 1971).
42. K. Mellanby, 'The Phoney Crisis', *Minerva*, July 1972, p. 501.
43. Some of the reasons for this are discussed in Chapter 6. See British submission to the 1972 UNO Conference on the Human Environment, Stockholm, 1972, and First Report of the Royal Commission on Environmental Pollution (H.M.S.O., London, 1972).
44. Warren Spring Laboratory (Department of Trade and Industry), *National Survey of Air Pollution 1961–71* (H.M.S.O., London, 1972).
45. Greater London smoke emissions decreased by over 80 per cent on the twelve-year period 1958–70, even though output must have risen by at least 30 per cent over the same period, implying a fall in the pollution/output ratio of 85 per cent. See also details of sharp cuts in air pollution in individual industries in spite of substantial increases in their output, over the last ten to fifteen years, given by Mr Eldon Griffiths in his speech in the House of Commons, December 22nd, 1972 (House of Commons Debates, Col. 1794).
46. Department of the Environment and the Welsh Office, *Report of a River Pollution Survey of England and Wales, 1970, Vol. 1*, and *River Pollution Survey of England and Wales, Updated 1972* (H.M.S.O., London, 1971 and 1972 respectively).
47. Report by the Assistant Scientific Adviser to the Greater London Council, in the G.L.C.'s *Intelligence Unit Bulletin*, January 1972 (London, County Hall).
48. *The Observer*, November 21st, 1971; report of findings by ornithologists from the London Natural History Society.
49. Council on Environmental Quality, Second Annual Report, *Environmental Quality* (Washington, D.C., 1971), pp. 212–15.
50. Written reply by Mr Peter Walker to parliamentary question, August 8th, 1972.
51. Royal Commission on Environmental Pollution, *First Report* (H.M.S.O., London, 1971), pp. 11, 12.
52. Statement by Mr Peyton, Minister for Transport Industries, House of Commons, June 14th and October 7th, 1972.
53. Mr Peter Walker, parliamentary statement, August 1st, 1972.
54. Joint Department of the Environment Circular No. 64/72 and Welsh Office Circular 127/72; *Vol. 2 of the River Pollution Survey of England and Wales*, July 10th, 1972.
55. See E.P.A., *Environmental Quality*, op. cit., (Washington, D.C., annual), and successive annual editions of E.P.A., *Economics of Clean Air*, in which targets implied in the latest programmes are given; and various press releases of the E.P.A.
56. See E.P.A., ibid., and numerous comments in the press and journals, such as the National Academy of Sciences Report, January 1st, 1971 (Committee on Motor Vehicle Emissions of the National Research Council) and the 'RECAT' report, *Cumulative Regulatory Effects on the Cost of Automotive Transportation* (February 1972). Sir Eric Ashby is reported as saying that the 'draconian' legislation that governments had been forced to draft in response to the outcry against car emissions would have been employed to much better social purpose in cutting road accidents, since there was no evidence that exhaust gases from cars had ever accidentally killed or injured anyone. He added that the more carefully one examined the impact of the gas carbon

monoxide, the more hesitation one had in giving it high priority in the pollution budget (Ernest Balsom Lecture to the Institution of Public Health Engineers, reported in the *Financial Times*, January 26th, 1973). Of course, British conditions are nothing like as bad as in the U.S.A. with respect to vehicle exhaust emissions.

57. There have been numerous reports in the English-language press on the plans of Japan and other countries, but most of these are also described in the official national submissions to the 1972 UNO Conference on the Human Environment at Stockholm. The Japanese legislation is also described in detail in English in the Report of the *U.S.-Japan Conference on Environmental Pollution* (Tokyo, October 1970), and in 'Japan Fights Environmental Pollution', *Fuji Bank Bulletin*, March 1971.

58. 'How to Keep Europe Clean', *Financial Times*, April 12th, 1972.

59. Meadows and others, op. cit.

60. Neil Iliff, *Man and Environment – The Future*, Lecture at University of St Andrews, November 15th, 1972; and Royal Commission on Environmental Pollution, *Third Report* (H.M.S.O., London, 1972), Chapter III.

61. 'Pollution Control', *Financial Times*, August 11th, 1971; *Bulletin of the Swedish Water and Air Pollution Research Laboratory* ('I.V.L. Bulletin'), 1972.

62. National Aeronautics and Space Administration press release, August 27th, 1972; and 'The Demand for Quiet Aircraft', *Financial Times*, September 20th, 1972.

63. *The Financial Times*, November 7th, 1972; *The Times*, August 23rd, 1972; *The Guardian*, August 7th, 1970; and *The Liverpool Daily Post*, December 15th, 1971.

64. Petr Beckmann, op. cit., p. 124 (see p. 258, n. 28).

65. Interview in *The Observer*, March 12th, 1972. See also reference to views of leading American nuclear engineers to the effect that the disposal problem is now soluble, with the aid of storage in insulated containers in bedded salt deposits (*New York Times*, March 14th, 1972).

66. Petr Beckmann, op. cit., p. 126.

Chapter 6. Pollution Policy and the Price Mechanism

1. See, for example, assertions to this in Howard Sherman, *Radical Political Economy* (Basic Books, New York, London, 1972), pp. 74-7.

2. J. de V. Graaff, *Theoretical Welfare Economics* (Cambridge University Press, London, 1967), p. 161.

3. See A. P. Lerner, 'Priorities and Efficiency', *American Economic Review*, September 1971. As Lerner points out, there are no grounds in equity for using the subsidy method for abating new pollution.

4. J. H. Dales, *Pollution, Property and Prices* (University of Toronto Press, Toronto, 1968).

5. A. P. Lerner, op. cit.

6. Such empirical evidence as is available also confirms that the charges system is cheaper than that of direct controls. The pioneer work, in this connection, is the famous Delaware study, the economics of which have been described

by Edwin Johnson in 'A Study in the Economics of Water Quality Management', *Water Resources Research*, Vol. 3, No. 2, 1967. See also Allen Kneese and Blair Bower, *Managing Water Quality: Economics, Technology, Institutions* (Johns Hopkins Press for Resources for the Future, Baltimore, 1968) and Kneese, *The Application of Economic Analysis to Water Quality Management, Some Cases*, International Economics Association (to be published), in which a similar analysis of the Potomac is described. A similar conclusion emerges from Ernst and Ernst (consultants), *A Cost Effectiveness Study of Air Pollution Abatement in the Greater Kansas City Area* (U.S. Dept. of Health, Education and Welfare, Washington D.C., 1969).

7. There are numerous examples of cost-saving technological progress in pollution abatement, such as those given by Paul Gerhardt (chief of the Economic and Science Studies Section, National Center for Air Pollution Control, U.S. Public Health Service), in 'Incentives to Air Pollution', *Law and Contemporary Problems*, Vol. 33, No. 2, 1968.

8. See reports on major technical advances in monitoring equipment in *The Financial Times*, October 12th, 1971, and *The Guardian*, June 25th, 1971, both of which related to the development of much more automatic instruments for measuring various parameters of water quality.

9. *Memorandum on National Policy on the Discharge of Trade Effluent into Public Sewers*, by the (then) Institute of Sewage Purification, 1952. The same advantages for the charging system have been claimed in a paper by Mr Goodman, Chemical Inspector, Directorate of Water Engineering, Department of the Environment, submitted to the Economic Commission for Europe, January 1972, p. 2. See also Simpson and Truesdale, *Methods of Charging for the Treatment and Disposal of Industrial Effluent in Municipal Sewerage Systems*, paper presented to the Institute of Water Pollution Control Symposium, London, November 1971.

10. *1971 Report of the President's Council of Economic Advisers* (U.S.A.), p. 119. However, not much progress has since been made in implementing this tax.

11. *Financial Times*, August 11th, 1972.

12. 'Taxing Polluters' in *Marine Pollution Bulletin*, Vol. 3, No. 7, 1972.

Chapter 7. The Economic Burden of Environmental Protection

1. See Lester B. Lave, *Air Pollution Damage*, paper presented to Resources for the Future Conference, June 1970.

2. See Lave, op. cit., p. 35.

3. See Marshall I. Goldman, 'The Costs of Fighting Pollution', *Current History*, August 1970; for some illustrations of technical progress in the chemical industry see Neil Iliff, 'Industrial Technology and Conservation', lecture to Second International Congress of the World Wildlife Fund (London, November 1970).

4. See Environmental Protection Agency (E.P.A.), *Economics of Clean Air* (1972 edition), Chapter 1.

5. *The Economic Impact of Pollution Control: A Summary of Recent Studies*, prepared for the Council on Environmental Quality, the Department of Commerce and

the E.P.A., Washington, March 1972, mimeographed. According to p. 12 of this source, 'real' GNP is expected to grow at 5 per cent p.a. from 1972 to 1976, so that total GNP over their whole five-year period would amount to about $6,100 billion, of which $127 billion represents 2·1 per cent. But clearly the order of magnitude of this figure is not sensitive to reasonable variation in the growth-rate assumption. The estimates exclude expenditure in connection with noise, land reclamation, and some other relatively very small items.

6. First draft (November 1972) of O.E.C.D. report: Table II.

7. Ibid.

8. O.E.C.D., *Report of Joint Ad Hoc Group on Air Pollution from Fuel Combustion in Stationary Sources* (PAC/70.72), Paris, May 1972, mimeographed edition.

9. Ibid.

10. E.P.A., *Economics of Clean Air* (1972 edition), Chapter 1, Table 1.1. SO_2 emissions will be reduced to about 5·2 million tons p.a. compared with the 1967 level of 30·3 million tons, and particulates will be reduced to about 4·3 million tons compared with a 1967 level of 15·5 million tons.

11. *The Economics of Environmental Pollution in the United States* (extract from a paper prepared for the Atlantic Council, December 1970).

12. O.E.C.D., *Report of Joint Ad Hoc Group*, op. cit.

13. Greater London Council Research and Intelligence Unit, *The Progress and Effects of Smoke Control in London*, February 1970.

14. There is already a very large and rapidly growing literature on the conceptual and practical problems of measuring concepts such as the loss of amenity resulting from certain kinds of pollution, and this is not the place to attempt to review this literature. The approach used by M. Clawson and J. Knetsch (*The Economics of Outdoor Recreation*, Johns Hopkins Press, Baltimore, 1967), consisted essentially of measuring the demand curve for certain recreational facilities by estimating how much people had been prepared to pay, in terms of travelling costs and time, in order to reach certain facilities, rather than by attempting to conceptualize the facilities directly in measurable terms. Some of the applications of this approach have given rise to a certain amount of controversy, as can be seen, for example, in David Seckler, 'On the Uses and Abuses of Economic Science in Evaluating Public Outdoor Recreation', *Land Economics*, No. 4, 1966, and R. J. Smith, 'The Evaluation of the Recreation Benefits: The Clawson Method in Practice', *Urban Studies*, October 1971. An excellent statement of the problem of evaluating health damage is contained in E. J. Mishan, 'Evaluation of Life and Limb: A Theoretical Approach', *Journal of Political Economy*, 1971. Another approach has been the use of property values as indicators of people's preferences for living in quiet as distinct from noisy locations, as for example in R. N. S. Harris, G. S. Tolley and C. Harrell, 'The Resident Site Choice', *Review of Economics and Statistics*, 1968, and 'The Determinants of Residential Property Values with Special Reference to Air Pollution', by R. G. Ridker and J. A. Henning, *Review of Economics and Statistics*, 1967. All these approaches are subject to great difficulties; for example, in the case of property values, houses that are near roads, and are hence more exposed to noise, will also tend to be seen by more prospective buyers, and therefore be easier to sell at higher prices. Many of the problems are admirably set out in the Roskill Commission Report on the Third London Airport (*Papers and Proceedings* [H.M.S.O., London, 1970], particularly Vol. VII); and a useful review of various

approaches to the noise-evaluation problem is contained in D. N. M. Starkie, 'The Costing of Disamenity', *Centre for Environmental Studies Conference Paper No. 2* (1972). The 'Roskill' approach has been criticized, notably by Mishan, in 'What is Wrong with Roskill', *Journal of Transport Economics and Policy*, September 1970.

15. *Report of the Committee on Air Pollution* (under the Chairmanship of Sir Hugh Beaver), Cmnd. 1322 (H.M.S.O., London, November 1954).
16. Op. cit., p. 11.
17. Ibid.
18. Ibid.
19. *Programmes Analysis Unit*, op. cit., especially tables VI-5 and VI-6. This report also contains extensive references to the more detailed technical studies on which they have drawn, such as those relating air pollution to health and so on, so that there is no need to repeat them here.
20. *The Economic Aspect of Pollution Control, A Summary of Recent Studies*, prepared for the C.E.Q., The Department of Commerce and the Environmental Protection Agency, March 1971, mimeographed.
21. *Final Report of the Ad Hoc Committee, Cumulative Regulatory Effects on the Cost of Automotive Transportation* (RECAT report) (Washington D.C., February 1972).
22. This figure is given in 'The Costs of Air Pollution Damages: A Status Report', which is reprinted as Appendix I-J of the RECAT report, and on which the main text of the RECAT report draws.
23. Environmental Protection Agency, *Economics of Clean Air*, 1972 edition (Washington D.C., mimeographed).
24. E.P.A., *Economics of Clean Water*, 1972 edition (Washington D.C., mimeographed).
25. Council on Environmental Quality, Second Annual Report, *Environmental Quality* (Washington D.C., August 1971), p. 108.
26. The study by Chase Econometric Associates Inc., which was carried out on behalf of the U.S.A. Council on Environmental Quality and the Environmental Protection Agency, reached the conclusion that the pollution-abatement programme would lead to a cut in jobs of between 50,000 and 125,000. This is because 'Pollution control costs are assumed to affect the economy in the form of higher product prices and new demands for investments in pollution control facilities by industry ... prices rise as a result of the cost–push impact of pollution control costs. In the absence of compensatory macro-economic policies, the effect of rising prices, which tend to slow the growth of demand in the economy, outweighs the stimulating impact of investments in pollution control facilities.' – *The Economic Impact of Pollution Control: A Summary of Recent Studies* (Washington D.C., March 1972), p. 11. But this is an unfortunate way of approaching the whole problem, which is best done in terms of the effect on GNP *at a constant pressure of demand*. Of course, if the authorities allow output to fall below capacity on account of their pollution-control policies, GNP will fall and unemployment will rise. But this is the consequence of *any* bad macro-economic policy; it is not the inevitable economic burden on the economy of having to devote more resources to pollution abatement, which is what we are concerned with in this book.
27. Characteristic of numerous statements along the same lines is the declaration by one of the top Confederation of British Industry officials, Mr Ian

Kelsall, in response to the Minority Report of the Third Report of the Royal Commission on Environmental Pollution (H.M.S.O., London, September 1972). The Minority Report advocated pollution charges, and Mr Kelsall's immediate response was: 'You will take away from companies the wherewithal for curing their problems. We are concerned about pollution. We are conscious of the need to improve the environment ... But we are worried by the effect on our costs in relation to our competitors overseas. The Government should encourage industry by additional grants in respect to effluent treatment plants.' This sort of reaction by industry is, of course, predictable and understandable, and more serious, perhaps, is that this fear of competitors is also expressed by the Chief Alkali Inspector, who is responsible for controlling much of the air pollution in Britain, and who recently stated: 'Preventing pollution is an international problem, for no country can afford to risk its international trade by progressing at a much faster pace than its rivals and thereby making its products uncompetitive.' (*Clearing the Air*, the George Davis Lecture, November 10th, 1970, published by the Institution of Chemical Engineers.) As pointed out already, exactly the same could be said of the pace at which a country proceeds to cover any other social costs. As for the C.B.I. representative's proposal that the government should subsidize installation of purification plant, there is no economic justification for subsidizing firms' output of, in effect, clean water by any particular means, and measures to do so would distort resource allocation. If it is thought that firms should be sheltered from the anti-pollution measures on income-distribution grounds, then a subsidy per unit by which the pollution is reduced would be the appropriate means.

28. Commission of the European Communities, *Communication from the Commission to the Council on a European Communities Programme Concerning the Environment* (SEC [72] 666) (Brussels, March 22nd, 1972).

29. 'The Community's Policy on the Environment', contained in *Industry, Research and Technology* (Brussels, July 27th, 1971), No. 109, Annex 1. See also 'Pollution Control within the Common Market', *Environmental Pollution Management*, Vol. 2, No. 5, 1972, and Laurence Reed, 'Britain's Role in Europe's Environment', *New Scientist*, June 29th, 1972.

30. The view expressed here is very much in line with the view expressed in the British submission to the 1972 UNO Conference on the Human Environment, *Basic Paper Contributed by the United Kingdom: International Standards for Pollution Control*, particularly paragraph 6. Fortunately the UNO Conference seems to have been of a similar mind, and 'Principles' 21–23 of *The Declaration on the Human Environment* which emerged from the Stockholm Conference are consistent with the view expressed here.

31. There are various bodies involved in the study of marine pollution, notably the International Council for the Exploration of the Sea, the GESAMP (joint Group of Experts on the Scientific Aspects of Marine Pollution), which includes representatives from many other bodies, the Intergovernmental Oceanographic Commission, and various other bodies under the auspices of UNO or its specialized agencies.

32. A useful survey of many aspects of the international implications of pollution policy is contained in Ingo Walter's, 'Environmental Control and Patterns of International Trade and Investment: An Emerging Policy Issue', *Banca Nazionale del Lavoro Quarterly Review*, March 1972. See also W. J. Baumol's Wicksell Lectures, op. cit., 1972; and O.E.C.D., *Problems in Transfrontier*

Pollution (1973), a report of a seminar on international problems of pollution held in Paris, summer 1972.

Chapter 8. Resources for Growth

1. E. J. Mishan, 'Industry's Impact on the Environment', *Financial Times*, August 7th, 1972.
2. John Stuart Mill, *Principles of Political Economy* (1848), Book IV, Chapter VI.
3. W. S. Jevons, *The Coal Question* (London, 1866).
4. William Page, 'Non-Renewable Resources Sub-System', Chapter 3 in University of Sussex, Science Policy Research Unit, op. cit., *Futures*, February 1973.
5. Ibid., p. 38.
6. International Bank for Reconstruction and Development (known as 'the World Bank' or the I.B.R.D.), *Report on the Limits to Growth* (mimeographed edition, Washington D.C., September 1972), pp. 38–9.
7. Ibid., p. 7.
8. 'Economists, Scientists and Environmental Catastrophe', *Oxford Economic Papers*, November 1972.
9. Estimate made by Commodities Research Unit, London, on the basis of data on concentrations of metals in the earth's surface in the latest edition of the *Encyclopaedia Britannica*.
10. I.B.R.D., op. cit., p. 41.
11. Metallgesellschaft AG, *Metal Statistics 1959–1968* (Frankfurt-am-Main, 1969); P. Ketzer, 'Copper from a Statistical Point of View', 1966 (both quoted in *Copper and its Alloys*, Proceedings of an International Conference organized by the Institute of Metals, Amsterdam, September 1970, published by the Institute of Metals, London, 1970); R. Allen, *Copper Ores*, Imperial Institute Monographs on Mineral Resources (London, 1923); F. Beyschlag, J. H. L. Vogt and P. Krusch, *The Deposits of Useful Minerals and Rocks* (Macmillan, London, 1916); UNO *Statistical Yearbook*.
12. W. H. Voskuil, *Minerals in World Industry* (McGraw-Hill, New York, 1955); E. W. Zimmerman, *World Resources and Industries* (Harper, New York, revised 1951), and UNO *Statistical Yearbooks*.
13. I.B.R.D., op. cit., pp. 43–4.
14. Ibid., p. 45. See also *Nature* (*Physical Science*), April 16th, 1973.
15. William Page, op. cit., *Futures*, February 1973.
16. John Maddox, 'Is the End of the World Really Nigh?', *Sunday Times*, June 4th, 1972.
17. A. J. Surrey and A. J. Bromley, 'Energy Resources', Chapter 8 of the Sussex University Science Policy Research Unit study, op. cit., *Futures*, p. 104. The World Bank also reports that oil resources in shale deposits and tar sands may be ten times conventional sources. And, recently, a consortium of oil companies has begun a development programme to produce oil from the vast shale deposits of North America, where it is estimated that the shale deposits of Colorado, Utah and Wyoming alone are probably about three times as great as the total oil reserves of the Middle East. (*Financial Times*, April 9th, 1973.)

18. H. R. Warman, 'The Future of Oil', *The Geographical Journal*, Vol. 138, 1972. Surrey and Bromley point out (p. 95) that the lower of various estimates available are still about three times as high as those given in *The Limits to Growth*.

19. A very interesting paper on 'An Economic Model of World Energy 1900–2020', prepared by Dr Michael Rothkopf for the Shell Petroleum Company, reaches the conclusion that even without new kinds of energy sources becoming practical, world energy-demand can be met during the next fifty years with only 'gradual increases in energy costs'.

20. 'The Case Against Hysteria', *Nature*, January 14th, 1972.

21. 'Where Will the Calories Come From?', *Nature*, December 1st, 1972.

22. See survey of estimates by Tom Bethell, *Financial Times*, February 8th, 1973.

23. E.g. Averitt's estimates and Hubbert's calculations therefrom, quoted in Surrey and Bromley, op. cit.

24. I.B.R.D., op. cit., p. 9.

25. Professor Fred Singer, 'The Predicament of Mankind', *Bioscience*, 1972; G. F. Ray, 'Energy: Resources and Demand' (paper presented to the 1972 meeting of the British Association); Petr Beckmann, op. cit., pp. 128ff.

26. Dr Alvin Weinberg, in *The Bulletin of Atomic Scientists*, June 1970.

27. Carl Kaysen refers to a calculation by Professor Socolow, of Princeton University, to the effect that, in terms of physical limits alone, the earth could support a population of at least 1,000 times the present one at the current U.S.A. *per capita* income levels; see Carl Kaysen, 'The Computer that Printed Out W*O*L*F*', *Foreign Affairs*, July 1972, p. 664n. A recent pamphlet by Neil Jacoby and F. G. Pennance, 'The Polluters – Industry or Government' (I.E.A., London, 1972), refers to the detailed studies by Resources for the Future which appear to establish that 'there are no foreseeable limits to supplies of basic natural resources including energy at approximately current levels of costs'.

28. W. Beckerman, 'Economists, Scientists and Environmental Catastrophe', *Oxford Economic Papers*, November 1972.

29. I.B.R.D., op. cit., p. 7. This World Bank report goes on to say that the authors of *The Limits to Growth* allow for the effects of higher prices on exploration for new reserves 'by the "generous" assumption that reserves could increase by 5 times over the next 100 years, but what appears to be an act of generosity turns out to be an unduly conservative assumption in the light of historical evidence and recent finds'.

30. The manner in which the Club of Rome has ignored all such favourable feedbacks was pointed out once by various commentators, such as John Maddox in 'Is the End of the World Really Nigh?', *Sunday Times*, June 4th, 1972.

31. Petr Beckmann, op. cit., pp. 68 et. seq.

32. Ibid., p. 89. As Beckmann points out, it is not true anyway that plastics cannot be destroyed in a virtually non-polluting manner.

33. Ibid., p. 87.

34. Ibid., p. 88.

35. Ibid., p. 82.

36. I.B.R.D., op. cit., p. 42.

37. H. H. Landsberg, L. Fischman and J. L. Fisher, *Resources in America's Future* (Johns Hopkins Press for Resources for the Future, Baltimore, 1963).

38. I.B.R.D., op. cit.

39. Ibid., p. 36.

40. See Carl Kaysen, 'The Computer that Printed Out W*O*L*F*', *Foreign Affairs*, July 1972.

41. William Page, 'Non-Renewable Resources Sub-System', University of Sussex Science Policy Research Unit, op. cit., Chapter 3.

42. W. Beckermann, 'Economists, Scientists and Environmental Catastrophe', op. cit.

43. F. Singer, 'The Predicament of the Club of Rome', *Eos*, May 1972. See also Professor Singer's excellent article on *The Limits to Growth*, 'The Computer as Pallbearer', in *The Nation*, March 13th, 1972.

44. I.B.R.D., op. cit., p. 5. Furthermore, the World Bank report, written from a position of unparalleled knowledge of the actual population-control policies being adopted in many countries of the world, specifically contradicts the Club of Rome assertion that the necessary birth-control policies will prove too expensive for the poorer countries (ibid., p. 27–9).

45. See reference to estimates by Professor Dudley Kirk of the University of Stanford, California, in *The Sunday Times*, June 4th, 1972.

46. The same point is made by others such as A. Kneese and R. Ridker, 'Predicament of Mankind', *The Washington Post*, March 2nd, 1972, or Beckmann, op. cit., p. 173, who writes: ' ... most of the relationships built into the doomsday machine simply do not exist on a worldwide basis, and in this sense it is futile to argue whether they are right or wrong. As far as its system levels and other variables are concerned, we do not yet live in one world. Industrial air pollution is worst in Japan, America and Europe. Rapid population growth now exists only in South America, Africa and Asia. If the feedback loops and other inter-connections of the doomsday machine were anything but a fiction, population growth in these parts of the world would lead to an increase in pollution in the industrialized countries, until it became so bad that the population of the underdeveloped countries stopped growing because the car exhausts of Los Angeles would shorten the life span of the inhabitants of Rawalpindi.'

47. They conclude that 'although there must clearly be physical limits to the world's capacity to produce food, the combination of technical progress and the rational use of the world's food-producing resources could put off these physical limits well beyond the time horizon of the World 3 (i.e. *The Limits to Growth*) model. However, we see the major problem of feeding the world in political rather than physical limits.' P. K. Marstrand and K. L. R. Pavitt, 'The Agricultural Sub-System', Chapter 5 of the University of Sussex's study, op. cit., *Futures*, February 1973, pp. 63, 65.

48. Lord Todd, *The Guardian*, January 26th, 1972.

49. John Cherrington, 'What the Alarmists Forget', *Financial Times*, April 4th, 1972.

50. Interview with Dr Borlaug in 'Are We Really in Danger?', *The Observer*, March 5th, 1972.

Chapter 9. Conclusions

1. Professor Kenneth Mellanby, 'Ecologists Who Ignore Technology's Successes', *The Times*, March 3rd, 1972. Professor Mellanby goes on to say:

'There are those who call themselves ecologists who appear to hate science as such, and to rejoice in its failures. They seem to get a nasty sort of pleasure from foretelling doom. Thus when a species of mosquito becomes resistant to DDT this is a subject for rejoicing, even if it means that thousands of babies will die of malaria.'

2. Meadows and others, *The Limits to Growth*, and J. W. Forrester, *World Dynamics* (Wright-Allen Press, Cambridge, Mass., 1971).

3. Rudolf Klein, 'Growth and Its Enemies', *Commentary*, Vol. 53, No. 6 (June 1972), p. 40.

4. 'Another Whiff of Doomsday', *Nature*, Vol. 236, March 10th, 1972.

5. Many other commentators have drawn attention to this basic flaw in *The Limits to Growth*, and in the Forrester model (*World Dynamics*) on which much of this was based. For example, H. J. Barnett writes that 'Forrester's model is unsound in basic structure. He fails to build in feedbacks whereby societies utilize knowledge to overcome resource depletion and pollution.'— *The Journal of Economic Literature*, Vol. X, No. 3, September 1972.

6. Allen Kneese and Ronald Ridker, 'Predicament of Mankind', *Washington Post*, March 2nd, 1972.

7. 'A Sober Look at Doomsday', *The Guardian*, March 6th, 1972.

8. John Kay, 'The Economics of Doomsday', *The Cambridge Review* (forthcoming).

9. Mr John Dore of the Association of Scientific, Technical and Managerial Staffs, at the T.U.C. Conference, September 1972, reported in *The Times*, September 8th, 1972. At the same conference, delegates from other unions attacked the 'academic excesses of some of the so-called spokesmen on the environment', and expressed concern that the environmental movement might follow the path it had taken in the U.S.A., where it had become a largely middle-class academic movement unrelated to particular working-class environmental interests. See 'Need for Balance between Environment and Jobs', report on T.U.C. Conference, *The Times*, September 8th, 1972.

10. Rudolf Klein, op. cit., p. 43.

11. Ibid., p. 44.

12. C. A. R. Crosland, 'Pollution – or Poverty', *The Sunday Times*, June 26th, 1972.

Index

absorptive capacity of the environment, 118, 119–20, 187
Agence des Bassins, 172
agricultural prices, 145–6
aircraft industry, 133
air pollution:
    absorption of, 119–20
    in Britain, 65–6; Beaver report on, 199–200; costs of abatement of, 200; decline of, 68, 76, 123–6, 132, 197; dispersal of, 187; legislation against, 76, 123, 125, 156n
    costs of, 199–200
    costs of reducing, 38–9, 190–95, 196, 200–201; as percentage of O.E.C.D. National Product, 193
    and health, 195
    measurement of, 122
    O.E.C.D. report on, 38–9, 191–5, 196
    from power-stations, 126–7, 197
    in Scandinavia, 211
    sources of, 46–7, 99, 127, 197
    in U.S.A., 129, 187; benefits of abatement of, 185, 201; costs of abatement of, 190, 194–5; damage done by, 190; decline in, 125; legislation against, 125, 127, 128–130, 130n, 132, 190, 194, 201; and see carbon monoxide, sulphur dioxide
Air Quality Act 1967 (U.S.A.), 129
alcohol, 116, 117
Allen, R., 274 n11
Almeida, Miguel Ozorio de, 109–10, 264 n3, 265 n14
aluminium, 229
ammonium sulphate, 197
anti-growth movement, 37–59; issue of, and real issues, 245–8; and see Limits to Growth, The, and references passim
anti-pollution policies, 125–31; in Britain, 125–8; and see under Britain; in major industrial

nations, 130; in U.S.A. see under United States of America; and see environmental policies; pollution, abatement of
Aral sea, 45
Ashby, Sir Eric (now Lord), 9, 114, 258 n1, 266 n21, 267 n33, 268 n53
aspirin, 115–16
Atomic Energy Authority, Programmes Analysis Unit of, 198n

Baikal, Lake, 44
Barnes, J. M., 259 n3
Barnett, H. J., 277 n5
Barre, Raymond, 259 n11
Barzel, Yoram, 264 n14
Baumol, W. J., 155n, 273 n31
bauxite reserves, 219, 229
Beaver Committee, 68; report of, 199–200, 272 n15
Beckerman, Prof. W., 262 n14, 275 n28, 276 n42
'Beckermanipus, web-footed', 111
'Beckermonium', 232
Beckmann, Prof. Petr, 41–2, 134–5, 228–9, 260 nn4,14, 267 nn31,35, 269 n61, 275 nn25,31,32
Bentham, Jeremy, 88n
Bethell, Tom, 275 n22
Bible, The, 90
Bienefeld, M. A., 72n
biochemical oxygen demand (B.O.D.), 158, 158n
biosphere, absorptive capacity, of, 99
birth-control techniques, 237
Blueprint for Survival, 42, 260 n6
Borlaug, Dr Norman, 117, 240, 267 n28, 276 n50
Boulding, Kenneth, 13, 37n
Bower, Blair, 270 n6
Britain
    air pollution in, see air pollution
    and air pollution in Scandinavia, 211
    anti-pollution policies in, 125–8